Unf*#!ing Believable

Unf*#!ing Believable

By Kay Matthews

ACEQUIA MADRE
P•R•E•S•S

162 El Valle Road
Chamisal, NM 87521

Copyright 2017 By Kay Matthews

All rights reserved, including those to reproduce this book, or parts thereof, in any form, without permission in writing from the Publisher

ISBN 978-0-940875-10-4

Library of Congress Control Number: 2017906958

Dedicated to Bartleby the Scrivener: "I'd Prefer Not To."

CONTENTS

About This Blog 13
Los Alamos National Laboratory 16
Developers and Designers 19
Capitalism 22
Hitchhiking 26
The Scourge of Computers 29
Civil Disobedience 32
Higher Education 35
Some Things are Relative 38
Invoking God 41
Israel 45
Health Insurance 49
Success 54
Enlightenment/Progress 59
Colorado Springs 62
Electoral Politics 66
Chatter 70
Consumer Culture 74
Westminster Dog Show 78
Hero Worship 80
Sustainability 82
Drug Company Advertising 86
Marriage 89
The Olympics 93
Dental Insurance, or the Lack Thereof 97
Global Domination 99
Self Image 102

White Men in Suits	105
Marginalization	108
Obfuscation	111
Funky Soul	115
My Summer Job	118
Baby Boom Regret	122
Productivity	125
The Best and the Brightest (According to the Sunday New York Times Style Section)	128
Diary of a Bad Year	131
Diary of a Bad Year, continued	134
Diary of a Bad Year, continued	139
Mothering	142
Power in the Middle East	145
Diary of a Bad Year, continued	148
Diary of a Bad Year, continued	151
Who Are These People?	154
Elegy for El Valle	157
Post-Marxist Humanist Pragmatist	160
Diary of a Bad Year, Ad Infinitum	163
Diary of a Bad Year: Invasion of the Bats	165
The Million Dollar Bone Mill	168
Unplugged	170
Diary of a Bad Year: Death or Philip Roth, I Can't Remember Which	173
Letter to Elizabeth	176
Guilty Pleasures	179
Christian Schizophrenia	182

Diary of a Bad Year: Mark and Steve	185
"When You Got Nothing You Got Nothing To Lose"	188
Diary of a Bad Year, The End	190
Stuff	193
Letter to Elizabeth, Number Two	196
On Not Watching Basketball1	198
On Not Being Able to Get a Job	201
The Swim Team	204
You Can't Go Home Again	206
Why I Live in Northern New Mexico	209
Death in the Afternoon—Or So I Thought	212
Pee Wee's Story: The Deaf Leading the Blind	215
Acequia Stories: The Democracy of Dysfunction or How Everyone is Equally Crazy	218
Butchie	221
"A sense of liberation"	224
Good Samaritans	227
Existential Thrill—Or Fear and Loathing—on the LA Freeways	231
A Dog's Life	234
"If I Can't Dance I Don't Want to be Part of Your Revolution"	238
The Phenomenon that is Scottsdale/Phoenix	243
Reflections on the Super-duper Bowl	246
Jamaica Kinkaid	248
Only in France	250
In Memory of Shulamith Firestone	253
Springtime in New Mexico	255

I'll Take You There 258
Role Reversal..260
Waiting for Lucia 262
Having Babies 264
I'm in love. With Alabama Shakes. With Brittney Howard 266
Entering the Affordable Care Act 268
Total Noise..270
Orwell Lives 272
Play that Rock Guitar 275
Fun and Fear at the Baseball Stadium....................................277
Rocky Mountain High, Colorado 280
"Get out of the new one [road] if you can't lend a hand
for the times they are a changin'. . . ."....................................285
New York, New York, it Used to be a Wonderful Town...................290
Is that Supposed to be Funny? 295
Russell Brand Tells it Like it is 297
Pilgrim and Waldo on the Appalachian Trail........................300
Tree Story 304
Babysitting..306
Insomnia...309
Berkeley Breathed is Back!..313
At the Malheur National Wildlife Refuge: There's More than
a Little Irony Here 316
Being Invisible 320
Sojourn to the Urban Landscape..322
You know, like, I just can't take it anymore!..........................325
It's Obscene...327
It's All Over Now Party Blue 329
Your Book That No One Reads..333

"Unf*#!ing Believable by Kay Matthews is a candid political and personal memoir, and one of the most intriguing books I've read in a long while. For starters, it's a prime example of activism with hope. It shares a tough analysis of our times, our culture, our overwhelming problems alongside an intimate discourse about life that often made me laugh or occasionally broke my heart. There's much love and some death, cherished community, raising kids, watching basketball, caring for the neighbors, and building your own house even as the memoir also rails against climate change, the destruction of rural communities, and elucidates many local struggles for social justice and economic equality in Northern New Mexico. The eclectic book shines with the joy of listening to rhythm and blues music, or snowshoeing the high country, experiences contrasted with the nightmares of American health care, the NSA, Los Alamos . . . and babysitting! Each blog makes you think. Kay does not hammer the reader with prophecies of doom, however she's not above flaying you occasionally with sarcasm, and you can't ever ignore the importance of her thinking globally and acting locally. (She and her partner Mark Schiller published the invaluable and progressive *La Jicarita News* for years and it still appears on the Internet.)

You can open *Unf*#!ing Believable* anywhere and read it forward or back because each blog is complete unto itself. That said, reading the book straight through from its start in 2009 until its end in 2017 comprises a thoughtful, inspiring, adventurous, and important memoir of a complicated, self-sufficient, and useful life well-lived. I think this is a New Mexico classic, so specific in its love of our state's northern communities, and universal in every wise story that it tells. Also, the book is a lot of fun!"

— John Nichols, author of *The Milagro Beanfield War*

About This Blog

It was November 17, 2005 and I sat watching the news about the debate in the U.S. Congress over torture in a state of shock. I always knew the American government trained others to torture at the School of the Americas, and that the CIA had secret prisons all over the world. I knew, as Naomi Klein says in her book, *The Shock Doctrine*, "Just as ecologists define ecosystems by the presence of certain 'indicator species' of plants and birds, torture is an indicator species of a regime that is engaged in a deeply anti-democratic project, even if that regime happens to have come to power through elections." But the fact that there was a public discussion on national network news about whether the CIA should be exempt from the Geneva Convention rules of prohibition was more than I could process.

After I cried awhile, I went over to lower the curtains and discovered, on our tomato plant sunning in the south window, a perfect tomato: round, bright red, barely soft to the touch, the repository of everything we deem beautiful and "good" in our universe. The dialectic of this tomato's relationship to torture expresses the dilemma of our daily lives. How does one live in the world we have created that embodies water boarding and the wonder and potential of a perfect tomato?

Suddenly, at 55, I found myself unable to navigate this terrain. While I am, by nature (the nature/nurture argument will be explored in due time), endowed with a personality that has kept me relatively calm and grounded over the course of my life—a life, like that of anyone else, filled with doses of success, disappointment, struggle, and happiness—I have previously suffered depression. In my early-twenties, after dropping out of college and moving to a funky airstream trailer in the South Valley of

Albuquerque, New Mexico, I was ready to admit defeat and buy a ticket to oblivion. I gained weight, I drank too much beer and tequila, and I brought home strangers from Okie's, Albuquerque's hippie/student bar, to try to assuage my loneliness. I wasn't on the course I'd set for myself as a believer in achievement, both personal and political, and therefore I, and the sixties revolution of consciousness, had no future.

Over the course of the next 30 years I of course learned that there is no penultimate achievement where we do or we don't arrive, personally or politically. But there are incremental steps, measured within the circumscribed time and place we find ourselves that provide enough reward and compensation to help define a life worth living. Personally, I built an entire house from scratch and made another livable. I bore two children who gave me enormous pleasure and a modicum of pain. I sustained a relationship with a life partner for 34 years, also with enormous pleasure and, I have to admit, more than a modicum of pain. Politically, I have been as true as I know how to be in disengaging from consumer culture and engaging in community efforts to smash the power elite. We knew the elite were vulnerable when the Cuban revolutionaries threw out Batista and embarked on a journey that revealed its own fits and starts, successes and failures.

But now, try as I might to not measure, I continually lose ground and I lose faith. The enormity of what is wrong in the world becomes the enormity of my daily life. Because I'm a writer, I find myself making copious lists of everything that has brought me to this impasse, with the idea of dissecting it, revealing it, indicting it, for some undefined audience that might actually listen and ultimately be moved by me. What that possibly can do to help me lift the daily burden is beside the point. Like the thousands of bloggers who have found voice on the Internet, I need the process of venting and the real or imaginary solidarity it elicits.

I started blogging the list in 2009 in no particular order other than the assault of a particular day. It is sometimes local in specificity but always global in application. It comes via all my senses: my eyes that read it on the computer screen or see it on TV; my ears that hear it on the radio and in many conversations I have with friends and acquaintances; and my gut, where everything gets churned up and viscerally spit out. It is all within the framework that Hannah Arendt, in *The Origins of Totalitarianism*, sees as "the process of never-ending accumulation of power necessary for the protection of never-ending accumulation of capital." I started this list before I read J. M. Coetzee's book, *Diary of a Bad Year*, but when I saw the explanation he gives for writing his great complaint, I knew I had mine: "An opportunity to grumble in public, an opportunity to take magic revenge on the world for declining to conform to my fantasies: how could I refuse?"

My younger son told me no one would read this book (or whatever it is), with its list of depressing evils, unless I offer some sort of solution (he calls me a hopeless communist). Of course, there is no fundamental solution other than smashing the system—and by system I mean the economic, political, and cultural one that denies our humanity—but I have added as a last sentence to some of the posts, something that might be done to perhaps move us along towards that goal. The rest of them just have to remain as is: honest, sometimes ironic, always irreverent.

Tuesday, June 9, 2009
Los Alamos National Laboratory

Every time our (former) illustrious senator Pete Domenici is quoted in the newspaper or appears on TV I am reminded of his legacy: Los Alamos National Laboratory (LANL), where the atom bombs dropped on Hiroshima and Nagasaki were developed and which today continues to poison our land, water, bodies, and minds. Everyone knows this, including Domenici, but believes that our economy is so entrenched in LANL that any cutbacks or movement away from arms production would result in statewide economic collapse. (He finally decided not to run for re-election in 2008 because of a brain disease.)

What they fail to acknowledge, however, is that our economy is already collapsed for everyone except the few hundred LANL scientists who live on "the hill" and get paid big bucks to pollute our lives and endanger the world. The rest of New Mexico—particularly northern New Mexico—continues to garner all kinds of claim to fame: highest teen age pregnancy rates; highest per capita heroin overdoses; highest per capita alcohol related deaths; highest poverty rates; worst paid teachers; etc., etc. An announcement by the Lab, after it renewed its management contract with the University of California and Bechtel Corporation, is illustrative of the disparity it helps engender: of the new 20 division managers named under a new administrator, not one has a Spanish surname. The Hispano people of northern New Mexico, who are the majority population, are LANL lackeys: they are the technicians, if they're lucky, and the grunt workers, if they're not. Two of my neighbors in the tiny village of El Valle get up every morning at five o'clock to drive the hour and a half to the Lab where they are outside maintenance workers, freezing their butts off in the winter and sweating in the overgrown forests they thin all summer.

The rest of us live with the consequences. What those consequences are became abundantly clear during the Cerro Grande fire in 2000. What started as a forest fire in the neighboring Bandelier National Monument (actually a prescribed burn that got out of control), the fire ignited the tinder dry, overgrown ponderosa pine forests that surround the town of Los Alamos, home to the Lab. The Los Alamos site, formally Hispano homesteading settlements and Native American hunting grounds on the Pajarito Plateau in the Jemez Mountains, was requisitioned by the federal government during World War II to develop the bomb in relative obscurity. During the cold war, the town of Los Alamos grew up to support the burgeoning bomb machine that ultimately became Los Alamos National Laboratory. Hastily constructed barracks provided instant housing for the scientists and their support crew (although most of the workers continue to live in the valleys surrounding the Lab in their traditional communities). Over the years, more suburban style housing became available but was primarily framed and flimsy. When the Cerro Grande fire roared through town, it destroyed over 400 of these houses and apartments and then began burning Lab facilities, storage pits, and contaminated canyons. Directly downwind, in El Valle and neighboring villages, the sky darkened and irradiated ash fell on our houses and fields. Those who could afford to leave fled: Mark took our son to Colorado to stay at my sister's while I remained at home to take care of the animals, closing myself in the house as much as possible. Communities like Chimayó suffered under a constant cloud of smoke and many folks had to leave for weeks in order to breathe.

While the Cerro Grande fire brought the dangers of the Lab literally into our homes and yards, we've all known for years that the Department of Energy has never enforced adequate protections. Radioactive waste has been dumped into canyons, contaminating groundwater and vegetation. Open incinerators have sent radioactivity into the air for us to breathe. For the past several years the Lab has been constantly in the news, as workers have been accused of security lapses, secret files have disappeared, funds have been misappropriated, worker morale has sunk to a new low, and the disparity of pay has been exposed. To address all these concerns, the Department of Energy renewed the Lab's management contract with the University of California, in partnership with the private weapons manufacturer Bechtel to make sure that these problems will continue to be swept under the carpet with corporate efficiency. Under this management, the Lab has been given the go ahead to start producing plutonium triggers (although it remains to be seen how many will be built) for nuclear bombs, work formerly done at Rocky Flats in Colorado, which was shut down and declared a Superfund site because of the contamination this work produced.

I often think that all of us who are activists involved in the many struggles we deal with in New Mexico—poverty, immigrant rights, resource protection, land grants, acequia advocacy—should probably all refocus our energies to shut-down the Lab in its current configuration. It is our most fundamental problem and the source of worldwide grief and suffering. It is an abomination.

Solution: Prohibit any weapons research and development and dedicate the Lab to environmental remediation and alternative energy development.

Sunday, June 21, 200

Developers and Designers

When Santa Fe homeboy Tom Ford decided to build a monster house on top of a hill in Santa Fe, a hill that had already caused a ruckus between the city and the previous owners when they tried to build a different monster house, the powers that be rolled over and died. I guess Tom's rationale, that he had to have a house big enough for his whole family to stay over, pulled at the heartstrings of the city councilors. They asked him to nip and tuck a little, here and there, which he graciously did, being the consummate designer that he is.

Tom Ford is the embodiment of two of the world's worst professions: developers and fashion designers. Technically, he's not a developer, he only hires them. His wealth underwrites their mad desires to build 15,000 square-foot what—mansions? manors? monstrosities? you can't really call them houses—that are the repositories of conspicuous consumption, from their jacuzzis and indoor swimming pools to their stainless steel refrigerators and Wolf stoves. The ones who build mansions for clients like Tom Ford probably think they're creating works of art. The ones who buy up vacant land and then subdivide it into gated communities so they can build many mansions at one time probably think they're the engines that drive the economic machine. The Santa Fe city fathers (city fathers everywhere, actually) certainly think they are. The bottom line is always that without the construction industry the economy of the city will crash: not only will the workers be laid off, but all the lumber stores, the paint stores, the hardware stores, the glass stores, the plumbing supply stores, the electrical supply stores, the fixture stores, the appliance stores, ad nauseam, will go bankrupt. It's as if nobody else already lives in the city and hires workers to restore, upgrade, and add onto houses already here and buys all the necessary stuff to do so at the lumber store, the paint store, hardware store, etc. There is no understanding that there is a difference between economic development and economic growth, that development means continued urban sprawl and expanded markets that eventually degrade the quality of city life. Managed growth is finding ways to enhance the opportunities for workers who want to increase their skill levels or find new jobs that contribute to the well-being of the communities. Sustainability is finding ways to create neighborhoods that allow people to work and shop near home and be less reliant on their cars, roads, and strip malls.

But who cares about all that? Certainly not Tom Ford. He only lives here part of the year anyway, and other than attending a city council meeting to defend his property wouldn't be caught dead at a community meeting to discuss why the State Engineer's Office is allowing the county to transfer almost 2,000 acre feet of water rights from Taos County to underwrite development in the Pojoaque Valley (but that's another story, saved for later). He's too busy designing the clothes for all the other Santa Fe second home owners who only fly in to attend the opera or chamber music series and then jet back to their penthouses (those monstrosities actually have a designated name) on Fifth Avenue. Have you ever watched a New York or Paris fashion show on TV and seen what guys like Tom Ford think women should wear? It's enough to make you anorexic from throwing up. Not only would the majority of women in this country not be caught dead in these get-ups, I can't imagine when the Fifth Avenue matrons actually wear this stuff. Actually, they don't even wear it to the Santa Fe Opera, where the favorite mode of attire is tight-fitting jeans and sequined tank tops. Do they wear it to the grocery store to buy foie gras? Do they wear it to their toddlers' $60,000 a year pre-schools when they go to pick them up (or do only chauffeurs do that?) Do they wear it to cocktail parties where they talk about bond trading and learning Spanish so they can communicate with their Salvadoran maid? I guess they must wear it to MOMA for openings. After all, it's art too, que no? Jackson Pollack must be rolling over in his grave.

Solution: Turn Tom Ford's business into a co-op, where the people who want to wear his clothes have to work in his sweatshops making them.

Monday, June 22, 2009

Capitalism

"If civilization is to go no further than this, it had better not have gone so far: if it does not aim at getting rid of this misery and giving some share in the happiness and dignity of life to all the people that it has created . . . it is simply an organized injustice, a mere instrument for oppression, so much the worse than that which has gone before it, as its pretensions are higher, its slavery subtler, its mastery harder to overthrow, because supported by such a dense mass of commonplace wellbeing and comfort."

William Morris wrote this in 1880. It could, of course, been written by any of us today. I read this quote of Morris, a British writer and social critic, in *The Essential E.P. Thompson*, and I've also read about Morris, as well as other writers, who railed against what capitalism and the industrial revolution were doing to the people and culture of 18th and 19th century Britain, in Raymond Williams' book *The Country and the City*. Historians Williams and Thompson take a look at how the notion of cultural materialism enhances—or detracts from—Marxist economic theory. This is a subject that any of us who were active in the 20th century's sixties revolution of consciousness had to deal with, whether we were conversant with the terminology "cultural materialism" or just knew, in our guts, that while we were intent on smashing an economic system we also had to be intent on smashing racism, sexism, homophobia, and hierarchy.

Now that it's the 21st century, it's both helpful and painful to read the comments of Morris or Samuel Taylor Coleridge or D.H Lawrence, who lament the losses associated with capitalism—the cultivation of our humanity—and its emphasis—the "forcing of all human energy into a competition of mere acquisition." It's helpful, of course, because it binds us to these historical figures in a way that ensures a continuum of caring and activism. It's painful in that we're still, 200 years later, struggling against the same system that consigned the British laborer to the stultifying slums of London, the African slave to the plantations of American, and the Mexican peasant to *las maquiladoras de la frontera*.

The fact remains that neither Morris' literary assault nor the Students for a Democratic Society's physical assault on the imperial bastions of Britain and the U.S. have done much to rein in the "organized injustice" of capitalism. Its reach is now global and threatens the last isolated societies that have somehow managed to maintain a semblance of communal or subsistence living. The one revolutionary society we have witnessed over the course of our lives—Cuba—will inevitably transition from its relative isolation and self-determination once Castro is gone. As soon as the U.S. lifts its embargo—which has caused enormous pain and suffering in that country—the exerted economic and political pressures may be too much for Cuba to withstand. Will its fate come down to a power struggle between the U.S. and Hugo Chavez' Venezuela? It's hard for most of us in this country to understand what is really happening in Venezuela; all we get are sound bites from the mainstream press and the occasional alternative reports that either glorify or criticize Chavez with a cynicism born of the history of too many Latino strongmen in too many countries with too many ties to empire.

So where does this leave us? The debate between revolutionary and evolutionary change that engaged us for so many years seems largely irrelevant. In his book *After Theory* Terry Eagleton reminds us "it is one thing to make a revolution, and another to sustain it. " What is it about this country, established by revolution (elitist as it was) that created the notion of the rugged individualist, the mentality of "pulling oneself up by his or her bootstraps," so pervasive and so ungovernable? In a pithy few sentences in Richard Russo's *Bridge of Sighs* the mother says to her son, "You don't identify with people worse off than you are. You make your deals, if you can, with those who have more, because you hope one day to have more yourself. Understand that, she claimed, and you understand America . . . ." Max Weber's theory, of course, is that it's the spillover of the individualistic Puritan ethic once the religious asceticism has escaped from the cage: "In the field of its highest development, in the United States, the pursuit of wealth, stripped of its religious and ethical meaning, tends to become associated with purely mundane passions, which often actually give it the character of sport," i.e., competition. In his brilliant book *Diary of A Bad Year*, South African writer J.M. Coetzee, who now lives in Australia, reminds us that it is not just Americans who embrace this philosophy, it's also true of Australians, who believe they live in a "no-class" society where "energy, hard work, and a belief in one's self" make us all equal partners in the global market. "If we don't compete, we will perish." Americans still set the standard, however, and even European countries that many liberals look to as better models of how to achieve prosperity and enlightened social policies were part of the "coalition of the willing."

I still believe there is a desire in humankind to live in societies that provide for everyone equally, but our lack of altruism, on any kind of organized level, and our admiration of the accumulation of money, which translates into success and power, are unabashed.

I find myself worrying about Malthusian disasters—mass starvation due to the complete loss of topsoil or the collapse of genetic diversity; global warming that melts the icebergs and raises the sea level whereby

New York City and Los Angeles drop off into the ocean—that leave those of us with access to clean water and land to grow food holding the proverbial bag. And it better not be a bag full of greed and competition and built-in obsolescence and material accumulation or the cycle repeats itself again. I don't really know if there is such a thing as progress (an upcoming blog called Progress/Enlightenment) but there has got to be a better way to ensure that all of us have access to our material, cultural, and spiritual needs.

Friday, June 26, 2009

Hitchhiking

When I was in college I hitchhiked everywhere. It was 1968 and everyone hitchhiked everywhere. A friend and I hitched from Antioch, which is in south-central Ohio, to a wedding in Kansas. I hitched to work every day on my co-op job at a private elementary school in Berkeley. Another friend and I hitched a ride to San Francisco in an 18-wheeler when our Volkswagen bug died in northern California. We hitchhiked down to New York City from another co-op job in New Hampshire with a series of truck drivers.

I also picked up hitchhikers. I drove with one of my workmates at the New Hampshire job to Antioch one weekend to visit our friends there and we got the last tank of gas paid for by the student hitchhiker we picked up on the interstate. I picked up hippies with dogs, Okies, drunks, students, people with broken down cars, dueling couples, just about anybody. There were a few rules I tried to follow, both as a hitchhiker and a giver of rides. If I was driving by myself I always gave rides to women, almost always to male-female couples, and cautiously to single men or groups of men. I accepted rides from women, mixed gender groups, and tried to avoid single men. Sometimes, however, you couldn't tell who was driving until they slowed down or stopped, and it was always a leap of faith to take the ride. You thought you could appraise the driver with a quick once over—older than a certain age, dressed beyond a certain style, and with a certain ambiguous look—were usually good indicators that you let this one drive by. But you never knew, really. The truck driver who picked us up in northern California had needle marks up and down his arms but insisted on taking us over the Golden Gate Bridge, down Van Ness to Market and then to the corner of 19th Street where our friends lived. "I wouldn't want my kids stuck out on the highway."

Now, everybody's afraid to hitchhike and nobody wants to pick one up. The descent into this condition was gradual. After college I moved to a New Mexico village named Placitas and the hitchhiking culture was still viable there, for a time. But as the nature of the community changed from local Hispano land grant peppered with back to the land immigrants, to commuter suburb of Albuquerque, hitchhiking became reduced to picking up only those on the highway from the freeway to the village—still assuming no one who had business in Placitas could be bad, and finally, to only those you knew, who were few and far between because we'd all given it up.

Why did it become unsafe to hitchhike in Placitas? As a microcosm of society in general, one would think that the gentrification of the community would translate to the gentrification of hitchhiking. People with more money and better cars could pick up the less fortunate with impunity and deliver them with grace. Those of us still out on the road could trust those behind the wheel to provide a ride in style. Alas, it doesn't work that way, of course. As we become more comfortable we become more afraid of those who don't share our comfort. Those who are still not comfortable aren't benign college students anymore (college students don't hitchhike to demonstrations in Washington D.C.; the few who go fly) but those perceived to be the losers who haven't bought into consumer culture to the extent necessary to avoid any kind of disruption or break down that necessitates hitchhiking. It's a vicious cycle: the perception becomes reality as those of us who still haven't completely bought in rarely have to look for a ride, and when we occasionally do, don't bother hitchhiking because we know they aren't going to pick us up. So the ones left out there on the highways are what Hank Williams called them, the ones from Life's Other Side.

    I recently picked up a hitchhiker, however, from Picuris Pueblo, hitching a ride from one small village to the next, and I was very glad I did. He asked me if I was coming to the buffalo dance at the pueblo the next day, and then he told me that he had danced in the previous day's deer dance. He said it was such an overwhelming experience that he couldn't remember much about it except who was dancing on his left and who was dancing on his right. He didn't know if there were people watching, he didn't know how long he danced, he only knew that he danced as a deer would dance and then he ran for his life as the hunters came after him for the kill. He had a big grin on his face throughout this whole story and I then I dropped him off at the post office, where he met another friend and got in his car for the next leg of his journey. The commuters rushing down the highway missed a great story, and missed the opportunity to remember that theirs is not the only way to live.

Solution: Car companies will discontinue the manufacture of any car that doesn't run on four cylinders and the government will run van taxis, like they do in third world countries, that stop and pick up all the people on the street who need a ride, for a minimal fee. They will also run the taxis out on the highways between cities so there are no more hitchhikers, only passengers.

Monday, June 29, 2009

The Scourge of Computers

This particular diatribe was written in 2004.

My El Valle neighbors drive the buses that deliver Forest Service fire crews to forest fires. Which is what they've been doing, quite successfully, for almost 20 years. This year, however, the first thing the Forest Service supervisor's office tells my neighbors is that they have to have a DUNS number, an official number assigned by Dun and Bradstreet, before the business can be listed in the official Forest Service file of available contractors. OK, they call the toll-free number and are assigned a DUNS number. Then the Forest Service gives them a website address where they must register their business in a centralized system (a system run by the Department of Defense) that lists every contractor in the country who does business with the government.

My neighbors do not own a computer, have never used a computer, and certainly have never registered for anything, bought anything, or browsed for anything on the Internet. So I log onto the site for them, which takes 20 minutes to access on rural phone lines that urban, broadband users wouldn't even deign to use. I should have known immediately what was in store when one of the first instructions on the site cautions me to save data so I can come back to it later. All in all, I "come back" to the site at least ten times as my neighbors and I struggle to find the information it requests on five different required forms: General Information; Goods and Services; Corporate Information; Financial Information; and Points of Contact.

All of these categories have pages of questions that request information on a marketing contact and alternate, sales contact and alternate, accounts receivable contact and alternate; financial institution, routing number, bank account number, bank contact, and e-mail address for direct deposit of checks; type of business; name and type of prior business, ad nauseam. If you don't fill out every single line, with every single name, address, e-mail address, phone number, and alternate, the registration is incomplete. None of these categories allow a simple "Not Applicable" answer for those of us registering sole proprietor businesses with one employee: the bus driver. There are no sales, marketing, and accounts receivable positions; there is no type of prior business or auxiliary business. And there is a healthy distrust of providing the government with a bank account number when for twenty years checks have been mailed to the post office or rural mailbox that has worked just fine.

When I finally realize just how long it is going to take me to finish this registration (besides the 20 minute wait to access the site, it takes at least 10 or 15 minutes to process the information in each category) I decide to find a computer with a broadband Internet connection. On a friend's Powerbook the site informs me that some Macintosh computers do not allow access to this Department of Defense site because of certain security set-ups. Does this mean that the DOE suspects that Macintosh users are generally not good security risks, or that Macintosh designers decided that the DOE is not user friendly?

Meanwhile, my neighbors, and many of their bus driver friends who are also bogged down in this debilitating process, decide they do not want to provide the government with their bank account numbers. When I call up the Forest Service and tell them this, the clerk says, "Then they won't get paid." When I ask to speak to the supervisor, he says, "Believe me, I know some people don't want to give out this information, but our hands are tied. This is a directive from Washington and we can't do anything about it." When I suggest that it might behoove the Forest Service to have a workshop for contractors who might be reluctant to supply some of this information, explain the procedure, and help them through the registration process, he says, "We barely have the staff capability to do our own work, much less theirs." I ask for his boss's number in Albuquerque, but she's out of town.

Two weeks later I finally finish the registration. My neighbors and their friends figure out a way to supply the government bureaucracy with the financial information it demands without completely jeopardizing their privacy. The process leaves all of us a mess: the website technology staff that listens to complaints all day long from frustrated contractors; the Forest Service staff that listens to complaints all day long from frustrated contractors; the frustrated contractors who believe the process is a total waste of time and an invasion of their privacy; and me, the friend of the frustrated contractors whose blood boiled and guts churned over the insensitivity and complicity of the bureaucrats who designed this system that demands the entire world buy into technology that makes our lives more complicated, more anxious, and less our own. Welcome to the world of techno-fascism.

Solution: Businesses will answer phones with real people, not automated systems run by computers; all new software systems will be compatible with older versions so we may avoid spending the bulk of our time dealing with technological problems instead of the problems they were supposedly invented to address; no one will be required to conduct any kind of business or communication online. Instead, if we so desire, we will conduct business and communication face-to-face, or voice-to-voice, with people, not machines.

Thursday, July 2, 2009

Civil Disobedience

"All men recognize the right of revolution; that is, the right to refuse allegiance to, and to resist, the government, when tyranny or inefficiency are great and unendurable . . . In other words when a sixth of the population of a nation which has undertaken to be the refuge of liberty are slaves, and a whole country is unjustly overrun and conquered by a foreign army, and subjected to military law, I think it is not too soon for honest men to rebel and revolutionize. What makes this duty the more urgent is the fact that the country so overrun is not our own, but ours is the invading army."

Henry David Thoreau was of course referring to the Mexican American War, but his words hold true for any number of our military incursions, either overt or covert, via the CIA, into the Philippines, Yugoslavia, Panama, Cuba, Chile, Sudan, and today, Iraq.

What form could Thoreau's exhortation to commit civil disobedience take today to actually be effective? The way I see it, every American soldier would have to refuse to serve in Iraq or Afghanistan. Bush and the neocons went to war despite the millions worldwide who took to the streets to express their vehement opposition to the invasion. They're certainly not going to end the war even if people are enraged enough to continue to stay in the streets or smash windows like they did in Seattle. During the Vietnam War we managed to stay in the streets, largely, I guess, because of a sustained youth movement fomenting on college campuses, the emergence of identity politics with Black Power and the Brown Berets, and the thousands of body bags that were brought home that touched thousands of other lives.

But what really ended the Vietnam War was when the soldiers there started to mutiny, refusing to fight the people the U.S. government told them were the enemy, and deciding the real enemies were their commanding officers. And oftentimes they were, literally as well as figuratively. For the past few years I've arranged for a group of Veterans for Peace from Santa Fe to come to the high school in Peñasco to make a presentation on Full Disclosure Recruiting. The Vets, who served in Korea, the Vietnam War, and the first Gulf War, try to provide the kids the kinds of information they need to make an informed choice when deciding to join the military. It's always disheartening when the first thing they ask is how many of the students have family or friends who are currently serving in the military, and 75 percent of them raise their hands. Military recruitment in northern New Mexico is extensive, and many of the kids have a long family history of military service.

One of the Vets who came was a woman named Joan Guffy. She served as an Air Force nurse in the Vietnam War, where she was exposed to Agent Orange and was twice raped by American military officers. She suffered from ovarian cancer and Post Traumatic Stress Disorder: "The military is a macho system where women are demeaned. I had to be afraid of my own soldiers." Joan died in 2007.

The soldiers who served in Vietnam were drafted, of course, and were there by default: their families weren't rich enough and they weren't educated enough or life-experienced enough (most of them were taken right out of high school) to be able to avoid the draft. The dehumanizing conditions fueled already existing feelings of futility and hopelessness, and their training to be killing machines backfired: there are stories of soldiers throwing grenades into their commanding officers tents and mutinying in the middle of battles, leaving the officers to make it on their own. Today, the men and women in Iraq and Afghanistan are military volunteers, but that doesn't mean they aren't from the same families and communities that supplied the Vietnam War. What will it take to raise their consciousness as to the futility of both their personal and societal positions, to "rebel and revolutionize" against their commanders and refuse to fight?

Maybe the straw that breaks the camel's back will be the gut wrenching returns to duty of those who thought they were only signing on for one tour—or the older, National Guard men and women who have families, jobs, and lives that are devastated by two or three tours. There just aren't enough of these volunteers, or guardsmen, to maintain a force that even the Bush administration begrudgingly admitted wasn't enough to "liberate" Iraq. There's a a movie about it playing right now, called Stop-loss, which all the critics say no one is going to attend because no one wants the war to be any closer than reading another article on the inside pages of the local newspaper.

In an interview we did with Ike DeVargas for *La Jicarita News* in the late 1990s, he told us how he had come to his activism. "Most of us went there [Vietnam] believing what the government told us, that what they were doing over there was good and necessary, and most of us came back knowing that if they were lying to us over there they were lying to us here, too." It took Ike only one tour to make the connection, and it led to a lifetime of civil disobedience. If only all the other soldiers would refuse to take up their weapons, just one time, all together, we could end these obscene wars.

Ike DeVargas

Monday, July 6, 2009

Higher Education

When my younger son called to tell me he'd just found out, via the Internet, of course, that he'd been rejected by Princeton, Yale, Harvard, Cornell, and Stanford, was on the waiting list at Columbia and Brown, and was accepted at Dartmouth and the University of Pennsylvania, my immediate reaction was, "What does it take to get into these fucking schools?"

Silly question, really. It obviously doesn't take overachieving by a white kid who attends a public high school in Santa Fe: a 4.60 GPA, between 750 and 800 on all his SATs, captain of his chess and tennis teams, an internship with the ACLU, a stint with Amigos de las Americas, fluency in Spanish, a writer for the teen section of the city newspaper, and on and on and on.

Neither does it take that special something that makes him stand out from other overachieving white kids. He was raised in El Valle, an Hispano village of 20 families in northern New Mexico by a couple of parents who dropped out of mainstream culture a long time ago to try to get real. He lived on 10 acres with a horse, burro, chickens, cats and dogs, vegetable garden, orchard, and hay fields. His neighbors were descendants of settlers from Mexico and indigenous Pueblo Indians. He helped clean the acequias—irrigation ditches—every spring and gathered wood in the fall.

That wasn't the path he wanted, however. By ninth grade he'd rejected everything rural, had picked one of the few sports that required proximity to concrete—tennis—and made it clear that if he wasn't more challenged in school he was going to quit and do it on his own.

So we moved him to the big (1,800 students) public high school in Santa Fe. For the first two years he lived with his dad's parents, whom we'd just moved out from Buffalo. When that became untenable because of his grandfather's Alzheimer's and his grandmother's inability to deal with a teenager, his dad (Mark) and I rented a house in Tesuque, a Santa Fe suburb (we totally lucked out through a friend of a friend with a cheap rent), and took turns living with him: we split the week between Tesuque and El Valle, where one of us had to be to take care of the animals.

Mark and I, of course, never wanted him to go to Harvard or Yale. We don't want him going to school with elitist rich kids—or what he aspires to be. Are there so many of these kids applying to these schools that there's no room at the inn? What about all the public school kids like our son who are their class valedictorians and captains of their cross-country and swim teams who deserve to go to these schools if that's what they want? And why are they convinced that they have to go to Cornell or Princeton to get a good education? Why are their parents spending thousands of dollars to hire tutors to raise their SAT scores to 800? Why are these kids applying to 10 or 14 schools, screwing up the admissions process and driving their parents crazy with admission and financial aid forms?

Seems like a vicious cycle to me. The Ivy League schools reflect the increasing disparity in our society between the haves and have-nots: prep school kids with money and connections and minority kids enrolled to fill quotas. The two kids from our son's high school who were accepted at Harvard are an Hispana and the daughter of an alumnus. The co-valedictorian, who got accepted at MIT, is Asian. For the prep school kids, it will be a validation of their privilege. For the minority kids, it will be a struggle, and many of them won't make it.

Our son will go to U Penn or New York University (where he got accepted in the Scholar's Program) or Oberlin or somewhere perfectly reasonable and he will have to figure out what to do with his life, just like the rest of us. This was his first real taste of how badly the system sucks; I hope that helps him make a life-affirming choice rather than a cynical one.

Solution: Make all higher education free, which will quickly pay for itself.

Friday, July 10, 2009

Some Things are Relative

When George Bush became president of the United States for the second time I remember lying on the floor in front of the TV sobbing uncontrollably. The wave of despair and misery that washed over me was palpable, even though I knew my life would go on, at least externally, in pretty much the same fashion as before. I would continue to live on my 10 acres in El Valle and irrigate my garden, orchard, and fields. I would continue to publish and edit *La Jicarita News* with my partner Mark, where we could pretty much print anything we wanted. Our kids would continue to attend public school and the college of their choice and pretty much say anything they wanted. When Mahmoud Ahmadinejad became president of Iran, I read a profile of a young Iranian writer who described sitting in his room in despair, holding his head in his hands. His life, already in a state of precariousness, would certainly not go on as before. If he continued to write what he wanted to write, he would probably end up in jail. If he continued to associate with those who believed in a secular, democratic Iran, he would probably end up in jail. And if his girlfriend continued to refuse to wear a hijab, she might be whipped or end up in jail.

His suffering is more profound. My suffering is complicated by my privilege. It's only because of where I live that I have the leisure and capacity to be writing this attempt to deal with what makes me suffer, the dichotomy of the tomato in the global society. While I struggle to reconcile my faith in the Marxist analysis of capitalism with a more postmodern exploration of how cultural conditions figure into the equation, the student in Iran is still very much aware of a systematic, historical process that controls and dominates his life, leaving not much room for worrying about how to appreciate the tomato.

Those of us who live in privileged American society, which is responsible for much of the oppression in places like Iran, seem incapable of figuring out how to smash the power elite after losing the will of the sixties and early seventies, when the political system seemed vulnerable, at least momentarily. Michel Foucault gave up the barricades for the San Francisco bathhouses and Abbie Hoffman killed himself. A young friend of mine, who is in her late twenties and graduated from Antioch, where I also went to college, doesn't like to hear my stories of the sixties. My best one, about the time in Berkeley the cops surrounded our house with a swat team, looking for a fellow Antioch student who was arrested in Cambridge at an anti-war demonstration, fled to Berkeley, and tied up the sheriff on Telegraph Avenue when he tried to arrest him, bores her silly. She bristles when we complain about the lack of young people out in the streets protesting the invasion of Iraq or the prison at Guantanamo Bay. She says demonstrations are useless, that the mainstream media subverts the intent by refusing to cover them.

But then, after a month of student and worker riots in the streets of France the government capitulates and rescinds the law that caused the riots in the first place (a labor law that would allow employers to fire workers younger than 25 without cause). It took ten years of demonstrating in the streets of the U.S. before this country pulled out of Vietnam (and it's debatable how much of our withdrawal was due to political unrest at home, see the Civil Disobedience blog) and millions of demonstrators in the streets of all the major cities didn't deter George Bush from invading Iraq. Why did the French government respond so quickly to its student uprising? In France labor unions remain strong and viable and a force to be reckoned with, while here in the states the unions have largely been eviscerated, through a calculated campaign by the power elite and because of internecine fighting and corruption in the unions themselves. So not only are we ignored in the streets, we have no organizations with any political clout that can actually threaten the status quo of the government. Our privilege extends only as far as the marketplace: We have the power to consume but lack the power to change anything. I can write and speak out about whatever I want but my words effect nothing. Internet blogs can appear on our computer screens in a blink of an eye but we can't stop the bombing in Iraq and we can't make sure no person goes to bed hungry.

A lot of us spend a lot of energy trying to figure out how this has happened and what we can do about it. That doesn't stop us from continuing our own struggles that manifest in a million different ways, but it's obviously not enough and periodically it results in the malaise that I am now struggling with. But, as the Mexican immigrants who took to the streets during the last election to agitate for immigration reform, like to remind us, "Si se puede"—if only fleetingly, if only temporarily, if only in the alleviation of the suffering of a few at the hands of many.

Solution: Hasta siempre liberación.

Saturday, July 18, 2009

Invoking God

Mark and I always manage to have a seder at Passover with whomever happens to be around and interested in attending: non-Jewish neighbors; Jewish friends from Santa Fe; family from New York, etc. One year, our friend Lisa, a Jew from Washington D.C., who was at the time living in a small Hispano village across the Rio Grande from us, decided to have a seder and invite all her Catholic neighbors. We downloaded a liberation haggadah from the Internet and went over to Servilleta Plaza to celebrate Passover in Lisa's run down adobe house. Besides being the only Jews there except for Lisa and her mother, who was visiting from D.C., we were the only gringos as well. Everyone crowded into the large kitchen while we went through the ceremony and took turns reading the passages from the haggadah before digging into a scrumptious meal of lamb, matzo ball soup, and frijoles. When it got dark we lit a bonfire outside, told stories, and danced.

Mark and I also attend Catholic mass in El Valle, on Christmas and special occasions, and at funerals (or rosaries, where the Penitentes sing on their knees in front of the alter). I'm not sure anyone in the village even knows we're Jews, but they don't care what we are as long as we come to show our neighborliness and respect for their religion and culture.

That being said, I truly hate organized religion. I hate the fact that certain friends find it necessary to "rediscover" their "spiritual" life (particularly after they become parents) that gets all tangled up in some form of religion, usually the one they grew up in, or sometimes, one they find more "liberating." Religion is not liberating: it is suffocating. It is about taking on faith certain precepts that have nothing to do with liberation or freedom or goodness. It is about believing stories that were devised to control people by keeping them ignorant and disenfranchised. And it is about fomenting hate and intolerance. According to Voltaire: "Papist fanatics, Calvinist fanatics, all are moulded from the same sh . . . , and soaked in corrupted blood."

This is the promo for a new video game:

> Imagine: you are a foot soldier in a paramilitary group whose purpose is to remake America as a Christian theocracy, and establish its worldly vision of the dominion of Christ over all aspects of life. You are issued high-tech military weaponry, and instructed to engage the infidel on the streets of New York City. You are on a mission – both a religious mission and a military mission – to convert or kill Catholics, Jews, Muslims, Buddhists, gays, and anyone who advocates the separation of church and state – especially moderate, mainstream Christians. Your mission is "to conduct physical and spiritual warfare"; all who resist must be taken out with extreme prejudice. You have never felt so powerful, so driven by a purpose: you are 13 years old. You are playing a real-time strategy video game whose creators are linked to the empire of mega-church pastor Rick Warren, best-selling author of The Purpose Driven Life.

Actually, they've got it wrong when they target "moderate, mainstream Christians" because they're just as insidious. This is author Sam Harris in his book *The End of Religion*, who is unafraid to state the obvious (although a certain political naiveté and latent Islamophobia shortchanges the impact of the book):

"The problem that religious moderation poses for all of us is that it does not permit anything very critical to be said about religious literalism. . . . Religious moderation is the product of secular knowledge and scriptural ignorance—and it has no bonafides, in religious terms, to put it on a par with fundamentalism. The test themselves are unequivocal: they are perfect in all their parts. By their light, religious moderation appears to be nothing more than an unwillingness to submit to God's law. By failing to live by the letter of the texts, while tolerating the irrationality of those who do, religious moderates betray faith and reason equally. . . . Religious moderation, insofar as it represents an attempt to hold on to what is still serviceable in orthodox religion, closes the door to more sophisticated approaches to spirituality, ethics, and the building of strong communities. . . . Moderates do not want to kill anybody in the name of God, but they want us to keep using the word 'God' as though we knew what we were talking about."

My son Jakob, who worked in Evansville, Indiana as a photojournalism intern, told us about the church on every corner and even attended some of them to get a feel for what Midwest culture is really like. At the last one he went to, a middle-class mainstream Christian denomination that houses thousands of worshipers every Sunday, the minister's sermon was singing a dirge for the church's younger generation, who were not attending services with their parents and apparently showed little inclination in becoming members. So there is still hope, that the next generation, which already embraces a much more culturally inclusive lifestyle that bends gender and class rules, will eschew the trappings of organized religion and celebrate their spiritual lives through their acceptance and celebration of all human diversity.

Solution: Give all churches to their respective communities to be run as halfway houses, homeless shelters and training centers, domestic violence retreats, and dance halls.

Sunday, July 26, 2009

Israel

When it comes to Israel and its position in the Middle East, there are no progressives in Congress, there are only cowards. I am an American of Jewish descent who has made it my responsibility to learn the history of the dispossession of 700,000 Palestinian people and the complicity on the part of the United States in the militarization of Israel to maintain our control of the region's resources. It's all there in the history books, but starting with the Woodrow Wilson administration and culminating with George Bush the Second's, there has been a very calculated campaign to pervert that history to keep the American people ignorant and fearful of the so-called "terrorists" who supposedly threaten the existence of Israel and our interests in the Middle East. In actuality, the U.S. has helped create those "terrorists" in every perverted move it has made, from supporting the Muslim Brotherhood against Arab nationalism to invading Lebanon in futile attempts to squelch guerrilla movements like Hezbollah, which gained the support of the Lebanese people in the conflict of 2006. The U.S., along with its other western allies who have allowed us to call the shots, are largely responsible for the abysmal situation in the Middle East and for the civilian deaths and destruction suffered by the Palestinians, the Lebanese, and the Israelis.

To my knowledge, not one Democrat (except for Dennis Kucinich) has had the guts to stand up and acknowledge the lies, distortions, and propaganda that are spewed out on a daily basis by every administration, by Congress, and by the mainstream media. How many Americans know abut the refusenik Israeli military pilots who have refused to fly bombing missions that kill civilians indiscriminately, or the editor of an Israeli newspaper who has provided a point by point analysis of how we have arrived at this insane moment in history when the Israeli government is perpetrating atrocities that turn the entire world against it (and its military supplier, the U.S.) and turn poor, disenfranchised, angry young Arab men and women into jihadists? What they do is tragic and counterproductive; what we are doing is obscene. And as one of the refuseniks pointed out, as he traveled around this country speaking out about what is going on in his country, what is equally obscene is that the majority of Americans are completely ignorant of the fact that there is a peace movement in Israel and in Palestine. That knowledge would not serve our purpose of controlling the Middle East.

Until Congress takes a stand against these policies, now threatening the stability of the entire world, and the media begins to do its job of giving voice to those who try to speak truth to power, the Obama administration will have a free hand to continue its control by force. Is Iran next? I saw a film clip of the 60 Minutes Mike Wallace interview of Iranian President Mahmoud Ahmadinejad. Or really, it wasn't an interview but an assault, the only way the arrogant octogenarian Wallace knew how to pretend to be a journalist. As Wallace asked his snide questions and acted out his grievances, Ahmadinejad, through an interpreter, actually tried to say something about the relations between his country and the U.S. in the larger context of Middle East politics, but Wallace was not about to have him appear as a statesman, with opinions based in historical context (and, unfortunately, in an Islamic fundamentalist vision of economic progress and social regression). He had to be demonized, like all the rest of the Arab leaders (except for Saudi Arabian kings and princes who cut off peoples hands as punishment but send their oil in the right direction), so that our invasions become liberations and our occupations become democratization.

How did the Jewish lobby in this country become so powerful? Why do otherwise liberal and progressive Jews sit on their hands when it comes to criticizing Israel or Zionism? Why did they allow Bush and Cheney to invoke the Holocaust at every turn in the road in their "fight against terrorism," which has suddenly morphed into a "fight against fascism"? Why do Jews continue to let a Holocaust culture excuse Israeli and American imperialism that continues to turn the world against us and create real antisemitism? Before he died, Columbia University professor, author, and activist Edward Said had come to the conclusion that a two-state solution to the Palestinian/Israeli problem would never work. The only hope was for a one-state homeland to both Arabs and Jews, where an elected government could actually represent the interests of the Palestinian population.

That will probably never happen in our lifetime. Palestinian political disorganization and lack of leadership are no match for the Zionist and Israeli guiding principle, aided and abetted by the U.S. Santa Fe author and activist Kathleen Christison, in her book *Perceptions of Palestine*, quotes Said complaining about the Palestinians' "historical inability as a people to focus on a set of national goals, and single-mindedly to pursue them with methods and principles that are adequate to these goals." And no American president and no American Congress, Republican or Democrat, will ever see Palestine as anything but an impediment to Israel. When as brilliant an advocate as Said becomes filled with such despair over any hope of solving the Palestinian/Israeli conflict, it makes us cynical as well. But I mourn the loss of his constant attention and passion to the situation. Without it, we are even further removed from a solution.

A Not Very Hopeful Solution: Create a one-state homeland to both Arabs and Jews, where an Arab majority will have to find the political will to create a democratic and just society.

Saturday, August 1, 2009

Health Insurance

I was fifty-six when I first got health insurance. Two years later, I'm wondering if it was more of a burden than a benefit. Here's the story.

I have arthritis: I've had it as long as I can remember and in as many places in my body as there are joints. Before Insurance, which I will refer to as BI, I did what I could with over the counter pain relief, an occasional shot of cortisone, slings for my arms to relieve tennis elbow, and hiking poles for the downhill stretches. When I tore my meniscus hiking the Grand Canyon (I probably already had a partial tear due to weak joints caused by disintegrated cartilage) and could barely walk down the stairs, much less squat in the garden, I shopped around for the most affordable orthopedic surgeon, who gave me a discount for cash, and under a county indigent fund got the hospitable bill paid off. The surgery was arthroscopic, and I was hiking the trails again within a few weeks.

So when I actually qualified for insurance, through a new state program that covers the under-employed and self-employed who can't afford private insurance, I figured I was home free, at least with the stuff that Western doctors are supposed to be able to deal with. I finally had the ugly subcutaneous benign something or other removed from my upper arm, a colonoscopy (ugh!), and a few other check-ups that I was supposed to have before fifty.

My left thumb was already in trouble before I got the insurance, but the bone spur that developed at the base of the joint became increasingly painful. If I accidentally banged it against a wall I almost fainted. So I got a referral from my doctor at the rural public health clinic, which is the only place I'd ever gone to see a doctor (other than the guy who repaired my meniscus) and off I went to the hand specialist, Dr. Chun, in Santa Fe (it wasn't really "off I went" because it took almost two months to get an appointment). He sent me for specialized x-rays, and another month went by before I got his pronouncement: I had a deformed bone between my thumb and wrist and the treatment is called arthoplasty—as opposed to an arthroscopic—surgery to remove the bad bone and either replace it with a small piece of tendon from my arm, fuse the bones together, or implant an artificial "spacer" between the bones. I opted for the tendon, and he told me I'd have to wear a cast for a month, then go to a removable brace so I could start physical therapy, and be good as new (with maybe a little less strength than before) in three months.

I kept putting off the surgery because my life kept getting in the way (should I go back east to visit our younger son who was obviously depressed as hell his first semester at the University of Pennsylvania, should I be able to make pies for Thanksgiving and Christmas, or should I not miss cross-country ski season?). But eventually I couldn't stand the pain, and I had the surgery January 16.

It is now the end of June and these past six months have been some of the most miserable of my life. After my cast was removed Chun's office sent me to a physical therapist who specializes in hands and arms. I didn't get any better: my thumb hurt horribly and my shoulder froze. I was treated by the actual physical therapist only once; subsequently it was by her aides, and nothing helped. I figured it was time to go back to Chun with my troubles, but each time you go see him you have to wait at least at hour for a 10-minute visit, so I procrastinated. When I finally told him my tale of woe he asked me if I wanted him to cast my thumb again. I told him no, I wanted him to figure out why it was taking me so long to heal. He offered to shoot up my shoulder with more cortisone, and I told him no on that one, too.

He told me to come back in another month, which I did, still miserable. My hand has not only not healed but has triggered a chain nerve reaction in my arm, shooting pain from my hand up to a frozen shoulder and across my shoulders and even down my back. Chun sent me off for an MRI for my shoulder, where they shove you into this tube that is inches away from your face and tell you to be sure not to move because then you'll have to start all over. They give you a panic button to push (and many people do panic, you can bet on that) and then the noise begins, the whirring and pounding and whining, despite the ear plugs. I closed my eyes and didn't move, so it was over in 20 excruciating minutes. When Chun saw the MRI he said I had a small tear in my shoulder tendon and some abrasion, but that it really shouldn't be causing me this much pain, so he sent me to his partner, the shoulder guy. The shoulder guy saw me for ten minutes, max, and said the same thing: these injuries shouldn't be causing your shoulder to freeze up, which we need to unfreeze. He didn't even want to look at my hand until I insisted: "That's Dr. Chun's business." But then he looked at my hand for a few minutes, asked me some questions, and said, "I'm going to go call Dr. Chun. So he spoke with him on the phone, came back into the room and said, "I think you have Reflex Sympathetic Dystrophy."

I, of course, had no idea what Reflex Sympathetic Dystrophy was, and he didn't enlighten me, except to say that surgery seemed to have set off some nerve problems in my arm, that he wanted me to get a bone scan for diagnostic validation, and then he'd send me to the pain clinic on the floor below where they'd give me a shot in the neck. "What kind of a shot?" I asked. "A local anesthetic," he said. "You may have to get it a couple of times but that should do it." I got him to write down the name of this diagnosis before I left, and I went home.

Notice that he said "A shot in the neck." What he didn't tell me was that the treatment he was prescribing is a shot in the spine, that Reflex Sympathetic Dystrophy is one of those autoimmune classifications that doctors dump illnesses into when they can't really figure out why you're in so much pain, that there is no definitive diagnosis (not a bone scan or a blood test or anything else), and that there is no effective treatment. I learned all of this on the Internet the next morning, of course. On one of the Internet sites the words "some people can have unremitting pain and crippling and irreversible changes in spite of treatment" especially stood out.

As soon as I saw that RSD, or as it's also called, Complex Regional Pain Syndrome, has a support group, like Sjogrens (which I already have) and fibromyalgia (which my younger sister has) and that I was consigned to a life of never ending pain and debilitation (as testimonials on the web site declared) I burst into tears.

After weeks of bitching and moaning and wishing that I'd never gotten the insurance and never had the operation, I decided to get a second opinion, which meant I had to be thankful that I could afford to do so—meaning that I had the insurance (fifty per cent of bankruptcies are triggered by medical bills). And I actually found someone who is trying to heal me. He's a sweet Jewish doctor from New York, which immediately made me feel better, who had me in his office for two hours reading the medical records I'd brought with me from Chun and the shoulder guy, listening to my story, asking me questions, looking at my whole body, recognizing me as a person with a medical history who might need some holistic treatment and gentle reassurance. He said, "Let's not assume you have RSD, doctors don't know everything," and sent me back to a different physical therapist, who is loosening up my arm. He also, without any request on my part, gave me a prescription for Valium, so I could sleep, and asked me if I wanted to try a new drug that might or might not work, to help relieve the pain.

So I took the drug, which does help, I'm loosening up my frozen shoulder with a physical therapist who also told me, "Let's not go there." I'm actually managing to fall asleep without the Valium, and the pain is diminished. So while I haven't "gone there," to the land of chronic pain and suffering, I still have a ways to go to the place where everyone experiences a little pain and suffering.

Solution: A complete revamping of the health care system, where everyone is covered by government, single pay, comprehensive insurance but also assigned a health care advocate who follows your course of treatment, informs herself about diagnoses and what treatments are necessary, possible side effects of treatments, what alternative treatments are available, etc. This person should be the doctor, but that probably ain't going to happen, so let's find someone else and pay them well to do it. The system would end up saving millions of dollars in uncalled for diagnostic tests, treatments, rehabilitations, etc. And patients might feel like human beings again.

Sunday, August 9, 2009

Success

I'm standing at the kitchen sink shelling shrimp for dinner and I'm thanking my lucky stars I'm not my famous (within certain political and literary circles) friend who is "terrified" (I know this because I've just got off the phone with her) at the thought of her reading later tonight in Santa Fe, where she will not only read to an eclectic group of unknowns but to her new boyfriend as well, who is also famous and flying in from out of town for the occasion.

I'm terrified only when I anticipate the nasty letters I might receive for the essay or newspaper article I occasionally write for a weekly Santa Fe paper that explore the political battles I deal with as a community activist. When the paper devoted an issue to the question of race and culture in northern New Mexico, where I live and work, I wrote about how the environmental movement fails to address issues of social justice. While I was careful not to call any particular enviros racist, I did identify the policies they effect as such. Surprisingly, I didn't get any nasty letters for that article, but the one I called "A Question of Semantics," which poked fun at these same environmentalists who co-opt language in an attempt to validate their positions (I questioned their use of the word "radical" to describe what I see as their reactionary politic) raised a lot of hackles.

However, this is merely a by-product of my default career, if one can call it that. With my "unmarried partner" (the box I checked for the 2000 Census) Mark I write a community newspaper and organize around issues of environmental and social justice. If someone in high school had told me this would be a career, I would have laughed in her face. I was destined for academia, perhaps the law, at least "great things." That I never got there is perhaps due to the fact that my concept of "there" was destroyed by the process of "getting," which is essentially the substance of mine—or anyone's—life. The "getting" took place in the late 60s and early 70s, when I and my fellow travelers were engaged in smashing the "there"—Vietnam, the military industrial complex, the nuclear family, etc.—as fervently as the times demanded.

But that's only part of the story. My famous friend, who is "terrified" in Santa Fe, came of age alongside me, but obviously decided at some point in her life that she would dedicate it to writing books. And part of the dedication would mean being part of a national (i.e., "famous") community that was writing and speaking to the same issues as she. I don't know if people who so dedicate themselves to certain causes consciously say, to be successful in my endeavor I must be willing to promote myself, so that my voice becomes part of the larger voice that is listened to, that makes a difference.

Whether or not this is a conscious decision, the effect remains the same, be it Scott Nearing or Andy Warhol. I just finished reading a memoir by Helen Nearing of her life with Scott, who in an interesting twist of fate was first famous as an academic and political activist until he was banished from academia and became even more famous as a homesteader who repudiated academia and the public life (although he remained steadfast in his political life). Although a certain air of self-righteousness permeates this book and several of those they wrote together, it seems that Nearing genuinely believed that in order to share his private and political vision of what constitutes a good and moral life (he never would have embraced poststructuralism) he needed to lecture, write books, travel, spread the gospel, so to speak.

Warhol, on the other hand, dedicated his life to being as notorious as possible for the sake of that notoriety. Whether this was motivated by the Nietzschean "will to give expression to one's personality" or simply the drive for "utter moral worthlessness," like Colette's first husband, Willy (from *Secrets of the Flesh*, Judith Thurman's biography of Colette), doesn't really matter. He procured his fame, just as Nearing and my friend did, and they all had or have to deal with what fame brings in our society: terror, unwelcome distractions, or attempted assassination (at least for Warhol).

It's easier to stay home, both physically and mentally. In one of my feeble attempts to actually get a book published with the local university press, I remember telling the editor that I lacked the chutzpah it took to promote myself, and that if her press didn't publish me this would be the beginning and end of that particular career (and it was*, if you don't count the children's book I wrote that was published by a Santa Fe house that took 10 years to sell 2,000 copies). I've written some national magazine articles over the years that chronicled life in northern New Mexico, which people in mainstream America find fascinating, but the few attempts I've made to sell articles of import, where my voice could perhaps make a difference on critical issues of environmental justice, were dismissed as too "local" or too hard to understand by an "eastern, urban readership." Thus I learned that one has to pay dues, like my terrified friend, before one's voice is heard.

I imagine that there are millions of us out here, voices that are knowledgeable, analytic, eloquent, profound (I'm not necessarily claiming all these qualities). Just like all the painters who may have been a lost link between cubism and abstract expressionism or abstract expressionism and Andy Warhol. Or composers, like the eccentric woman who hitchhikes around Taos in her mumu and straw hat and is occasionally acknowledged for her operas that are locally performed. I once wrote a short story (which sits in my bottom drawer+) about her called the "Woman as Artist" (I turned her into a painter). In my story she sits on an old car seat on her back porch with her legs stretched out onto an adjacent chair to rest her varicose veins: "I'll never be a huge success, honey," she sighs to the narrator. "It's not in the cards. Or should I say, it's not in my blood. I can't sell myself to the highest bidder to get there, like the cold-blooded ones do. Do you have any idea how many talented people there are out there in the world—painters, musicians, composers, writers, philosophers—living in places just as obscure as this crumbling adobe in El Rancho, who will never, ever see even the modest success that I've had in this fucked up society that defines your worth by how much you sell yourself for? Then once you're sold they have to keep investing in you because so much money is at stake. Doesn't matter if you're old, stale, hackneyed and worthless—if some investment banker on the upper West side bought you for thousands of dollars to hang on his wall, by God you better double or triple by the time he's ready to sell you to an investment banker on the upper East side to hang on his wall. 'All the world's a stage and we're only the players.'"

Maybe some of this is sour grapes. I don't have the talent that I give my Taos character, and I often lack her equanimity. But I do share her devotion to her old car seat on her back porch where she can see the Sangre de Cristo Mountains across the fields of irrigated pasture that have defined this view for 300 years. We also share a love for our neighbors, whose ancestors have lived here for 300 years. And I appreciate their regard for the work I do to help maintain these pastures and lives. That it is a way of life, not a career, is what I mean by "default." My friend who is terrified and famous also experiences this way of life, but it is within a different context, with an edge that, at least for me, spoils the quietness, the safety, the sameness. I don't buy the adage that only things that terrify you are worth doing.

One day my almost grown son calls to ask me what I'm doing. When I tell him I'm working on my book about environmental justice, he says, mom, why don't you publish your stuff. Ah, hito, if you only knew. But I tell him that I'm going to get down to work and finish up my memoirs of life as a norteño activist, my second novel, and edit my book of short stories so he and his brother can read it all when I'm dead. Mom, I'm going to publish all if them, he says. Good luck, I tell him, you have my blessing. I won't be around to be terrified.

* My memoir of life as a norteño activist was published in 2015 (*Culture Clash: Environmental Politics in New Mexico Forest Communities*).
+ My book of short stories called *Stories From Life's Other Side* was published in 2016.

Sunday, September 6, 2009
Enlightenment/Progress

Sometimes, when I'm stuck in city traffic, wandering the grocery store isle dedicated to high fructose corn syrup products, or fruitlessly trying to wend my way through recorded messages on the telephone, I imagine that Henry David Thoreau, Jean Jacques Rousseau, or Simone Weil were risen from the dead and there beside me to commiserate. The shock would probably kill them again, however. Despite all their prescient warnings that have been passed down in inspired writings over the decades and centuries, even they would not believe what we have wrought.

In his famous *Discourse, The Origin of Inequality*, Rousseau asks what it is that created the difference between "men and brutes," and came to the conclusion that it is the "faculty of self-improvement," why man alone is liable to grow into a dotard and makes him "at length a tyrant both over himself and over nature." Not a great endorsement of progress, reflection, or our entire historical record. He and Voltaire are credited with bringing Enlightenment to an 18th century European world defined by tyranny, but Voltaire didn't believe, any more than Rousseau did, that there was much hope for the dotard: "Enlightened times will only enlighten a small number of honest men; the common people will always be fanatical."

Apparently the American founding fathers didn't think much better of the common people than Voltaire when they created our representative republic and established the electoral college so the common people's vote could be overruled by the aristocratic vote. They may have thought they were throwing off their European shackles during the American Revolution, but they were quick to identify themselves as the new elites of the vast American continent, ready to conquer the "savages" (Native

Americans) and the wilderness, not to mention expanding their agricultural economy on the backs of their slaves.

While the abolitionists and Transcendentalists of the 19th century sought to enlighten American society to the evils of slavery and European religion and culture, Thoreau also talks about humanity distinguishing itself from the "brute beasts" through an unsuccessful striving for "purity." I can just imagine him, more than Rousseau or Voltaire, who both led what he would probably have called "impure" lives, plunked down in the middle of a shopping mall in Los Angeles, crying out, "Simplicity, simplicity, simplicity!"

All my life choices have been based on finding that simplicity—avoiding consumer culture by living in the closest thing to its last vestige in northern New Mexico. Then I get here and I end up fighting the environmental "purists" who tell me that the indigenous folks who live up here aren't pure anymore because they want to continue to harvest trees for a living and graze their cattle on public lands that used to belong to them. The only thing pure is their environmentalism *sin gente*, which would like to consign everyone to town and consumer culture so we don't pollute the wilderness. Civilization becomes the scourge of nature.

Raymond Williams said, in his essay "Problems in Materialism and Culture," "It will be ironic if one of the last forms of the separation between abstracted man and abstracted nature is an intellectual separation between economics and ecology. It will be a sign that we are beginning to think in some necessary ways when we can conceive these becoming, as they ought to become, a single discipline."

Thoreau, these environmentalists, and even the postmodernists fall into the trap of assigning progress an a-political, historically sweeping definition that negates the need to continually pursue a just and equitable world with small, but insistent victories. As I said in my introduction, there are incremental steps, measured within the circumscribed time and place we find ourselves, that provide enough reward and compensation to help define a life worth living. You don't have to label it progress, but you do have to constantly evaluate it as a kind of enlightenment that allows an increasing number of us to flourish.

Saturday, September 19, 2009
Colorado Springs

I grew up in Colorado Springs, Colorado, a town I wouldn't recommend to anyone. Colorado Springs is the home of NORAD (North American Air Defense Command), which is located under a mountain outside of town where at the touch of a finger the missiles will fly towards whomever our current enemy is. It is also home to Peterson Field, an Air Force Base, and the Air Force Academy, where male cadets have harassed and raped female cadets with impunity. As if that weren't enough, in the early 1990s the town also became the headquarters of Focus on the Family, the reactionary Christian organization that lobbies against equal rights for everyone except themselves. James Dobson, the founder (who George Lakoff uses as his example of the "strict father figure of the family" that the Republican right has been so successful in promoting) is carried on thousands of radio stations and has published millions of books. Not surprisingly, Ted Haggard, another Colorado Springs-based evangelical minister, who was one of the loudest denigrators of equal rights for homosexuals, was not too long ago outed by a body builder in Denver who said the minister had paid him for sex.

My mother, who lived in Colorado Springs until her death in 1997, was a member of the Unitarian Church and used to threaten to shoot Will Perkins, a big-name car dealer who had been one of the organizers of the initiative to get an anti-gay amendment on the state ballot. She figured since she was already in her eighties, if they arrested her it was unlikely they'd execute her, and she was prepared to die in jail. She had joined PFLAG (Parents, Families, and Friends of Gays and Lesbians) after my younger sister revealed she was a lesbian, but being a Unitarian was probably enough impetus on its own. She was a Jew, actually, but came from an assimilated family, and my father, raised a Methodist, called himself an agnostic. So they joined the Unitarian Church when we were kids, and both my sisters and I became members of the youth group, LRY (Liberal Religious Youth) and learned all about sex and drugs and rock 'n roll there. When some members of the Jewish Conservative temple in town decided to break away and form a Reform congregation, their kids came to the Unitarian Church for Sunday school until their building was finished. So there is that element in Colorado Springs as well, but the casual observer would never be aware of it.

Most people go there as tourists, to enjoy its spectacular setting at the foot of Pikes Peak, and visit all the sites: the cog railroad to the top of the Peak, Cave of the Winds, Seven Falls, Manitou Springs, etc. When I was in high school I was a lifeguard at one of the motels in Manitou, where tourists from Kansas and Texas all stayed. The motel was owned by a husband and wife, who were probably in their late fifties at the time, and unlike other motel owners in Manitou or anywhere else, considered it their responsibility to guard their guests while swimming. But you know how it is at motels. Families go off to sightsee during the day and come in for a dip in the late afternoon, and that's about it. So I spent a lot of time sitting around an empty pool playing gin rummy with the owners' son, who was about fourteen and who cultivated a weirdness that manifest itself in black clothing and an encyclopedic knowledge of cult horror movies. I was also his designated partner for meals, at various restaurants around the neighborhood, as his parents never seemed to leave the motel. But I was compensated for being saddled with the weird kid by being allowed to have my friends come swim in the pool, getting all my girlfriends hired as maids, and essentially becoming a member of the family.

But Colorado Springs isn't what it used to be, and the motel, actually made of Spanish-style adobe, with individual rooms and suites centered around a central plaza-like area where the original owner, the kid's grandmother, hosted great barbecues and parties for guests who came every year to vacation at her establishment at the foot of Pikes Peak, was losing business to the more modern motels and hotels that were being built by the developers taking advantage of the booming economy. The coup de grace, however, was when the wife died of cancer and the husband didn't have the heart to keep going. He sold the motel to investors from Texas, and the first thing they did was tell me they wouldn't be keeping a lifeguard. They offered me a job as a maid instead. But a week into my new job I put a bedspread on sideways and they fired me.

I left Colorado Springs right after high school, although when I dropped out of college I ended up back home for a stint until I left for good for New Mexico. But I often go back to visit, of course. My mom was there, my older sister eventually came back, and my younger sister ended up living in Denver. Also, my best friend from high school, who I got hired as a maid at the motel, also came back and lived there for a long time. There are some good thrift stores, and the downtown, although rather deserted these days, is still beautiful, with its wide, tree-lined streets that run north into the neighborhood of old mansions that were once owned by those who made it rich on the gold and silver mines. Now the town sprawls to the east, subdivision after subdivision, dividing the land into tracts of ranch style or split-level houses where I guess all the evangelicals live. Or maybe I'm kidding myself. Maybe they now live in the mansions with their new-found wealth along with their new-found religion.

But I still hate the town. On one visit Mark and I went back to my high school, Roy J. Wasson, where mediocrity ruled and the sensitive suffered.

I had him take a picture of me standing on a wall in front of the school name giving it the finger. Silly, but somewhat cathartic.

Solution: You can't go home again.

Wednesday, October 14, 2009
Electoral Politics

Only two days after the presidential election of 2008 Barack Obama hired as his chief of staff Rahm Emanuel, whose father, an Israeli physician, was quoted as saying now that his son is in the White House Israel will certainly have the ear of Obama. Why shouldn't it? After all, his son is no Arab, scrubbing the floor.

It just descended from there. Obama picked an economic team comprised of the current masterminds of unfettered capitalism who are responsible for our economic meltdown (if Milton Friedman were still alive Obama probably would have assigned him some job). He picked a secretary of agriculture who favors the development of genetically modified organisms, a secretary of defense who's going to take more troops into Afghanistan, and Hilary Clinton as secretary of state, who is in favor of anything that keeps the Clinton dynasty alive.

Why do progressives fall for these figures like Obama who promise "change" and redemption. I guess because there's not much of anything else to believe in. The sixties revolution of consciousness, that promised, and to a certain degree delivered, changes in how we view and relate to issues of gender, race, and postcolonial freedoms, had no lasting political effect, really. The same political elites are the ones getting elected to state and national office, with an occasional moderate swing from right to left. They're still threatening to overturn Roe versus Wade. They're still sending young men and women (mostly minorities) all over the world to kill and be killed. They're still complicit in the capitalist system that continues to increase the disparity between rich and poor. And they're still the only vote in the United Nations defending Israel's incursions into the West Bank or the blockade of Gaza.

Our children see how our efforts failed to effect any kind of real political change, so what are they supposed to do? There are still young activists out there, like my nephew, who belong to radical anti-war or anti-capitalist organizations that protest and demonstrate and scream bloody murder. I don't know how much community organizing they're doing, but after the failure of my efforts in that capacity, I'm not surprised they don't bother. We marched by the millions against the war in Vietnam. How much did that actually undermine the U.S. role and bring about our withdrawal? I don't really know. People all over the world marched by the millions against the U.S. invasion of Iraq, and look where that got us.

So what motivated them to get out and vote in the 2008 election? Bush's abysmal record on everything, of course, but what made them think that electing Barack Obama was going to really change anything. By the time you're in a senate race, yet alone a presidential race, you're already bought and sold. There's no way around it. To be one of the elite you have to be able to raise the capital to compete in enormously expensive campaigns that get your face on the TV screen and your voice on the airwaves. You have to make promises to interest groups and you have to pay them back so they don't abandon you in the next race. Here's how J. M. Coetzee puts it in *Diary of a Bad Year*: "We do not choose our rulers by the toss of a coin—tossing coins is associated with the low-status activity of gambling—but who would dare to claim that the world would be in a worse state than it is if rulers had from the beginning of time been chosen by the method of a coin?"

In a recent issue of *The New Yorker* there was an article on Arthur Fisher Bentley, who wrote a book called *The Process of Government: A Study of Social Pressures* back in 1908 that claims all politics and governments are the result of the activities of interest groups (pluralism) that are engaged in a constant struggle for advantage. His argument gained traction after World War II because of people's fears about the "big ideas of government," i.e., Hitler and Stalin. Bentley himself was a progressive who advocated using government to curb the power of big business, but maybe he was right: reforming government, as it's actually constituted, will never be possible.

I sometimes fantasize about what would happen if someone who got elected actually decided they would never run for office again and see what they could actually accomplish without fulfilling promises to anyone except their own conscience. This may be the collective fantasy that got Obama elected. So if Nobel Laureate in economics Paul Krugman can write an open letter to Obama detailing what he thinks he should do about the failing economic situation, here's my open letter about what he should do about everything else. (Unless Obama is in favor of the violent overthrow of the government, which I doubt, he's not going to change our economic system from capitalism to socialism, but some of the points I make in my letter may make us a bit more like Sweden or even Germany, economically speaking.)

Dear President Obama,

> The first thing you have to do is bring all American troops home from Iraq and Afghanistan. Emergency negotiating sessions, involving every country with any kind of involvement with either county must begin immediately so as to deter reprisals by the warring religious factions in Iraq and the Taliban in Afghanistan.
>
> The second thing you have to do is shut down Guantanamo and provide civilian trials for all those remaining who a case can actually be made against (the Center for Constitutional Rights has

to be consulted, along with every other NGO or human rights lawyer who is working on individual cases). Then you have to replace Robert Gates with a Defense Secretary who will look into shutting down other military bases around the world based on the reduction of our military industrial complex, and who will pursue nuclear disarmament. You will get rid of the Reliable Replacement Warhead Program and begin to reduce the stockpile of nuclear weapons at all our nuclear facilities in order to comply with the Nuclear Non-Proliferation Treaty. You will order a mission change at these labs to develop a renewable energy policy that will develop cars that run on alternative fuels, that develop local renewable energy grids that rely on solar, geothermal, or biomass, and you will redirect highway funds to subsidize mass transportation, in whatever forms are best suited for city, town, or rural area. You will rewrite an economic stimulus package that includes universal health care, whether it's based on expanding what we currently have, such as using Medicare to cover all the uninsured and letting those with private health insurance keep theirs (which is probably the only way you'll get it passed) or scrapping the entire system and doing away with private insurers altogether. There's a ton of other stuff I could tell you to do, but I think I'll finish by saying you can get rid of the Forest Service and manage our vast western public lands with what Daniel Kemmis describes in his book, *This Sovereign Land*, watershed-based local coalitions of citizen democracies.

So best of luck, and when you're done, in 2012, if you last even that long, you can go back to Chicago and Michelle can go back to being a college administrator and you can write some more memoirs. Sounds like the good life to me.

Monday, October 26, 2009

Chatter

I'm sitting on the Chinatown bus in Philadelphia waiting to go to Washington D.C. after visiting my younger son at U Penn. The man in the seat behind me is on his cell phone talking to his wife/girlfriend/partner who just dropped him off and is herself driving home in their car. I know all this—which I don't want to know—because I can hear every word he says through the crack in the seats. As soon as the bus leaves Chinatown and heads south along the river, he's on the phone again, this time to someone he's meeting in D.C. They proceed to have a 30-minute conversation about how the third person they're meeting in D.C. screwed up by not getting in touch with them sooner so they could coordinate everyone's arrival better: "I'm counting on the bus to not take more than two and a half hours or I'm going to be late for the meeting. So and so should have made her reservations weeks ago so we could have arranged to come in on our flights close to the same time. I know, I know, it's too late to do anything about it now but . . . ." and on and on and on.

About half way to Baltimore (the guy is still on the phone) the bus pulls into a rest stop and we sit there for awhile until some of the passengers start wondering aloud if this is a scheduled stop or what's going on. An Asian gentleman then approaches the rear of the bus where we're sitting and explains that he's having to translate for the two people who were on the bus from New York but slept through the stop in Philadelphia where they were supposed to get off. When they woke up and realized where they were they approached the bus driver and asked him to take them back to Philadelphia. The translator says, "We're trying to decide whether to turn around and take them back to Philadelphia or continue on to Baltimore where they can catch a later bus back."

Up jumps the cell phone guy who starts in, "There is no way this bus is going to go back to Philadelphia. I'm already late as it is. These people need to take responsibility for themselves." That's right, a chorus of voices ring out. We've paid good money (the Chinatown bus costs $15, as opposed to Amtrak's $60 to $80) to get us on time to D.C. and we can't go back because two passengers missed their stop! The woman in the seat in front of me wakes up and asks what's going on. I explain the situation and she says, "I heard them come through the bus when we stopped and yell out 'Philadelphia, Philadelphia,' at least a couple of times." I answered her, "I wish I could sleep that soundly."

Several days later I'm sitting in the Philadelphia airport waiting for a flight that's two hours late, knowing I'm probably going to miss my connection home. Sitting next to me is a young woman waiting for the same flight who decides to pass the time talking to her sister, who is also sitting in an airport waiting for a flight. They are both going home for Thanksgiving. No one wants to give up their seat in the waiting room because the room is packed and you'll end up on the floor if you do. So I listen to her tell her sister every excruciating detail of her trip to the airport, what's going on in the airport, what she's got in her suitcase (five pairs of shoes for her four day stay), how her sister can possibly survive four days with only a backpack for a suitcase, etc., etc.

I actually need to talk on a phone because I have to call Mark and tell him to cancel my surgery for the next day (how crazy was I to schedule hand surgery on the day before Thanksgiving and then actually try to get home on time) and give me the phone number of our friends in Chicago who I'm probably going to have to stay with when I miss my connecting flight home. I pile all my possessions on my chair while I go find a pay phone, for which my calling card company charges me ten times what they charge from a regular phone, and hope all my stuff is still on my chair when I return.

I do end up staying the night in Chicago with our friends, who can't believe I don't have a cell phone so I can call them when I get off the train at the stop near their house, The next morning I'm back again at O'Hare waiting to catch my plane to Albuquerque. A young man in his late twenties or early thirties is pacing the floor with his cell phone, speaking loudly in what I think is an Australian accent, talking to his wife/girlfriend/partner about the fact that he is about to get on the plane and that the plan for New Year's Eve at the hot springs outside of Denver is just "awesome" and that it's going to be so powerful, the best celebration yet. Then he tells her goodbye, and as we're walking down the ramp onto the plane (he's right behind me) he's on the phone with someone else explaining that the celebration at the hot springs is going to be truly "awesome" because 30 of his closest friends have already said they're coming and can you believe how fabulous it's going to be, better than last year, truly outstanding.

Of course, there he is when we get on the plane, sitting right in front of me and he tells two more people about the hot springs gig before they make everyone turn off their cell phones. But do I finally get a reprieve from the constant chatter than has taken over every public place and ruined it with private bullshit? Not on your life. It turns out that the guy sitting next to him is a student at a seminary and that the hot springs gig that the Australian (turns out he's from New Zealand) has been raving about is some spiritual gathering that he and his "closest 30 friends" have been going to for the last few years. So naturally, their conversation turns to religion and they are off to the races. For the next hour they engage in a spirited dialogue regarding the church doctrine espoused by the seminary student and the freewheeling Christianity celebrated by the New Zealander. There's a lot of scripture quoting, scripture interpretation, discussion of the merits of various popes, discussion of dogma regarding who's going to heaven and hell, ad nauseum. While the New Zealander challenges the seminary student on a lot of his fundamentalist rap defending the church, it's within the context of the sanctity of Christianity, and I'm hoping (I don't pray) there's not a Muslim or a Jew across the isle.

Finally, after a free bloody Mary from the airline attendant, who I've consulted about airplane etiquette, I've had enough. When the seminary student starts in about homosexuality being an abomination I stand up and say, "That's it. I've listened to this crap for almost an hour but I'm not going to sit here and listen to offensive talk about homosexuality. You've offended any number of people on this plane, particularly me, and it's got to stop."

And it did. They listened to their iPods for the rest of the flight, and the guy sitting next to me bought me another bloody Mary.

Solution: Never leave home.

Thursday, November 5, 2009

Consumer Culture

Somehow the idea of intellectuals deconstructing Enlightenment values that failed to enlighten and liberate while mindlessly participating in privileged consumer culture seems absurd. And the idea becomes more than absurd when it declares that the values that determine how I try to live my life are mere constructs based on style, not substance, that there is no rationality and truth, progress is a myth, and pluralism and heterogeneity are alternatives to mainstream, normative life. Of course, all of us who came of age during the sixties revolution of consciousness were creating and living these rejections and assumptions. But the hope was not that, in the inimical words of Terry Eagleton, "A radical assault on fixed hierarchies of value [would] merge[d] effortlessly with the revolutionary leveling of all values known as the marketplace." In the rush to smash hierarchy, it seems the postmodernists forgot that it is necessary to smash capitalism as well.

The juxtaposition of two halves of page A12 in a recent *New York Times* couldn't have been a more revealing testament to just how decadent, how obscene, really, our consumer culture has become. On the left side of the page was a Bloomingdale's advertisement with an anorexic model decked out in a "dyed sheared mink double breasted coat." On the right side of the page was an article detailing the incursions of Sudanese Arab gunmen into Chad, where they were killing and wounding hundreds of civilians.

How do these mink coated people live with themselves? I know that money buys you protection from things you don't want to know or think about, but they do pick up the *New York Times* occasionally and see page A12, don't they? Even if wealth is equated with success, isn't there some line over which the excesses begin to bother them, just a little? Like "dyed sheared mink double breasted coats?"

Apparently not. Maybe this blog can't really be separated from the one on Capitalism—cultural materialism is inextricably linked to an economic analysis—but there is still some part of me that believes there must be a human, gut level connection that transcends these analyses. I know, I know, this has been wrestled with by the likes of Rousseau, Voltaire, Locke and Weil and everyone one else worth his or her salt, but there's just something about conspicuous consumption that baffles me. One clichéd answer is that once shopping and accumulating goods becomes the focus of your life, you can never have enough because then you wouldn't have anything to do. But why does one think that shopping and accumulating goods is fun? I hate shopping: clothes shopping, household goods shopping, even food shopping. I rarely end up with any piece of clothing I truly like, buying toilet paper is boring, and I race through the grocery store as fast as possible so I can get home as fast as possible.

Maybe that's my problem. I don't particularly like leaving home. Home is my life's work, essentially. It's where I surround myself with everything, or almost everything (I can't make my kids stay home forever) I value. Inside my passive solar adobe house I have access to an incredible music collection (Mark is an incomparable audiophile and our record collection is comprehensive); books I've read once, am waiting to read, and will probably read several more times before I die; a lifetime collection of art and photos on the walls, ranging from John Wenger's spaceship landings, Mark's contemporary santos (Emily Dickinson, Rene Magritte), and Alan Labb's fat-bellied men to collages of each of our children from infancy to public school; our two dogs Django and Sammy, and Mavis the cat (who also belong outside, but seem to want to stay inside as they age alongside

My El Valle house

us); and various lifelines out—telephone, satellite Internet, and satellite TV. Outside I have ten acres of pasture, orchard, vegetable garden, flower gardens, casita, river frontage, and small village life, which is both colorful, comforting, and fraught with annoyances, just like any other place one decides to call home.

Why do I need to go out other than to see some of my friends occasionally, go to a movie theater to see a first-run movie instead of waiting for it to appear on DVD (although I can barely stand the commercials and booming sound in the theater), hear some live music (there's always Youtube), or god forbid, actually have to attend a meeting to cover it for La Jicarita News, the alternative journal we publish monthly. When we first started producing the paper we were caught up in the immediacy of the battles among the Forest Service, environmentalists, and community people over access to forest resources. Those battles, at least for the communities, were largely lost, and the Forest Service barely has a budget left to mark enough trees for community firewood. The environmentalists went on to other issues like wolves and salamanders, which fortunately don't live in northern New Mexico (it was the spotted owl that started all the ruckus in the 90s when the enviros insisted it lived in our woods). While other battles still rage, over the commodification of water and the nuclear mission at Los Alamos National Laboratory, we see that our fourteen-year newspaper run may be nearing its end. We don't even want to attend the few meetings we've determined must be attended to maintain our viability.

So because I don't go anywhere, I certainly don't need to shop for clothes. If I happen to find a good deal on a shirt or pair of shoes at the thrift store, which I do like to cruise through for additions to my cow collection or a file cabinet for 30 years of collected papers, I make it a policy to give away a shirt or pair of shoes I already own. One of my favorite entertainments is to periodically go through my closets and cabinets and throw or give things away. With tremendous delight I watch files of battles I've had with the Forest Service since 1985 burn up in the wood stove. I sigh with satisfaction when I've depleted a closet enough to be able to push hangers from end to end to see what I actually still own.

I chose time over money. If through some fortuitous circumstance I ended up in a life with both, maybe I'd like to shop, too. But if the "me" in that life was still the "me" in this life, I would hope I knew where to draw the line in the sand. And a "dyed sheared mink double breasted coat" wouldn't even be in my cultural vocabulary.

Sunday, November 29, 2009
Westminster Dog Show

"Best in Show," which is one of the funniest movie spoofs ever made, really doesn't do justice to the absurdity and pathos of the Westminster Dog Show. The contrast between beautiful dogs (we'll talk about the distastefully groomed and ugly ones later) and their handlers is almost too much to take. Do you ever notice the women handlers' shoes? They sparkle. Remember those flats we wore to high school in the sixties, with our matching lime green and pink sweater and skirt outfits? Well, most of them wear flats like that but they actually sparkle. Usually they're black, but in this year's show one handler was actually wearing silver ones. Is there a dress code for women handlers that for some reason says that to run around the floor of Madison Square Garden with a dog on a leash you have to wear the ugliest shoes ever made?

Are they also required to wear these weird suits that have little flairs at the waist over tight skirts that show off their bottoms? And a lot of the bottoms are of ample proportions in the Westminster Dog Show, as well as bosoms, which when their owners run around the floor with their dogs do a lot of jiggling. To be fair, there are plenty of heavy-bottomed men handlers at the show as well, but their bulk is more discreetly hidden in your typical street suit (although one guy this year wore a tuxedo!). I didn't see one handler who looked like that cute little Parker Posey from "Best in Show."

But enough about the handlers. The huskies and terriers and St. Bernards and spaniels are all beautiful, of course: pampered, indulged, and treated like children rather than dogs, but still beautiful. Even the standard poodle, before grooming, is kind of cute. But what they do to the poor poodle—this year's Westminster finalist was black, the one in Best of Show is white—is beyond the pale. First they shave all the hair off its skinny little legs except for these puffballs at the ankles. Then they attack the poor dog's rump with the clippers until the only hair left on its body is around the ruff. Then they shave the dog's face, where any semblance of its embarrassment could be hidden, and tease it's topknot into a beehive. Finally, they produce a puffball at the end of its tail, and voilá, you have the ugliest, most humiliatingly desecrated creature one could ever create. I don't have the heart to do the research to find out who started this hideous practice, but they're all complicit, as these poor poodles seem to win more Best in Shows than just about any other breed. This year, a cute old Sussex spaniel named Tiger Woods won Best in Show. I'm not quite sure how this happened, as the woman who is the judge for the final award not only wore sparkly shoes but a sparkly dress and arrived in a limousine after being sequestered in a hotel without a TV so she couldn't see any of the previous Best in Breed winners before she picked the Best in Show. She stood imperiously on the floor in her sparkly high heels and diamonds while little old Tiger Woods ran his little old legs like spinwheels down the length of the floor, ears flapping, to the roar of the crowd. Yeah, Tiger Woods!

Sunday, December 13, 2009

Hero Worship

Ironically, my Westminster Dog Show blog, which ends with the phrase, "Yeah, Tiger Woods" (the dog), was posted just before the golfer Tiger Woods' escapades were aired in public. The following piece, also written before the airing of Woods' troubles, seems particularly appropriate to the situation.

They stripped Michael Phelps of his Wheaties gig for smoking pot. Gee whiz. He's twenty-three or twenty-four, doing what most other twenty-year olds do at some point in their lives and he gets taken off the back of a cereal box. But the question is, why is he, or Alex Rodriguez or Mark McGuire or O.J. Simpson, on the back of a cereal box in the first place? I assume being on the cereal box means that kids are supposed to look at the picture and want to be just like you, meaning they want to be born with the physical attributes and the psychological ambition and drive that allow these guys to make it to the top in their respective sports, where they are paid millions of dollars to single-mindedly pursue success in a very narrow field of interest. What is heroic about that? Is making millions of dollars heroic or simply what our society equates with success? If it's heroic, why don't they put the pictures of corporate CEOs on the back of cereal boxes. Or do you have to earn millions of dollars and play a sport to be a hero. Is it the single mindedness (or simple mindedness, as the case may be)? Then why aren't members of the U.S. House of Representatives on the back of cereal boxes. One certainly has to be single minded to disrupt your life every two years to raise the money for re-election.

Don't get me wrong. I'm not shedding any tears for Michael Phelps. He knew what was expected of him when he signed up to make millions by selling Wheaties or Nike sneakers. It's us I feel sorry for. Apparently our lives are so bereft that twenty-something swimmers (swimmers, for Christ sake) are the people we find most interesting and want to spend time with by reading People Magazine and joining fan clubs. I could understand wanting to spend a day with, or wanting to know better, Emily Dickinson or Che Guevara or Raymond Williams, but what on earth are you going to talk about with Michael other than the finer points of the breast stroke or how to get the most out of your turn?

While this kind of hero worship reveals the bankruptcy of our intellect, raising a good Samaritan to the status of hero reveals our emotional bankruptcy. Shouldn't we expect any and everyone to stop to help someone on the road who is broken down or been in an accident? Why then do you see the letter to the editor telling everyone about the "hero" who stopped to help his wife change her tire, calling it "beyond the call of duty." No, it *is* the call of duty to help your fellow man or woman. Poor "Sully" Sullivan, the pilot who set the plane down in the Hudson River last year. What a reluctant hero he was. Or rather, was his wife, who, when interviewed by every TV and radio station in the country said, "I really don't think Sully is a hero." With the skills and judgment he had honed over a long career, and with the luck of the day, he saved a bunch of peoples lives as well as his own skin. Do we elevate him to hero status because we're wrapped in our cocoons of self-concern and self-doubt and worry we would fail the test?

Thursday, December 24, 2009

Sustainability

Sustainability is a word often bandied about by environmentalists, economists, and politicians trying to establish a platform. I don't remember ever using the word myself when I decided to live in rural New Mexico for the rest of my life. Whatever we were after was more along proletarian lines, or the opposite of whatever we defined as bourgeois. There were plenty of other words to describe these goals: hippie, back to the land, alternative generation, or counter culture, but they all somehow missed the fundamental motive of wanting to discard any notion of being part of consumer culture while advocating for the overthrow of the government. How we could achieve the second goal in Placitas or El Valle, New Mexico, I don't know, but we certainly could be non-consumers when we couldn't afford more than a weekly trip to town or anywhere you could spend money. Did that mean we were living a sustainable life? Not really, but it was probably as close as we could come to being self-sufficient without being labeled Luddites and maintaining some semblance of normalcy for our kids.

We weren't prepared to live like our Hispano neighbors had only fifty years ago, when they grew all the food they consumed except for coffee and sugar. They grew all their vegetables and fruit and canned it for the winter. They raised sheep, pigs, cows, and goats and dried the meat for the winter. They grew and milled their own wheat for bread. They made most of their own clothes and musical instruments and actually spent time at each other's houses talking, singing, dancing, and being neighborly. That's the most important thing we learned in our El Valle lives: becoming buen vecinos.

I was surprised to learn recently that writer Jack London moved to a 1,400 acre ranch in northern California in 1905 where he could "leave the land the better for my having been." He wrote in his journal, "My work on this land, and my message to America, go hand in hand." He said he spent two hours a day writing, which is how he supported himself, and ten hours a day farming.

I thought if I worked on the land then I could have a message for America, that there was a better (whoops, not a poststructuralist word), more equitable way to live, if not sustainably, then at least consciously and lightly. Like building your own house, cutting firewood to heat your house, growing some of your own food, fixing, or at least maintaining, your cars, learning how to take care of yourself. If we could do everything the pioneers did, we could at least get a taste of a day in the life where everything was tended to: your body out in the garden, your mind at the computer, and hopefully your soul, the melding of the two. I try to never sit at the computer for more than a two-hour stretch (except when I had a deadline to finish the index for Malcolm Ebright's book, *Witches of Abiquiu*, after which I gave up doing indexes) or I won't have a body left to sustain a mind.

Perhaps the agenda calls for watering the vegetable garden or garlic field, which is really not that difficult as almost everything is on a drip irrigation system—I turn a few valves on and off and the plants are wet in a matter of hours. Of course, because everything is so sufficiently watered, things grow in abundance, and more and more of my time is devoted to dealing with the harvest. Some days I'm on my hands and knees thinning the carrots that have to be thinned in stages, rather than one fell swoop. Other days I'm stooped over searching for string beans hiding on dense vines only a foot high. At least the sugar snap peas grow six feet tall, although that means I'm constantly adding new string to the trellis to catch the incessant growth. Every day I search for the disgusting green tomato worms that if left un-squished would soon look like the caterpillars in Dune.

El Valle orchard and hay fields

Irrigating the pasture is not so easy. One of my neighbors calls the corner of the field to which he can never get the water "Arizona." We have a Sahara, a Gobi, and a Death Valley. No matter how many feeder ditches we dig off the main acequia, no matter how fast we get the water, or how much water we get, there are bare, brown spots that will never receive the sparkling waters of the Rio de Las Trampas. Too bad for them.

On the days when I do have to go to town, I always anticipate with great relief the final turn onto the dirt road that leads two miles to this village of twenty families. I find myself playing a game, pretending that this is the first time I have come here, that I have never before seen the lush, green valley or mountain peaks that are the setting for the village homes. I try to remember what I felt years ago when we first stumbled upon this place on one of our periodic, wistful trips to northern New Mexico when we still lived in Placitas, where we no longer wanted to live. I distinctly remember saying to myself, "You'll never be able to live here," as we made our way along the road of tin-roofed, handmade adobe houses painted lovely greens and pinks, sitting in fields of timothy grass, grazed by cows and horses, with at least one mandatory junked car on display. I thought at the time that it was probably the most beautiful landscape in New Mexico, if not the world, and I still do: the 13,000-foot peaks of the Sangre de Cristo Mountains provide the backdrop, the piñon-juniper hills rolling to sandstone cliffs the vista. Now, as I drive down the road, I never fail to marvel that I am able to live here, surrounded by all the things that are meaningful and comforting to me. I lead a privileged, if not sustainable, life.

Tuesday, January 12, 2010

Drug Company Advertising

Even though we have satellite TV, which we got for our younger son and so Mark could follow the NBA, I don't watch it much, and when I do I am continually astounded by the commercials. Instead of seeing the U.S.A. in your Chevrolet and getting your wash sparkling clean with Tide and Cheer, we can now ingest drugs for erectile dysfunction, arthritis, constipation, osteoporosis, high cholesterol, fibromyalgia, dry eyes, and depression. The commercials all end with a list of potential side effects for each drug—dizziness, weight gain, blindness and heart attack—along with the caveat, "Ask your doctor if this drug is right for you," but what do we need doctors for? The drug companies have identified the diseases, designed the drugs, and have apparently bought off the doctors who now prescribe the medicine. The patient just needs to tell the doctor, "I saw Viagra advertised on TV and I want some," and voilá, he's got an erection.

I'm old enough to remember when doctors not only diagnosed and prescribed the drugs, they actually came to your house to do so. When I was in grade school, our doctor in Colorado Springs came to the house when we were too sick to go to his office. Which usually meant we had the chicken pox, measles, mumps, or the flu. Now, of course, they have vaccines for all of these diseases, but in those days all the kids got them and were down for at least a week or two. I remember when I had one of them, and the doctor wanted to give me a shot, I ran out of the bedroom and into the closet in the kitchen that went under the stairs. This was a very deep closet, full of all kinds of things besides clothes, and required a major extraction by my parents, with a lot of kicking and screaming on my part. But the good-natured doctor waited until I quit screaming and still gave me the shot.

Even with the new vaccines there are plenty of diseases out there that need a drug—mainly all our new "lifestyle" diseases—ergo all the drug advertising on TV for all the couch potatoes watching it. Everyone over 60 seems to be on medicine to reduce their high blood pressure and cholesterol. Type II diabetes is epidemic, but weight loss medication will allow you to drop the pounds without ever trying to adhere to a healthy diet. Environmentally caused auto immune diseases like fibromyalgia are bringing once active people to their knees with chronic pain and loss of energy. Lyrica, however, will help you do all those things you used to love to do, like watering your plants and going on vacation to Bermuda. Baby boomers are dropping like flies with hip, knee, and even shoulder replacements, after years of pounding their joints by running on pavement or climbing across all those scree fields on their mountain ascents. But boniva once a month will keep those bones strong and sturdy, and ativa once a year will keep that "on the go woman" going.

After being bombarded nightly by these unfulfilled promises no wonder everyone is depressed and can't sleep. But there are plenty of drugs for that, too. No more of those hard core barbiturates, you can take ambien and lunesta, which will lull you into a gentle sleep and make you fresh and alert the next day, assuming you don't have any of the potential side effects like walking in your sleep and falling down the stairs or falling asleep while you're driving, which a former Santa Fe county commissioner did, claiming ambien made him crash into that parked car on the side of the street. If you're depressed you can take zoloft or prozac and get rid of all that anxiety and worry about whether you're going to have to spend the last of your paycheck on a tank of gas or enough groceries to get you through the week. You may even have to cancel your high-speed Internet connection, or god forbid, your satellite TV service that allowed you to find out all about prozac in the first place.

So we're all going to live to be 90 as long as we take our daily regimen of 20 or so different medications every morning and night that are probably working against each other to counteract each one's desired effect, leaving us all demented. But hey, we're not dead, and apparently that's all that matters.

Thursday, February 4, 2010

Marriage

I recently reread Shulamith Firestone's book, *The Dialectic of Sex*, and while I reject the cyber solutions she posits, her description of marriage is right on the money:

"A second cultural prop to the outmoded institution is the privatization of the marriage experience: each partner enters marriage convinced that what happened to his parents, what happened to his friends can never happen to him. Though Wrecked Marriage has become a national hobby, a universal obsession—as witnessed by the booming business of guidebooks to marriage and divorce, the women's magazine industry, an affluent class of marriage counselors and shrinks . . . still one encounters everywhere a defiant 'We're different' brand of optimism in which the one good marriage in the community is habitually cited to prove that it is possible."

I'm guilty as charged. While I'm not married, per se, I've lived with a partner for 33 years and have two children with that partner—Mark. I didn't exactly rationalize our relationship with the thought that we could do it "better," at least at the beginning. It was fraught with difficulty from day one, as I had no idea how to live with a man and he'd already spent nine years living with his first wife. Ours was more of a partnership by default (a common theme in my life). We were both living in Placitas at the time, a little village at the north end of the Sandia Mountains near Albuquerque, when our mutual friends Anne and Charlie decided to move to Arkansas where Charlie could go to Physician's Assistant school. Mark and I both claimed that they'd told each of us we could move into their cheap little house. He was living in a leaky dome up in Dome Valley and my landlady was moving back into her house and kicking me out. We were having an affair, but it was new and I certainly was not ready for a commitment beyond that. I suggested we move into Anne and Charlie's house as roommates. Mark would have none of that, so we moved in as lovers and I did a lot of crying those first couple of months, as I learned what it meant to live intimately with a man.

We started out keeping our finances separate. There was never any doubt that I wouldn't marry him. But we became a couple, partying with all the other couples and families in Placitas, some of whom had previously been members of communes but had eventually drifted into more traditional relationships. The months somehow turned into years. We were both so poor we eventually pooled our resources. And we started building a house together on the land I had bought outside the village before we were together. (I'd borrowed the down payment from my mother and made monthly payments; in those days, land was cheap.) Five years later, we had our first child. Seven years later we had our second one.

Before we had the first one there was talk of extending our family to include a female friend of ours who I had known since college. She was single, she and Mark got along well, she loved New Mexico, and we didn't want to be a nuclear family. We talked about having two mothers, but I don't think we talked about our being two wives—at least with her. I always thought it would be a good idea. But we had lots of good ideas in those days and few of them came to fruition. So I ended up in a nuclear family situation, rationalizing like all the rest, that we wouldn't make the same mistakes our parents made, that our generation was more enlightened and better able to avoid the pitfalls of marriage, particularly with regard to a woman's position in society. I don't know why we made those assumptions, as on a daily basis we had to deal with all the cultural issues that had never been resolved, particularly the woman's issue. I fought like hell to maintain a position of equality and independence, both circumstantially and psychologically. It made for a very combative relationship that ultimately elicited resentment and regret.

But for some reason we stayed together. Inertia? Money (we never made any)? The kids (our older son once told us he'd kill us if we ever broke up)? Fear of being alone (it is a travesty in this world that our two choices are living in nuclear families or living alone)? I've thought about it a lot over the years, and even discussed it once with a therapist who I went to see when the built-up resentment over the battles I'd had to fight to maintain equality was making me hateful. And I finally figured out what it comes down to is loyalty. I know that Mark, as a white male who grew up in a culture of dominance against which we all have to struggle, has made that his struggle as well, and I know that he has tried, to his best ability, to shed those shackles. I also know that despite his foibles and insecurities he has been incredibly loyal to me and continues to try to make me happy.

So here I am, more than 30 years later, rereading Shulamith Firestone (I've searched for information about what ever happened to her after the publication of *The Dialectic of Sex* and have come up with nothing). My older son has been in a series of monogamous relationships since he was in high school and is now marrying a lovely and independent woman. My younger son is still in college and to my knowledge has never had a serious relationship with anyone. Both of them at least had a less traditional upbringing than Mark and I did, were less pressured in high school to pair off and become part of a couple, and have been exposed to an array of peers and friends who function quite well outside mainstream society. But they also have the weight of the marketplace on their backs and have less opportunity to slip through the cracks that Mark and I managed to navigate because the cracks aren't there anymore. I don't know if either will ever have children, and although Mark and I would be doting grandparents, that may not be such a bad thing. But I fervently hope that they both find some way to live with other men and women who will care about them, be intimate with them, and create a family for them, not necessarily based on marriage between a man and a woman with two kids.

Solution: To recognize and encourage—socially, legally, economically—everyone's personal choices about how they want to live with other people.

Mark and Kay

Monday, March 1, 2010

The Olympics

It's Olympics time again, the Winter Games in Vancouver, where we're already experiencing the "heartbreak" of Lindsay Vonn, whose entire life has been building towards this moment when she was expected to win as many gold medals as Michael Phelps did in the Summer Games. The heartbreak being, of course, that she was injured just before the games began, that she failed to win multiple golds, and wiped out completely in several races. The list of injuries that led to this disappointment, however, is just as heartbreaking: uprooting a family, a divorce, and not speaking to her father for the last four years. But hey, if that's what it takes to produce a world-class athlete, who am I to quibble. As these games come to an end, this post is about the previous Olympics, where there was just as much hype and heartbreak.

I was turned off to competitive sports a long time ago when I was on the YMCA swim team as a preadolescent. So when the Olympics roll around every four years I usually don't bother to watch much, even—or especially—the swimming competition.

During the last summer Olympics, however, it was hard to avoid the hype about Michael Phelps and his quest for eight gold medals, more than anyone has ever won in a single Olympics game. I ended up watching him easily win several freestyle events, then swim the heart-stopping butterfly event where he was behind and won only by one-hundredth of a second, and finally swim for his eighth gold medal in the medley relay event, where he had to depend upon his three other teammates to also swim their best race. Now, at 23, he can sit back and watch the endorsements come rolling in. But what does he do with the rest of his life?

I also watched some of the gymnastic events, mostly the girls' team competition and a few of the individual events. It's much more difficult to watch a sport like gymnastics as opposed to swimming: the subjectivity of the judges and the opportunity for costly mistakes make it excruciating for me as a spectator and, I imagine, excruciating for a competitor to have to experience. Several times during the course of the competitions the TV cameraman stuck his lens in the face of some poor young woman who had just made some momentary, but irreparable, mistake that cost her a medal in her event. Her tears and anguish were on display for millions of people around the world to witness. It's just another example of the lack of privacy any public figure must relinquish, but you feel sorry for her, nonetheless. And per usual, there were complaints that the judges unfairly awarded a medal to the host country's Chinese competitor, despite the major error she committed in one of her individual events.

Of course these athletes, with their flag waving and anthem singing gestures of patriotism, complicitly agree to participate in these games that are political games as well. They interviewed Serena and Venus Williams about coming to the Olympics despite having to rush back to the States for the U.S Open, and they delivered the expected paean to patriotism: we're so happy to be representing our country and participating in one of the most exciting and important events in the world. What else could they say? We'd get accused by the media of being unpatriotic and selfish if we didn't come to play so we have to do this for our careers? We have to show the Chinese that despite their dominance of gold medals, America is still the most powerful imperialistic country in the world and intends to remain such no matter what it takes? Neither Serena nor Venus won an individual gold medal (they won in the doubles) but neither did the Chinese. Kobe Bryant of the Los Angeles Lakers was also there to do his patriotic duty by telling the interviewer that his team was a special team that appreciated the significance of representing your country, doing damage control for previous basketball teams of NBA superstars who were accused of not taking the games seriously enough, and damage control for his own reputation as an accused rapist and renegade.

Then there was Dara Torres, the 41-year old wonder who was participating in her fourth or fifth Olympics (not in consecutive order) who was out to prove that with millions of dollars in endorsements to pay for the state of the art training and attention it took to get her body into shape to beat 20-somethings in the 50 meter freestyle, anyone could be in the Olympics at 41. They showed pictures of trainers walking on her muscles for massage, while others hovered over her weight-lifting routines, and still others directed her Pilates, yoga, and meditation sessions. All for her eleven seconds of fame, where she came in second. She was very gracious and smiled her toothy grin, but you can bet she was devastated.

So back to what you do with your life after the gold or silver. Mark Spitz became a dentist, of all things (see the blog piece Dental Insurance, Or the Lack Thereof). Michael Phelps gets caught smoking a hookah on camera. Some of the ice skaters join the Ice Capades, a few become sports commentators, but most of them join the rest of us in obscurity, where we have to generate our own sense of self worth without the aid of the TV camera. I finally threw out all my swimming medals from when I was a kid when my own children were still kids. Max was appalled, and made me give him several golds to put in his pile of accumulated junk. Now his chess trophies line the top of the dresser in his former room, and when he comes home for xmas/hannukah this year we're going to make him put them away somewhere so we have more room for our accumulated junk.

A postscript about the Winter Olympics. Because NBC overbid for the rights to broadcast the games and had to make as much money as possible, the frequency of commercials ruined my already lackluster attempts at watching even the interesting sports, like figure skating. After two hours of commercial bombardment during prime time at night, like most baby boomers I was already nodding out by nine, when they showed the skaters in contention for the medals, and asleep by ten (only for a couple of hours, though, as that's all I get at one stretch these days; if they aired the show at midnight, I might have seen a few triple axels or double salchows, whatever they are). Ah well, it's finally over, the Canadian hockey team beating the Americans. Amen.

Tuesday, March 9, 2010

Dental Insurance, Or the Lack Thereof

Seems like the medical industry would be quite happy for us to revert back to the days when George Washington had wooden teeth and Michael Bakunin didn't have any. He probably ended up having some kind of teeth—I don't know what kind—after he lost them from scurvy in the infamous Peter and Paul fortress in St. Petersburg, as he went on to marry a young woman when exiled to Siberia and enjoy a long career as an anarchist after his return to Europe. Hardly anyone's health insurance policy covers dental, so when you go into the dentist's office for a simple filling: $300. Need a root canal, which probably won't work anyway and you'll end up losing the tooth: $1,500. A tooth implant or bridge? I don't even know because you lost me back at the $1,500 for the root canal. I just have them pulled and leave a space. So far, those spaces have been at the back of my mouth, but I'm sure the day will come when it's one of my front teeth and I will be consigned to being either a toothless old hag or bankrupt.

When Mark had an appointment with his urologist, who, by the way, is a very nice man and a very competent doctor, I started wondering why anyone would want to be a urologist. Or a proctologist. Or even a gynecologist who gets to deliver babies as a bonus. But I know why someone wants to be a dentist: money! I recently had fillings put across the top of my three bottom teeth, worn down by wear and tear. No Novocain was administered, I was in the dental chair for half an hour tops, and bingo, I owned $575. A few customers like that every day, even with the office overhead, and you're taking home a big bundle.

I suppose some of this dentist vitriol also comes from the fact that they hurt you—almost all the time. During one of those great root canal experiences where I ended up losing the tooth anyway, the dentist injected Novocain into a nerve that went all the way up into my cheek and had the entire side of my face tingling for months. Or they're drilling away and suddenly hit a nerve that wasn't deadened by the Novocain and you're Dustin Hoffman being tortured by Lawrence Olivier. And every time they put those rubber blockers into my mouth to isolate teeth for x-rays my gag reflex makes me spit the thing out of my mouth and then they make me do it all over again.

I have to pause here, however, to exclude a very special dentist from this rant. Michael worked for the local clinic right out of dental school and my whole family used him and liked him enormously. Then he moved on somewhere and I lost track. But I found him again, in a small practice where he does his own billing as well as take care of people. He works to save my teeth, we talk politics, and he almost never hurts me. (I apologize to other nice, competent dentists as well.)

Why isn't dental care covered by insurance? Do they figure the rich people are just going to pay for it no matter how much it costs out of vanity, and the poor people will, after enormous pain and suffering, go to Juarez for a set of false teeth they can afford? In a time when the advertising industry has everyone convinced that the path to success requires a set of big teeth—remember those big white smiles of Hillary Clinton and Barach Obama plastered across our TV screens for months—we've come up with an entire category of haves and have-nots: the ones who can afford to buy the veneers and the rest of us with the crooked, slightly yellow teeth of character. Before advertising I never particularly noticed teeth. Now I see that all my friends are in the same character category as me, and it's comforting, really. Except that none of us want to be hags.

Sunday, April 4, 2010

Global Domination

The day after I posted my Electoral Politics blog the local newspaper ran a column by conservative pundit Rich Lowry, in which he tells Barack Obama he should be "insulted" by getting the Nobel Peace Prize because it means he agrees with the Nobel Committee that America needs to be put in its place as a member of the world team, not its dominating leader: "The apologies for his country, the embrace of the U.N., the ridiculous talk of global disarmament, the distance from Israel and kid gloves for Iran, the slaps at American hegemony—are all the stuff of shame-faced American weakness and retrenchment, uttered by the most powerful American on the planet." Another conservative, this time the chairman of the Republican National Committee, said that his nomination was proof that "the Democrats and their international leftist allies want America made subservient to the agenda of global redistribution and control."

Obama wants this? Never. The international and domestic leftists? Yes and yes! It's hard not to read these guys with a certain amount of incredulity—do they actually believe this stuff they write—until you remember that they rule the world. George II liked to talk about invading Iraq to spread Democracy, with a capital D, to the rest of the impoverished world. Even if pundits actually use words like "hegemony," they still cop to Bush's excuse for this global domination: that because we're a so-called democracy and our standard of living is the highest in the world, it's our moral obligation to spread this largess and allow capitalism to bring everyone into the twenty-first century.

Hannah Arendt, in *Imperialism*, explains perfectly the real reason for our push for global domination:

"Since power is essentially only a means to an end a community based solely on power must decay in the calm of order and stability; its complete security reveals that it is built on sand. Only by acquiring more power can it guarantee the status quo; only by constantly extending its authority and only through process of power accumulation can it remain stable. Hobbes's Commonwealth is a vacillating structure and must always provide itself with new props from outside; otherwise it would collapse overnight into the aimless, senseless chaos of the private interests from which it sprang. . . . [The] ever-present possibility of war guarantees the Commonwealth a prospect of permanence because it makes it possible for the state to increase its power at the expense of other states."

Globalization is changing the face of imperialism but not its basic function, the spread of capitalist accumulation. In his book *The New Imperialism* David Harvey talks about how imperialism has changed from nationalistic control over foreign territory (Britain in India, France in Algeria, etc.) to an economic imperialism based on production and finance (oil and Wall Street). The success of the U.S. in this new age of imperialism is what Lowry and his ilk are defending, of course. As Harvey explains it, "From the late nineteenth century onwards, the US gradually learned to mask the explicitness of territorial gains and occupations under the mask of a spaceless universalization of its own values, buried within a rhetoric that was ultimately to culminate . . . in what came to be known as 'globalization.'" Therefore, Wall Street/Treasury/IMF, all one thing, can do no wrong in opening up capital globalization, by whatever means necessary, because it is simply spreading our democratic values and standard of living to all those poor countries who resources would just be sitting there without benefit to anyone without our intervention.

What the U.S. failed to anticipate is that if financialization is the key to accumulating more power, as Arendt talks about, and if our internal and external deficits, largely held in Asia, continue to skyrocket, then we may just find our hegemony "slapped upside the head" by China. To come back to Lowry's complaint, it makes perfect sense for us to invade Iraq and Afghanistan, to threaten to invade Iran, to refuse to reduce our nuclear arsenal, and to arm Israel to the teeth when that may be all we've got left: our military prowess, our "exploitative domination," as Harvey calls it. So in our fight to the finish with China to maintain global domination we'll just keep sending those soldiers to protect the world from "terrorism" and bring those infidels into the twenty-first century. It's reminiscent of Marie Antoinette: let our schools continue to fail our students, let our transportation systems crumble, let the global corporations drill for oil on all those offshore shelves, and let the insurance companies make a profit from our ill health. In other words, let civil society be damned as long as those in power can continue to acquire more power.

Solution: Off with their heads!

Friday, April 16, 2010

Self Image

I am completely schizophrenic when it comes to my self image. I hate having my picture taken because I hate the way I look: long nose, thin mouth, chicken neck and all. Sometimes I catch myself thinking that if I were just a little better looking I wouldn't have to worry so much about it and could focus on being a better person (just like Madonna and Angelina Jolie—not!).

Yet at the same time I find myself outraged that anyone would dare judge me on my looks and I plow ahead through the forcefulness of my personality to do what I want, say what I want, and expect results. I rarely let anyone get away with anything against what I think I can achieve. If, as society has conditioned us to think, our physical appearance matters as much or more than our character, where does this chutzpa come from? I recently came across this passage in a Joanna Trollope book: "I do not long for beauty, she told herself resolutely in the glass in the hall coat stand, but I do require some significance. I am not in any way ready or prepared to be rubbed out. I do not agree—or submit—to being invisible merely because my outward self, lacking the required drama for contemporary life, gives no indication of what is going on inside."

My mother always thought I was wonderful and could do no wrong, but my father, who was emotionally crippled, belittled me (and my mother and my two sisters) about my appearance and behavior but bragged about my supposed IQ. He insisted that somehow he'd gotten the results of the IQ tests they'd administered to my sisters and me at school and that they were grand. I knew I wasn't particularly brainy, just that I had to do well in school to get my ticket out of Colorado Springs into some less provincial world where I'd be a "professional," whatever that meant. In the meantime, I had to deal with a plain face sometimes broken out with acne that would never land me a spot on the cheerleading squad or a position in school government. Of course, I was always disdainful of these social networks and longed to be one of the jet setters, which is what we called the kids who were just beginning to become the potheads and daytrippers of the late sixties and early seventies whom I would join in college.

Was this disdain sour grapes or was I somehow able, from a very young age, to see through the crap and know what to value? My parents helped me along this path by joining the Unitarian Church (she'd been raised an assimilated Jew, he a Methodist, and neither were believers) where LRY (liberal religious youth) turned me on to sex and drugs and rock 'n roll. And I didn't have to wait too long after high school to see what happened to the cheerleaders and student council members who got married young, divorced young, and stayed, as the Dixie Chicks sing, "in the same zip codes where their parents live."

Of course, not many better things happened to many of the pot smoking, LSD dropping jet setters I emulated. Some over dosed, some ended up in dead end jobs, and some eventually found God. I ended up dropping out of college, never even getting a bachelor's degree, and never becoming a "professional."

So what did I become and how did I become so full of it? I became not so much something but an amalgam of some things: a house builder, a gardener, a writer, a partner, a mother, a community activist, a publisher, an acequia commissioner, and a buen vecino in a tiny little village in northern New Mexico. In other words, I learned how to get along with lots of kinds of people, how to sustain relationships, and how to fend for myself. It was an attempt to be whole in the postmodern world increasingly fragmented by specialized work and paying someone else to take care of your necessities. Becoming whole builds assurance, and so I acquired mine—or at least enough to weather being relatively poor and anonymous except within a small circle of folks I care about. I'm never going to publish a best selling novel and I'm never going to get a humanitarian award for devoting my life to a cause. But I figured out a way to live with the choices I made, which in and of themselves define my character: kind of schizophrenic, but defiantly so.

Friday, April 23, 2010

White Men in Suits

I sat in a room all day yesterday with white men in suits, and I'll tell you, I can't take it anymore. On my way home in the car I rolled down the windows, turned Aretha on full blast, and stopped for an Oreo ice cream bar to cleanse my soul and restore my sanity, or what's left of it.

My poor compañera, the director of the anti-nuclear community group on whose board I sit, had to be in the same room with these white men in suits for two weeks straight while they bickered over the hazardous waste permit the state will be issuing to Los Alamos National Laboratory. How has it come to this, that these white men in suits can tell us it's OK to burn chemical waste in the open air to rain down into our soil and water? How can they deny their fiduciary responsibility to clean up the mess they've made making bombs? How can they insist that their monitoring wells that have numerous structural problems can adequately tell if our aquifers are being contaminated?

Of course, I've also sat in many rooms with white guys in green uniforms telling me it's OK to use herbicides on noxious weeds in the forest, that acequias need to get special permission from them—our friend the Forest Service—to work on our headgates or diversion dams even though the acequias predate them, and that ski area expansions are good because they provide jobs.

These white guys in suits and green uniforms are the professionals. Just because they've built enough bombs over the past 55 years to blow up the world a thousand times over and clearcut enough forests and suppressed so many forest fires that we now live in a tinder box waiting for catastrophic fire to burn us to smithereens doesn't mean we have the right to question their authority or judgment. I can see it in the paternalistic roll of their eyes when we (brown people, women, white men in jeans) sit across the table from them, meaning, oh Christ, here we go again, what a waste of time. They're thinking, these people just don't get it, they don't live in the real world, while we're thinking, these guys have created a world no one in their right mind would want to live in.

It's a perpetual impasse, of course. It's nothing new. It's just the consequences are now so enormous and we all know they're so enormous that apparently it renders us helpless. That's not really a fair analysis, but that's how it seems sometimes. Is our postmodern world so fragmented, so transient, ambiguous, and fetishized that we can't figure out how to take unified action because we can't figure out who the enemy is? Capitalism? Consumerism? Neoconservatives? Religious right? (Unrepentant Marxist that I am I think it's all about capitalism.) Arundhati Roy talks about this dilemma often in her activism—"To contemplate its girth and circumference, to attempt to define it, to try and fight it all at once, is impossible"—but hopes that we can all take on our individual, localized battles that remain connected to each other despite the power elite's attempt to identify our common ground as the market place.

Occasionally there are signs of hope. Everyone is down in Bolivia right now at the World People's Conference on Climate Change and the Rights of Mother Earth, where President Evo Morales, who never wears a suit, said to the crowd, "Death to Capitalism!" Of course, some of his own people are concurrently demonstrating in the streets of San Cristóbal against the continued mining of silver by a Japanese corporation, the capitalist signifier of Bolivia's colonial history. He has a tough row to hoe, figuring out how to nationalize foreign industries to benefit Bolivians while at the same time function in a global economy where capital accumulation continues to define how business is done. But apparently Bolivians have figured out who the enemy is and aren't afraid to remind their fearless leader when they think he has forgotten. So keep wearing those brightly colored woven shirts and wool sweaters, Señor Morales, to keep our hopes close to your heart.

Thursday, May 27, 2010
Marginalization

I've acknowledged before that living in El Valle involves both privilege and deprivation. The privilege is the fact that we're not dependent on wage labor, i.e., a nine to five job in a designated location, and can therefore live where we want, in a relatively isolated community that is beautiful, friendly, and restorative. The deprivation comes from living on a very limited income, where we don't enjoy the luxuries most middle class folks take for granted—that is, until the economy tanked again and lots of middle class folks have lost their jobs, their new cars (I've never owned a new car), and even their houses. So while I wouldn't wish any of this on anyone, except the bankers, Wall Street traders, and complicit politicians who brought us to this point (that comes to a lot of exceptions), the trade off has definitely paid off.

But as the years go by, the privileged part of getting to live someplace out of the way is being assaulted by a world that, in its march toward collective consumerism (cities) and globalization (see Global Domination blog), apparently would like nothing better than to marginalize us out of existence. As the "home becomes a private museum to guard against the ravages of time—space compression" (David Harvey), it seems we spend way too much time on the phone trying to tell a computer that there really is a little village in northern New Mexico where you can send a package to our mailbox or door. We have this rural mailing address that says Box 6 El Valle Route, Chamisal (where the post office is located), New Mexico. This address gets rejected by computers that recognize only addresses that have numbers and streets or P.O. Box numbers. So we tell the computer —or very rarely, a person—that it's OK, just let the computer change our address to P.O. Box 6, because as long as the name of the town, Chamisal, is in the address, the postmistress, who knows who everybody is, will make sure it gets delivered by the highway contract mailman to that green mailbox number 6 sitting at the head of our driveway.

Even she can't compensate for some confusion, however. We were once given a subscription to the Sunday *New York Times* by a friend. After finally verifying that we did indeed exist, we got our first issue on the Monday after the Sunday it came out. We were ecstatic. The next Monday, there it was again in the mailbox. The next Monday there was no paper, and it didn't come Tuesday, Wednesday, Thursday, Friday, or Saturday, either. But there it was on Monday morning, along with the new issue that actually came the day it was supposed to. From then on, Mondays we either had no paper, or two papers, but I guess the Book Review and Arts and Entertainment section are never really dated for us, as we have to wait for new books to get to the library anyway (and take our turn on the request list, usually about thirty spots down) and we don't often get to New York to go to the jazz clubs (I think the last time was around 1995).

United Parcel Service is another story. The main artery for northern New Mexico deliveries is in Santa Fe. There used to be a branch center in Española, the town of any size closest to us, and the man who made the deliveries to all of our little villages picked up his truck there. He, like the postmistress, knew everyone on his route. It didn't matter how mangled the address was, even as UPS tightened up its requirements on rural addressing, if the name was on the package Wilfredo got it to the right house. Alas, Wilfredo eventually retired. I think it took us a year to figure out what the current UPS regulations required for shipping, but once we got it right it didn't mean we got our packages on the stipulated delivery day. The package may get sent out from Santa Fe, but if there's no other delivery in El Valle that day, the driver doesn't want to drop by. If it's been raining or snowing, which is usually the case nine months out of the year, and our well maintained dirt road is wet, the driver may decide not to stop by. If we finally get the phone number of UPS in Santa Fe (they only list a central 800 number in the phone book, where you end up talking to someone in India) and tell them to just keep the package there until we come in to get it, they send it out anyway and the driver doesn't deliver it because we're not home, we're in Santa Fe getting the package that isn't there.

But I have no right to complain, really, because if I have these expectations that means I should move to town where the rest of the folks in the industrialized world conduct business, buy things, and communicate with people around the world without worry or complaint. Except for when the U.S. Postal Service deconstructs, which it did a couple of years ago, and everyone in Santa Fe started getting everyone else's mail, getting mail two months after it was sent, or not getting any mail at all, and went ballistic. The New Mexico congressional delegation had to intervene to demand better service for its constituents. While all this wasn't as bad as the current meltdown of the entire financial system, it's another reason I think I'll just stay here.

Sunday, June 6, 2010

Obfuscation

I sat down to read the local paper today and it hit me hard in the head how every story—from the health care bill to Afghanistan to the Mexican drug cartels—was only that, a story made up to obfuscate the issues that lie not so deeply buried beneath the rhetoric and lies. These issues cannot be talked about in public (language is institutionalized) because the house of cards that has been carefully crafted to keep the powers that be in power would crumble like salted crackers into the deep wounds they have inflicted upon our society. Maybe then things would change.

Let's take a look at today's stories, one by one: 1) health care "reform"; 2) Hillary Clinton's meeting with Felipe Calderon on stemming the flow of drugs from Mexico to the U.S.; 3) sex abuse in the Catholic church; and 4) the war in Afghanistan.

Health Care Reform

There can be no equitable health care reform until it is taken out of the hands of for profit insurance companies. During the long and excruciating "debate" on fixing the health care mess in this country a few people talked about health care as a "right," not a privilege, like education, police and fire protection, and social security. Well duh, who pays for those rights. Society does, that's who, through taxation for teachers, cops, firemen, and so the elderly don't starve—just barely. In Canada, where they have nationalized health care, the cost is 10 percent of the gross domestic product. In the United States, where insurance companies cover only those who they think are healthy enough to not rack up too many hospital bills—by denying coverage for preexisting conditions—we pay 16 to 18 percent of GDP towards health care. That's for all those folks who don't have insurance and end up in public financed emergency rooms and hospitals, all the enormous bureaucracy that goes along with all the complicated billing, denials, referrals, and appeals that should be covered by a single payer, we the people. That's what a society is and does: it levels the playing field by helping those who need it and by regulating those who don't.

War on Drugs

The war on drugs was lost before it ever began. As long as drugs are illegal there will be an underground market that will stop at nothing to keep the flow of money across *la frontera de los Estados Unidos y Mexico*. Yes, while the drugs flow north, the dinero flows both ways: to Mexican drug lords and their hordes of couriers and into the country's economy (the second largest money maker next to oil); and to the U.S. border guards, DEA agents, prisons, and Homeland Security. The illegal drug industry is big business over here, too. When NAFTA was implemented during Bill Clinton's reign, making the price of tortillas sky rocket as Mexico had to import subsidized corn the U.S. was selling, destroying the local agricultural economy, how was anyone in Mexico supposed to make a living other than selling drugs or leaving for the U.S.? Hillary recently admitted that the U.S. does bear some of the responsibility for the violent deaths of thousands of Mexicans caught in the drug war crossfire because of U.S. drug consumption. When she puts up a sign in her office that says, "It's the Mexican economy, stupid," we may actually get somewhere.

Pedophile Priests

I can't really talk about this one without devolving into a diatribe about the evils of organized religion (see Invoking God blog), but in an attempt to be more specific and to the point I will state the obvious: the Catholic church could go a long way towards reducing priestly pedophilia by allowing priests to marry, by recognizing women priests, and forcing priests to be prosecuted for child molestation in civil courts. Let the priests marry and at least have a chance at gratifying their libidos, even if marriage itself isn't going to entirely solve the problem of sex and/or relationships (see Marriage blog). And, of course, marrying a woman isn't going to do much for the priests who prefer men (can you imagine the day the Church ever let men marry men??!!), but maybe the latent pedophiles who currently fill the priestly ranks wouldn't be so attracted to the profession. Maybe they would be less inclined to preach their homophobia from the pulpit as a distraction from their deceit. It's hard for me to understand why so many women want to become priests, and why they think they can deconstruct church hierarchy without abandoning the church altogether. If it's faith and observance they're after, why can't they do it outside the confines of a church that has abused and ignored them since it's inception? But you have to admire their persistence and their desire to bring down the priests who have done so much harm to so many.

The War in Afghanistan

I thought we'd already won the war in Afghanistan. Isn't that what the neocons told us when they said it was time to invade Iraq? The Taliban were on the run, the Afghanis had elected a great guy who would do the U.S. bidding, and the women there could walk around town without covering their heads. Of course, a few of us on the left were not in favor of that first war in Afghanistan, either, including Susan Sontag who caught all kinds of shit in the pages of the *New Yorker*, and Professor Ward Churchill, who lost his job, for daring to point out that maybe we should first look at the political and economic reasons for jihad against the U.S. before we started bombing Afghanistan back into the stone age. Of course, western society thinks Afghanistan never left the stone age. So now, after more than seven years of occupation in Iraq Obama decides its time to send "our good men and women" back into Afghanistan, in greater number, because surprise, the Taliban is back (seemingly the only ones capable of providing goods and services to the poor villages in the hinterland), President Karzai is more corrupt than ever and an anathema to his people, and women are still abused and repressed and kept out of mainstream society. I guess because we're a postmodern society we can't factor Afghanistan's long and unfortunate history into any decision making process where it's recognized that imperialist countries are never going to "save" or "liberate" it. But that's not really the goal, is it. This poor, volatile, and oppressed country is necessary to our geopolitical goals in the Middle East (see Globalism blog) and that trumps everything.

So the obfuscation keeps getting written and the wars on drugs and people keep being waged.

Solution? Just what I quoted Rick Lowry saying in my Global Dominance post: " . . . the embrace of the U.N., the ridiculous talk of global disarmament, the distance from Israel, the slaps at American hegemony." Thanks, Rick, for putting it so nicely

Thursday, August 5, 2010

Funky Soul

If you don't start dancing or break down in tears when you hear Jimmy Ruffin sing "What Becomes of the Broken Hearted" or Ben E. King doing "Stand By Me" (there's also a breathtaking video on Youtube of street musicians all over the world singing it) then you ain't got any funky soul.

I know, this is ageism speaking. Who under 50 (or 60 maybe) knows who Jimmy Ruffin is (remember, this is a white girl speaking, who can never speak for the black community, who I'm sure know Jimmy Ruffin and Eddie Kendrick like they know their abc's)? Their loss, I would say. They would say, in the person of my 29-year old son, what about Rage Against the Machine or Orishas? I happen to love Orishas—a great hip hop band from Cuba—but the rhythm and blues we grew up with came from a different place and time and evokes a different response.

When I was in fifth and sixth grade I watched American Bandstand on TV every day after school. My mother was at work, and this was my time to see the whole weird mix of acts Dick Clark brought to the stage: Stevie Wonder, Lovin' Spoonful, Rascals, Shirelles, Bobby Rydell, Beach Boys, and Marvin Gaye. When the show was broadcast from Philadelphia, the teenagers who came to dance were all Italian kids with names like Carmen, Dominick, Michael, and Loretta. I could tell by who was dancing with whom whether they were still going steady, whether they had just broken up, and whether there was any hope that they would get back together.

When I was a teenager, the music I listened to, locked in my room doing homework or lying on my bed daydreaming, came from the KOMA airwaves all the way from Oklahoma City (I was in Colorado Springs, remember). For some reason K-O-M-A had this powerful frequency that broadcast Motown, Philly soul, Memphis soul, the British invasion, and bubblegum pop all over the Rocky Mountain West to the bedrooms of fourteen- and fifteen-year olds like me, dependent on the radio to know what was going on musically. I was just starting to buy 45s, but albums were still too expensive for my measly weekly allowance. When I got my first job at sixteen—lifeguard at a motel swimming pool in Manitou Springs at $1.10 an hour—I still couldn't afford many LPs.

But I did get to see a lot of groups at the Colorado Springs City Auditorium, like the Rascals (called the Young Rascals back then), the Beau Brummels (remember "Laugh Laugh"?), Spanky and Our Gang, and even Eric Burden and the Animals. I never wondered at the time how come these groups came to little old Colorado Springs, Colorado, for some unheard of cheap ticket price, but in retrospect I assume they played the big venues in Denver and drove the sixty miles down to the Springs for a little extra cash before flying out to Phoenix or Salt Lake City.

I was fourteen when the Beatles came to New York and played on the Ed Sullivan Show. The radio had been playing "I Wanna Hold Your Hand" and "She Loves You" but I was unprepared for the thrill I felt when I saw them bouncing their heads and tapping their feet to the screams of the fourteen-year olds who were actually in the TV audience. Their musical debt to rhythm and blues was evident in this visceral response. My father always ate dinner on Sunday night on a TV tray in front of Ed Sullivan, but this time we were all there: my mother, my two sisters, and me. And when he said, "They'll never last," I knew he was utterly, and irrevocably, wrong because anyone who could touch my soul the way they did, the way Marvin Gaye did singing "Sexual Healing," the way the Shirelles did singing "Will You Still Love Me Tomorrow," Curtis Mayfield and the Impressions singing "You Must Believe Me," Aretha Franklin singing "Prove It," and

Jimmy Ruffin singing "What Becomes of the Broken Hearted," would last forever in the heart and mind of a fourteen-year old going on 60.

Saturday, August 28, 2010

My Summer Job

I was listening to NPR the other day and there were these people describing what their summer jobs, oh so many years ago, meant to them in terms of life lessons. It seems that NPR is running a series on summer jobs and soliciting stories from all of us nobodies out in radioland. But rather than go through that process—I already know what it takes to get on NPR's Click and Clack show, which my son did with his story about the time we were driving down from Mount Lassen and he decided to toot his horn at the slowpoke ahead of us . . . but that's another story—I'm going to post my story here, where I don't have to audition. (I've already touched on this job in the Colorado Springs blog.)

I learned to swim at the local YMCA and by the time I was 16 had my Red Cross Life Saving and Water Safety Instructor credentials under my belt. So now that I could also be legally employed, there was no question that I would try for life guarding at a pool; no bussing, waitressing, or housecleaning for me. I don't remember how I got the job, but it was a lifeguard's dream: a motel swimming pool in Manitou, the resort community "nestled at the foot of Pikes Peak," where hardly anyone ever swam. The motel was owned by an older couple, who I'll call Harvey and Helen Oakley, probably the only motel owners in town who provided a lifeguard for their guests. The motel had been in the family for a couple of generations, and apparently Harvey's mother had run it in grand style, with evening barbecues and weekend square dances for the Midwest clientele that came back every year to enjoy the Rocky Mountains. After Harvey and Helen inherited the place, though, tourists seemed to prefer the newer motels with hot tub jacuzzis, and their old fashioned lodge, with no attendant restaurant or fancy features, was losing business.

But this meant nothing to me, at least at first, because all I had to do was show up in my bathing suit and sit out in the sun waiting for the occasional guest to take a dip. Helen never emerged from inside the motel where she smoked Camels and kept the books, but Harvey would come out periodically to check on me, apologize that there wasn't much for me to do, I must be bored, and bring me sandwiches from the restaurant across the street.

Then Edward showed up. Edward was Harvey and Helen's 14-year old son and was truly weird. He had pale, peaches and cream skin and jet-black hair that fell across his forehead and over his ears. He dressed only in black: black pants, black turtleneck, black fedora. I learned later that several of his bedroom walls were also painted black, while the remaining ones were covered with posters of Bela Lugosi and Lon Chaney. At first Edward wouldn't talk to me, he'd just come out and walk around the pool and look at me and act really annoyed if one of my friends was there hanging around with me. That was another perk that Harvey provided; permission to have my friends come swimming while I was on duty. I was just getting involved with one of the jet setters, what we called the older boys in high school who were the first to smoke dope and drop acid, and I was beside myself with nervousness when he began to show up at the pool to smoke cigarettes with me and laze around in the water. One day while he was there Edward showed up and jumped into the pool with all his clothes on; Harvey had to come out and apologize for his behavior, finally convincing him to get out of the water with the promise of a new guitar.

I was a kind person, even back then at the mixed-up age of 16, and I quickly befriended Edward, as I knew he desperately needed one. He used to show up at noon, after staying up late playing guitar or watching old horror movies, and Harvey would come out, lock up the pool, and send us across the street for lunch, which he paid for. Then Edward and I would play gin rummy all afternoon around the pool, waiting for guests. I finally persuaded Edward to swim without his clothes on (with trunks and a T-shirt) and I helped him practice his strokes. He'd still get pissed off when my boyfriend showed up on his way to work—he watered one of the local golf courses in the evening after everyone had left and would often take me for rides on the golf carts racing through the sprinklers—but resigned himself to going inside and bothering his parents until the boyfriend left. Then, unless I had to be home early or was going on a date, Edward and I would head back across the street to dinner.

This scenario played itself out over the course of two summers. For the second summer I got Harvey to hire all my girlfriends as maids. But also during that second summer Helen became ill and died of lung cancer. Everything quickly fell to pieces. After the funeral, Harvey took the night shift so he could drink without anyone knowing. Edward spent more and more time locked in his room with his stereo blaring, adrift at a tender age when he especially needed loving, involved parents. At the end of the summer Harvey sold the motel to a couple from Texas, who promptly fired me, having no intention of providing a lifeguard. They kept me on only long enough to teach them how to backwash the filter system, which I did every morning before opening the pool. Then, in a moment of contrition, they hired me as a maid. That lasted about a week, until one day I apparently put a bedspread on sideways, and between the time I left for the afternoon and drove home they called my mother and told her I was again fired. When she told me, I immediately got back in the car, drove back to the motel, and told the Texans that if they were going to fire me they better do it to my face, which they did.

So did I learn a life lesson from this? As I said in my blog post called Self Image, maybe this experience helped me learn to "do what I want, say what I want, and expect results." While I didn't get the result of getting my job back (who wanted to be a maid anyway), I did get the satisfaction of telling someone what's what, and knowing how to do that, my friends, is indeed worth learning.

Sunday, October 3, 2010
Baby Boom Regret

What follows is based on anecdotal, not empirical, evidence, at least the part about my baby boom cohort. But by the time I'm done you may want to eschew empiricism with the same abandonment we eschewed feudalism, monarchy, republicanism, and social democracy (at least those of us who think *The Nation* is wimpy).

My partner Mark is 62 and has pancreatic cancer. Our friend Richard is in his early sixties and had surgery for prostate cancer. Our friend Alan, who is in his fifties, lost a kidney to cancer. Gilbert, our neighbor, who in his sixties and a former Los Alamos National Laboratory subcontractor, also had kidney cancer. My friend Emma's sister, who is fifty, has colon cancer. I am 60 and have an autoimmune condition called CREST syndrome. My brother-in-law has suffered from psoriatic rheumatism, another autoimmune disease, since his fifties. My sister was diagnosed with fibromyalgia in her late forties. The local postmistress, in her fifties, has lupus.

The list goes on and on, but what stands out about it are the predominant ages: fifties and sixties. Cancer and autoimmune diseases have been around for a long time, of course. But the frequency of their occurrence in my generation, the baby boomers, seems to me to indicate a causal relationship. Our post-World War II generation was largely bottle-fed, as the formula industry, in concert with the gynecological industry, convinced mothers (and fathers) that breast feeding was unnecessary. So our first line of defense—mother's milk—was compromised right out of the womb (and now we know cancer causing chemicals leach from the plastic used in bottles). The formula industry, of course, was just part of the food industry in general, which proceeded to package our food for mass consumption by adding artificial colors, preservatives, and flavors made with cancer causing chemicals. The farms that produced the food also became highly industrialized as well, and the cancer causing pesticides and herbicides necessary to support that industrialization entered the food chain in massive doses.

This has all been documented in books like *Silent Spring*, *Fast Food Nation*, and *Omnivore's Dilemma*, so I won't belabor the point. Combined with an exponential increase in air pollutants, as urban areas became clogged with cars and the entire country was contaminated by energy and manufacturing development, baby boomers were clobbered from all sides. I'm afraid the environmental safeguards that were promulgated in the 1970s with the passage of government regulatory laws (the Clean Air Act, Clean Water Act, etc.) were too little, too late.

So what we've been exposed to by scientific (chemical), medical (gynecologists), and industrial (power plants) development, all in the name of progress, seems to be killing us. Whereas previously we died in massive numbers because of the lack of scientific discoveries like penicillin and medical inventions like angioplasties, now we're dying in massive numbers (when you count the number of people who are dying not just from cancer and autoimmune diseases but industrial pollution and accidents, the number is massive) because of technological poisons. I can't take the long view on this, that every generation has suffered its particular burdens, because this is my generation Most of our parents lived into their seventies and eighties (never exercising, drinking martinis). Many of us will not. That may not be such a bad thing, when I see the individual suffering of those kept alive by medical intervention and the burden that places on society as a whole. But we're suffering, too, both physically and emotionally. We'll probably be the butt of many jokes regarding our slogan—"Don't trust anyone over

30"—and our delusions of immortality, but despite our excesses and self-indulgence, we developed a conscience and decided as adults to breast feed our babies, grow organic food, and riot for revolution. We were too preoccupied being active, political, and creative to see this coming.

Thursday, October 21, 2010

Productivity

"Without productivity, life is worthless and unbearable." This is Friedrich Nietzsche, who, remember, went completely mad (I'm reading *A Philosophical Biography* of Friedrich Nietzsche by Julian Young). He did get to live on in posterity, both worshiped and maligned, but I wonder how things might have turned out for him if he'd spent a little less time trying to figure out the meaning of life (to be fair, he was also trying to figure out how to have a peaceful and pleasant life).

My partner Mark used to tell me that my "productivity" intimidated him. I'm not sure he meant productivity in the sense of "producing" things, like novels and magazine articles or gourmet dinners and cherry pies, but my "busyness." Because here's the thing. Even though I've almost always worked at home, setting my own schedule and creating my own agenda, I've also had a rule that during the day I do not sit down and read a book. Now, that doesn't mean I don't read things during the day like information related to whatever article I'm writing, Environmental Impact Statements for whatever issue I'm dissecting, other people's books that I'm editing, etc. But reading a novel, biography, or philosophical treatise is reserved for in the mornings with my coffee and after dinner until bed. I manage to get a lot of books read in those hours, but what in the world makes me think that there is something wrong with sometimes sitting down during the day and reading a book?

I don't have weekends for reading books, either. Because of my self-employment I don't really have Saturday and Sunday off. I take days off here and there, to go for a hike or ski or go to town for a movie or lunch, but there's no designated day for lying around the house reading or watching TV, heaven forbid. Does it mean that I think life is worthless without productivity? Sort of. If productivity means using your individual talents to the best of your ability to create something that is uniquely yours or contributes to the common good or taxes your brain and body, then I'm definitely a fan of productivity. Again, according to Nietzsche: the well being of society is better promoted by everyone pursuing her own "highest good," or becoming an "enlightened egoist." If productivity means feeling that you have to constantly be doing something to prove your worth, then I think you've got a problem. Or I've got a problem.

This has become more obvious to me as I've gotten older. It's a byproduct of having to look back instead of forward and make certain assessments about the outcome of your productivity. If an assessment of the outcome makes you say, "I never really did the things I wanted to do" or "I was never able to effect the changes I wanted" or "what I produced is a pile of shit," then you better adopt the postmodern position immediately that all things are relative and there is no ultimate achievement or progress. That way your life can't have been meaningless because there's no such thing. You need to watch Casablanca again and listen to Rick when he tells Captain Renault, "Our lives don't amount to a hill of beans."

It was easier to live with that kind of attitude when I was younger. I have a kind of plodding personality that once I decide upon a course of action, say that of my organizing work that led to *La Jicarita News*, the radical rag I've written and edited with Mark for 15 years, I stay the course no matter how many battles we lose, no matter how many allies fall by the wayside, no matter how many nasty letters and e-mails and phones calls we get from the opposition. And there's been plenty of that. But somehow I always manage to see what I do is in my "self-interest" to further the "common good."

But now, as I face the fact that I'm going to retire *La Jicarita News* because of health issues and the fact that my energy has flagged with age, I can't keep those nagging assessments out of my head. While I doubt that I would have ever made the choice to be a "professional" so that right about now I'd be looking at a well deserved retirement along with the rest of my baby boom cohort, I could have made other choices: committing much more time to creative writing and publishing, learning how to play the piano really well, traveling much more often to Latin America and speaking fluent Spanish (a more peaceful and pleasant life),

But I do appreciate the small changes I did effect, even if they only amount to changing someone's life by knowing me or sharing in the work we did. And I don't think I produced a pile of shit. I could have spent more time perfecting what I produced and been more confident about it, but I guess I had no burning desire to "prove" my self worth and leave something to posterity. So I guess I'll muddle through this new phase in my life with the same mulish behavior that got me here, for better or worse. And maybe, just maybe, I can finish the Nietzsche biography and start that John Berger book in the middle of the day lying on the couch. Oh, what possibilities.

Friday, November 12, 2010

The Best and the Brightest (According to the Sunday New York Times Styles Section)

Synchronicity! On the very day I sat down to start writing about all the beautiful people announcing their marriages in the Sunday *New York Times* Styles Section I happened to read the Opinion Section where the Public Editor addressed a question from a reader that was the very same question I wanted to ask: "How do editors select which announcements to publish, and why don't editors make a sustained effort to include different types of couples?"

OK, I only wanted to ask the first part of this question about how editors select which announcements to publish because I know better than to ask why they don't make an effort to include other kinds of couples besides lawyers who graduate magna cum laude from Harvard Law School and now work for Wall Street investment firms or doctors who are doing their residency at the University of Pennsylvania in gastroenterology. In the intense competition among all these power couples who want their announcements to appear in the NYT Styles Section I figured it's the beauties over the uglies, the Harvards and Yales over the Oberlins, and the Greenwich parents over Newark who get the nod.

But lo and behold, according to the Public Editor, the criterion is none of these: it's achievement. "The only truly fair way to select one submission over another is on the basis of achievement." Nietzsche lives! (You have to excuse me, I'm still reading his Philosophical Biography). The elite are defined by their will to power, especially those who manage to make their way out of the herd and end up at the "top of their medical school class at

Yale or Stanford," as the Public Editor explained it.

So I decided to submit a marriage for publication that might give the Weddings/Celebrations editors pause, at least in terms of their definition of achievement, and might give the rest of us out here in the herd someone we can identify with.

"On March 20, at the lovely farm of the groom's family in upstate New York (I guess one of the criteria for publication is that the couple has some connection to New York, but I'm really talking about anywhere in rural America) so and so and so and so married themselves with their extended family members, their intimate comrades in arms, their three dogs, two cats, and tank of tropical fish in attendance (the cattle, horse, and chickens were confined to the field). They both will retain their own names even though they are their father's names but it's too late to do anything about that and anyway, everybody has always known them by those names.

So and so's parents own the local grocery store where they have kept accounts for as long as twenty years for the down and out folks in the community who live month to month on their social security or disability checks. The other so and so's parents drove in from New Mexico where they work as farriers and create magnificent iron sculptures on the side.

The happy couple has a long employment history that includes waitressing at a swank restaurant in the neighboring town, working for the Forest Service as seasonal patrols telling people to put out their campfires during times of drought, substitute teaching in the local high school while reporting on sports for the local newspaper, writing articles for various other local newspapers about whatever they can come up with on a day's notice, canvassing for the Service Worker's Union, growing great garlic that they sell to the local food stores, working construction on all their neighbors' houses so their neighbors will work construction on their house, and most recently, and thanklessly, as members of the school board even though they don't have any kids yet and might not because as anyone with a brain can see things are getting worse, not better.

They love to tell the story of how they met. One day so and so went over to a friend's house down the road for a visit with her/his dogs and the other so and so was also there visiting and had to run into the house when the first so and so's dogs started barking at him/her, which kinda pissed him/her off, but he/she also kinda liked the first so and so and thought she/he had an especially nice butt. He/she started dropping by the first so and so's house around breakfast time but she/he rarely invited him/her to eat, so they didn't make much progress. Then he/she got up his/her gumption, however, and invited the first so and so on a real date: they went to the State Fair. But then when they got back to the first so and so's house, where the second so and so had high hopes for a kiss, they got into an argument on the nature of inspiration and the first so and so kicked the second so and so out of her/his house. But the second so and so was tenacious, and when the first so and so started working in the fire lookout for the summer he/she went up to visit and those Desolation Peak fantasies were too much for both of them and they kissed. The rest is history."

Sunday, January 30, 2011
Diary of a Bad Year

I'm stealing the title of J.M. Coetzee's book because I can't actually steal the book, or come close to writing with the intensity, intelligence, and grace of which he is capable. And my subject matter is more literal: while it's actually been 17 months, my bad year dates back to the beginning of Mark's illness, when it became obvious that he was seriously sick. The diagnosis of nonresectable (meaning inoperable) pancreatic cancer came in August 2009, with a life expectancy of one to two years. He died on November 27, 2010.

I haven't really kept a diary. I've written tangentially about the abysmal state of the medical industrial complex, much of it gleaned from experience in emergency rooms and hospitals and chemotherapy clinics, but I haven't documented the day-to-day reality that was our lives. Or unreality, whichever it is. (In one of the last group e-mails I sent out to family and friends I said, "I find it's increasingly difficult to write these updates. It's almost as if Mark and I are in a separate reality—I use the term 'reality' in all its subjectivity, although as a pragmatist I have to assign some meaning to it.") So the question is, how does one live with one's mortality staring him in the face? I can't answer that question, obviously, but I can try to describe how I lived with his staring me in the face.

Before I take that leap, however, let me make a list of all the other things that happened during this bad year. In October of 2009 my younger sister killed herself after years of suffering with fibromyalgia. In November Mark and his mother had a falling out and he decided he wanted to terminate any relationship with her and he did. In January of 2010 I was diagnosed with CREST syndrome, an autoimmune disease that affects connective tissue and causes a lot pain in my neck and hands. In May I had a recurrence of vertigo, which I've had intermittently for 30 years. While in the past it's always been the positional type, where particles in the inner ear come lose and cause you to become dizzy when you move your head too quickly from side to side, this time the dizziness was constant, no matter what position my head was in, and it lasted most of the summer, in varying degrees of intensity. The ear, nose, and throat doc thinks I may have Ménière's disease, which is caused by fluid in the ear, as well as positional vertigo. In September our dog Sammy, who is completely deaf, almost died when one of his benign fatty cysts got infected and spread venom throughout his system. But it broke and drained and he lived. In October, our cat Mavis, who slept with us every night and provided much love and comfort, didn't come in one afternoon and disappeared forever. During the entire 17 months I watched our dog Django, who is 14, become increasingly crippled with arthritis, wondering, "Is she going to last through the summer?" and then, "Is she going to outlast Mark?" She also has a weak bladder and has to take estrogen to keep from peeing all over the house. I'm sure I'm missing some other events, but these are the salient ones.

Sammy and Django

Thinking about all this has kept me from thinking about Mark and how I want to go about telling our story. I know I don't want it to be another cancer lament, using words like "battle" and "valiant fight" to describe what happened over his year and a half of living, filled with much sickness but also energy, connection, and good feeling. I know I want to protect his privacy, as I did in my group e-mails, which detailed the bare facts of his illness and the course it took. But I do want to talk about how I lost a partner of 34 years slowly, and incrementally, as he withdrew into a world no one else could share despite our physical closeness and frank conversations about his dying and my living.

This is the first posting of Diary of a Bad Year, which I will continue with over the next few months, interspersed with other postings more in the vain of what I've been doing since I started blogging in 2009.

Monday, February 7, 2011

Diary of a Bad Year, continued

As a precursor to the bad year I started having orthopedic problems due to arthritis and my as yet undiagnosed autoimmune condition in my mid to late 50s, and in 2008 I had thumb surgery for a painful bone spur (see Health Insurance blog). My recovery was slow and agonizing: a hand that wouldn't heal and a frozen shoulder that went along with it. I finally found a sympathetic orthopedist and a talented physical therapist (hard to come by I discovered) who worked with me for over a year and finally referred me to a rheumatologist, who diagnosed my autoimmune condition, which was the underlying reason for my slow recovery. During all this time Mark nursed me, did all the chores around the house that I couldn't, did all the driving (which is considerable, seeing as how we live an hour away from Santa Fe and 45 minutes from Taos), with very little complaining. He'd always told me that my "productivity" was intimidating (see Productivity blog) and I think he enjoyed being depended on. I was still recovering from a second surgery to loosen up my arm when we assembled a crew to help us build our hoop house in April of 2009, where we planned to grow raspberries and all the warm weather crops we had trouble bringing to maturity at our 8,000-foot elevation. We have many pictures of Mark lifting, drilling, pulling the plastic sheeting over the frame, and reveling in a job well done.

By May Mark was experiencing significant stomach distress—pain and indigestion—and finally went into our local clinic in Peñasco to consult with the physician's assistant who was his primary care doctor. Here I need to momentarily digress to discuss the one enormously lucky thing about this bad year: health insurance. Right when we started to hit our medical brick walls we found out about a state-sponsored health insurance program called State Coverage Insurance that was designed for low income and self-employed people who didn't qualify for Medicaid or Medicare—Mark and me, in other words (see Health Insurance blog). We got on the plan and quickly told all our friends about it and they, too, got on the plan, which in its infancy was under enrolled (it hasn't accepted any new enrollment in over a year). It covered all hospitalization, doctor visits, and prescriptions. If we hadn't had this insurance I would now be over $100,000 in debt.

To continue the story, Mark was tested and treated for a common bacteria called H-Pylori with two antibiotics that wrecked his stomach even further. He continued to have stomach pain and weight loss and had to lobby both the PA and a substitute doc to forget about another course of antibiotics and send him for an endoscopy (coupled with a colonoscopy, although the pain was in his stomach, not his colon). If we hadn't had insurance, I'm sure he would have suffered through another course of antibiotic treatment because we couldn't have afforded the endoscopy.

The gastroenterologist conducted the colonoscopy first and found nothing unusual. Mark told me later that when they told him everything looked good in his colon he thought he was home free. When they brought me into the recovery room after the endoscopy and the doc told us both that he had been unable to get the scope beyond Mark's stomach into his duodenum, which is the beginning of the small intestine, we entered our separate reality of vocabulary, procedures, and protocols we'd never heard of and struggled to understand.

The gastroenterologist never used the word tumor when he told us something was obstructing the passage of the scope. But he did convey a sense of urgency that we needed to go directly to the hospital or imaging service to have a radiologist try to see what was going on. He told Mark not to eat anything but liquids until he got a diagnosis. I remember walking out to the car with one of the cheery recovery nurses, who didn't know about the obstruction, who told Mark, I bet you're hungry after all that fasting today so go enjoy a good meal.

That was the beginning of almost three weeks of a diet of Ensure and mounting weight loss and depression. Mark was always a skinny guy, with no extra body fat to get him through an emergency, but this was more than an emergency, it was the beginning of a long decline that would literally end in starvation.

We spent the rest of the day in the radiology department at the Santa Fe hospital where they made the mistake of giving him barium to drink, which they routinely do so they can see what's going on inside. The barium couldn't get through his system, however, because of the obstruction and obscured any decent x-rays of his digestive tract. There followed days of other kinds of scans that were also obscured, but a Santa Fe surgeon eventually came on board and confirmed that the most likely cause of the obstruction was a tumor on Mark's pancreas, in the worst possible place, the head, where all the veins and arteries are located, and that he was referring Mark to the Cancer Center at the University of New Mexico Hospital. I really can't remember whether he was the one who first mentioned the Whipple procedure, or whether we Googled pancreatic cancer and found out about it ourselves (oh, using the Internet as a source for medical information opens up that proverbial can of worms and takes you down a dangerous path of too much uninformed information, if you get my drift). The Whipple procedure is what everyone suspects Steve Jobs got when he was sick and treated in Houston, Texas (he also got a liver transplant). It's a highly technical procedure to remove a tumor from the pancreas that involves removing parts of the stomach and bile duct and then putting everything back together. Only very specialized surgical oncologists are capable of performing it at a few places around the country.

That's where we thought we were headed, but in the meantime we were at home, waiting for the surgical oncologist at the UNM Cancer Center to work us into his schedule. Mark continued to lose weight and we were still without a definitive diagnosis. Although we were using the words "tumor" and "cancer," without a biopsy we still didn't know if the tumor was benign or cancerous. We found out later that an acquaintance of ours in a neighboring village ended up getting the Whipple procedure for a pancreatic tumor that was benign.

Those were some of the darkest days of the 17 months. Mark couldn't endure not knowing whether the tumor was cancerous and having to wait for entrance into the UNM medical industrial complex. When doctors or nurses didn't call back immediately, he made me call them again and again or he would call again and again until he spoke with someone to impress upon them that he was starving and needed to be dealt with now, not tomorrow or next week. They assured him that the surgeon was seeing him as soon as he could work him in, and that as long as he was able to keep the Ensure, or other liquid foods down, he wasn't starving.

Both of our sons were in Albuquerque. Jakob, the older, had moved back to New Mexico after years of working around the country as a photojournalist, was living with his partner Casey, and enrolled in a PhD program at UNM. Max, the younger, was renting a place in Albuquerque for the summer before heading back to Claremont McKenna College in California for the fall semester. They both came up to El Valle as often as they could during those dark days to be with us, but when I was alone with Mark his depression was almost more than I could bear. He watched TV and played solitaire endlessly. He didn't want me to play music. He wouldn't talk to anyone, including me.

Finally, I confronted him. I told him if he couldn't make an effort now, to maintain some equilibrium, to maintain a relationship with the kids and me while we waited for a diagnosis, there was no hope of us getting through this without irreparable emotional damage. We still didn't know if the tumor was cancerous. Even if it was, there was the hope of surgery and follow up treatment. It was going to take all of us, in concert, to work our way through this medical maze and he was the linchpin, the one whose behavior would make or break us.

Jakob, Max, Kay, and Mark in the late 1990s

Sunday, February 13, 2011

Diary of a Bad Year, continued

Mark heard me (see previous posting) and made an effort to lift the black veil, but then we were again caught up in the maelstrom of the medical industrial complex, with two trips to the emergency room, a terminal diagnosis, a nine-day hospital stay, and finally, a stent surgically placed in his duodenum.

All the horror stories about emergency rooms are true. To UNM Hospital, the only public hospital in the city, go all those who have no health insurance. There, too, go those with emergencies that are not dealt with by urgent care centers or doctors' offices but are not dire enough to require an ambulance delivery, with entry through a different door (although when we were there several people who had been brought in by ambulance and seen in triage were then deposited into the waiting room). There are those who have insurance but can't get doctors' appointments at UNM in any timely fashion so they have to go to the ER to get the treatment they should have been getting from a doctor who would then admit them to the hospital. One of the ER doctors actually told us that his wife had been waiting four months for an appointment at one of the UNM clinics. And then there are those who are very confused and don't know why they are there.

Once you actually get out of the waiting room and into the examination room, in this fancy new ER wing that was recently added on to the hospital, you may find yourself there for three days. We were there for 16 hours our first visit, then sent home. On the second visit we were there for about 10 hours before Mark was admitted. If he had actually been admitted during the first visit we wouldn't have had to visit the ER twice, for a combined visit of 26 hours, for the same illness that finally got us admitted the second time. But the ER must adhere to a strict hierarchy of diagnoses that allow the most critically ill admission first, while the rest linger in exam rooms (or on the floor, where many prisoners in orange jumpsuits and shackles spent many hours) because there are not enough beds in the hospital.

Why are there no spare beds in the hospital? Because the health care system is broken beyond repair. People with preventable diseases end up in the hospital for any number of reasons. They have no insurance so they don't go to see doctors or health care specialists who might be able to screen for early detection of these preventable diseases. When they do see a doctor, it's not like the doctor we grew up with (those of us over 50) who came to the house, treated everyone in the family, often socialized with the family, and was able to integrate medicine with lifestyle choices and an intimacy that no longer remotely exists. When they do see a doctor, it's usually at a for-profit clinic where the doctor's salary is based on how many patients he or she can see in a day. So it's in and out the door, no follow up to see if the patient is taking the doctor's advice, taking his or her medication, or seen by whatever specialist he or she might have been referred to. And if the patient is referred to a specialist, that specialist might say to the patient, you need to go back to your primary care doctor and get a referral to see a different specialist, but no one checks up to see if that happens, either. In other words, there is woeful communication between doctors and woeful care for patients who cannot successfully navigate the complicated primary care/referral/specialist terrain of the medical industrial complex.

Even when you act as your own advocate, or have someone act as your advocate, and make every effort to work through the system as efficiently and expeditiously as possible, you are out of luck. You can't get through by phone to doctors who are already overworked and not inclined to return phone calls. If you question their diagnosis or prescription for tests, such as the enormously expensive CT scans and MRIs, you are labeled a troublemaker and sent off to someone else or just dropped from the system. If you happen to get sick on a Friday, you know you're going to spend your weekend in the ER. You have to get authorization from your insurance company for procedures you and your doctor decide are necessary, and if they turn you down—because, after all, don't for-profit businesses know more about health care than you do?—you have to appeal the decision while days or weeks go by when you should be getting treatment. Health insurance rarely covers alternative treatments that patients have discovered work for them and they end up paying out of pocket fees that certain doctors or HMOs would much rather put towards a diagnostic test from which the HMO or doctor gets a kickback.

During the debate on the health care bill all of this dysfunction was argued out in Congress, in the White House, in the mainstream media, on blogs, and among those of us who have to work through the system, which is all of us at some point in our lives. But until health care is not managed by for-profit HMOs and insurance companies the argument is moot. The ER doc who told us about his wife having to wait four months for an appointment summed the situation up very aptly when he said, "There are two kinds of health care being delivered in this country: the kind Steve Jobs gets and the kind everyone else gets."

Sunday, February 20, 2011

Mothering

Everyone is in a complete tizzy over the Chinese-American mother who wrote *Battle Hymn of the Tiger Mother* about the strict and expectant raising of her two daughters, presented as a philosophy in direct opposition to contemporary American mothering where the child is the center of the universe and can do no wrong because that would lower his or her self-esteem.

But I don't get it. Since when did the millions of mothers over there in China who are struggling to feed their families from subsistence farming or sending them off to work in factories 10 hours a day become Tigers? And since when do the millions of mothers here in the U.S. who work all day and then come home to cook and clean have time to be soccer moms?

This is all nonsense because of course we're talking about the privileged few. China may have a Confucian culture that cherishes education, and this country a Protestant ethic that believes anyone can lift themselves up by their bootstraps and succeed, but without a discussion in the context of class these mommy wars (it's always mommy wars, not daddy wars) are irrelevant. So I'm going to talk about mothering—and fathering—from a different point of view: just a regular Jill, the female equivalent of a regular Joe, trying to raise her kids in a loving, nurturing environment while at the same time make a living and have a life (more than a room, Virginia) of one's own.

Mark and I, as I've talked about before, chose time over money so our kids essentially had both of us as almost fulltime parents. When they were younger we each had part-time or seasonal jobs that allowed both of us to parent together some of the time and at least one of us to parent all of the time. While there were days in their infancy when I wanted to run screaming out of the house to the nearest bar, the Konrad Lorenz argument that infantile features trigger nurturing responses in adults and that this is an evolutionary adaptation that helps ensure adults care for their children seems pretty accurate. They were so cute, loving, and interesting that for the most part I didn't feel constricted or confined by spending a lot of time with them. I often viewed the rest of my life—writing guidebooks for a living, fighting the Forest Service over inane management decisions that impacted the community, and fighting the developers who wanted to smash the community—as obligations, not engagements, even though they were all of my own choosing.

When the kids were older we worked at home so were both around during the difficult preadolescent and adolescent years when they didn't particularly want us around. But things changed over time for us as well, as we got pulled into more interesting work or more intense struggles and we didn't have the time, or the interest, really, in being as intense caretakers as we'd been. I can't imagine trying to exert the kind of attention and influence the Tiger mother describes on children who start functioning more independently while we parents get on with our lives. We always expected our kids to do their schoolwork (even though a lot of it was just busy work) and get good grades (so they could have that illusory option of Harvard or Yale), we became more of a consultant than a programmer in our kids' lives.

Jakob was just here to visit and told me how scared he was as a kid of the attack rooster when he had to go out and feed the chickens (we gave him an attack broom). We once left Max behind in the forest (momentarily) when he threw a fit about cutting one more tree to load into the truck for firewood. This was how we traumatized our kids instead of how the Tiger mother did, calling one of her daughters "garbage" when she made her an unexceptional hand-made card, or Lang Lang's father did hanging him upside down from their apartment balcony when he told him he wanted to quit playing the piano. (Or am I getting that story confused with Michael Jackson and his hanging baby? I know Lang Lang's father did something terrible to him.) So who's the worse for wear? It's hard to say, but in terms of finding their way in the world, my kids haven't done too badly, despite the fact that they can't play the violin or the piano—well, that is. Jakob asked that he be allowed to quit taking lessons for his 14th birthday present. Sometimes you just have to let it be and hope that everyone, including your kids, can just have a life.

Thursday, March 3, 2011
Power in the Middle East

We all watched with joy and a certain amount of trepidation as the citizens of Egypt rose up in revolt against the Mubarak dictatorship. Seeing, and listening to, so many articulate (speaking English, no less) and passionate people from all walks of life demanding an end to the corruption and poverty that pervades Egypt after thirty years of totalitarian rule allowed us to focus on hopeful feelings rather than fearful ones.

Now that the military has reasserted its control (remember, since 1952 the military has essentially ruled the country), promising a transition to a freely elected government, the fearful feelings start creeping in. As much as I try to ignore what I've learned regarding institutionalized power, I can't help but worry about how that transition will take place, who or what will be the beneficiary, and whether it will translate to a "democratic" government. I put "democratic" in quotes because I'm not sure what that means. If the U.S. is taken as an example of a functioning democracy, where citizens participate in "free" and "fair" elections, we're in trouble. All you have to do is look at the incomes of our elected officials, or the billions of corporate dollars used to elect them, to remember that it's the elites who run the country.

Michel Foucault is the go to guy about how society has transitioned from sovereignty, the rule over a territory, to governmentality, or the rule within our institutions, or "micro-power structures." Unfortunately, in modern western democracies, this form of governmentality often takes the form of neoliberalism, based on the predominance of market mechanisms and of the restriction of the action of the state. We now live in a globalized society, and the revolutions in Egypt, Tunisia, Libya, and perhaps the entire

Middle East, will unfold in that context.

There is no comparison, of course, between the lack of personal freedom and dire economic situations in the Middle East and the U.S. If the people there achieve freedom of speech, assembly, and the press, and slave wages and benefits are improved, their lives will be enormously better. But if the revolution is "hijacked" by the neoliberals, rather than the Islamists, we will see, just as we are seeing in this country and in Europe, an institutionalized divide between the rich and the poor and an assault on government's basic function in society, that of providing access to basic needs and services. While the divide between the rich and poor in Egypt is already enormous (and already neoliberal, to a certain extent), will global capitalism just allow better access to a more efficient system of exploitation than the one perpetrated by the U.S., which has long worked behind the scenes in that country to ensure both political and economic dependency.

I went to the rally on February 22 at the Roundhouse in Santa Fe to show solidarity with the public employees and teachers in Madison, Wisconsin who are under assault by their Republican governor who wants to do away with collective bargaining. Private unions in this country have already been eviscerated, so now the neoliberalists are after the public unions like AFSMCE and teachers unions. The ultimate goal is to put more money in the hands of the corporate elite, and unfortunately, they've not only been successful in this goal but through the "power of consent" have convinced many of the working class that their interests are the same as the capitalists.

But the thousands of protesters in Wisconsin, those of us supporting them on the streets of Santa Fe, and many of the protesters all over the Middle East, understand that it is power imposed by economic coercion. We must break free of that control in the western world if there is to be any hope of breaking free in the Middle East. But in the meantime, off with their heads!

Sunday, March 20, 2011

Diary of a Bad Year, continued

Once Mark was admitted to the hospital, via the emergency room, when he could no longer keep any food down, they biopsied the tumor, which was malignant. It was, as we had previously been told, at the head of his pancreas and therefore nonresectable, or inoperable. The surgical oncologist came into Mark's hospital room to tell us—the kids and I were there—while a drug addict in the next bed kept moaning for medication and turning up the TV to unbearable levels. He glared and muttered at me when I turned it down every time I passed by. Once the surgeon left after giving us the bad news they moved Mark to a private room. I remember going back to Jakob and Casey's house about ten that night and collapsing on the bed in the guest room, sobbing, while the kids sat there helplessly with me.

It took nine days in the hospital to get a stent put in his duodenum with an endoscope so he could eat (it took two tries). Everyone there was incredibly kind. We made friends with all the nurses, the aids, the interns, the housekeepers, etc. and heard all their stories: how many kids they had; what school they were attending to improve their situation; where they were born and raised; how they liked (or hated) their job. You don't have time to make friends with the doctors; you only see them when they have news to deliver (I never did see the gastroenterologist who put the stent in).

Chemotherapy was scheduled once we could get our insurance company's approval. Mark was initially given dispensation for treatment at the UNM Cancer Center instead of Presbyterian Hospital, which was his medical insurer, because of the specialized surgical team at the Cancer Center. Once it was clear that surgery wasn't an option, we had to again get approval through Presbyterian for oncology treatment. That took about a week, and I was grateful for the time. Mark was able to eat, albeit a restricted diet (no fresh vegetables, chewy meat, or anything that could conceivably get stuck in the stent), and gain a little strength before starting once a week chemo treatments.

We've all heard the horror stories about chemotherapy (and seen them, if you follow the HBO series Breaking Bad, ironically filmed in Albuquerque): losing weight, losing hair, throwing up, spiraling down. Mark's physical wellbeing improved, however: he gained some weight, never lost any hair (he didn't have much to begin with but what he had stayed on his head), never threw up, and maintained the energy to go for a daily walk. After a few months of weekly chemo, if he felt well enough, he even drove himself down to Albuquerque for his session, spending the night at Jakob and Casey's or even driving himself back the same day. Max had made the decision to take a leave of absence from college, and stayed in Albuquerque, so he was there with Mark when I wasn't.

Every six weeks we both went down for a CT scan to monitor the size of the tumor and see the oncologist for an evaluation. (By the way, all those TV shows and movies where they show cancer patients going into the oncologist's office for a consultation are a complete fabrication. Those docs run from exam room to exam room and barely have more than 15 minutes for a look at the lab work, a quick physical check-up, and to answer a few questions we manage to squeeze in. Then it's off to the races.) We tried to make it festive, had dinner with the kids, watched movies, and spent many hours in front of the fireplace on cold, winter nights.

Amazingly, Mark was also able to pay considerable attention to his intellectual work. For many months during his illness he edited and serialized in our non-profit community newspaper *La Jicarita News* an article he had written concerning the adjudication of land grants in New Mexico. The article was intended to be the introduction to a book dealing with this sordid period in New Mexico's history, where indigenous people were dispossessed of millions of acres of land that had been granted them by the Spanish and Mexican governments. Titled "Brief History of American Imperialism" it chronicled early American expansionism, Manifest Destiny, the Mexican-American War, the Treaty of Guadalupe Hidalgo, and racism in the New Mexico Territory.

Not only that, but he spent two or three hours several days a week spread out on the floor of the bedroom finishing the article evaluating the effect George W. Julian's tenure as Surveyor General of the New Mexico Territory (1885-1889). He had received a grant from the New Mexico Historical Records Advisory Board to do the research and writing in 2009, and he finished the work by the spring of 2010.

So from about October through April Mark had a pretty good run. Then, as we headed into late spring and early summer, and as my work in the garden and fields intensified, his work to stay alive became all encompassing.

Friday, April 8, 2011

Diary of a Bad Year, continued

Marriage, or a long-term partnership, is in part a power relationship (see Marriage blog), and ours was emblematic of how that power shifts and flows through the many years of individual and relational change. For some crazy reason—part masochism, part curiosity, I guess—I started reading a book by Rafael Yglesias called *A Happy Marriage* that was a fictionalized account of his wife's cancer death. I'd read Yglesias many years before, and I must have seen it on the new bookshelf at the public library, but what possessed me to pick it up at that stunningly complex moment I don't know. Once I started, however, I couldn't put it down, and while I faced the latest manifestation of Mark and my relational shift I became intimately involved in the details of Yglesias' topsy-turvey marriage and their descent into cancer hell.

Although we arrived there along different paths, Yglesias's marriage and my partnership had settled into a less confrontational pattern, where jockeying for power had receded in the face of a need for peace and calmness between us as we came to terms with diminishing returns in the rest of our lives: less intensity in our political work, less need to prove ourselves artistically, and less parenting as our kids were fledged. We, like they, looked forward to some time to do things we hadn't done in awhile, like work on projects for our own enjoyment, visit our friends more, see some places we had never seen (albeit for us on a marginal income). But then we entered our separate reality, which manifest in both spacial and temporal terms.

As Mark's illness progressed, the past, present, and future took on entirely new meaning. He couldn't look forward to anything (no becoming in Nietzschean terms). To look back was an exercise in too much painful nostalgia. So his life became the present, which meant a focused attention to the details of his health/illness with little room left over for attention to much else. He had to center every fiber of his being on his being. I began to lose him incrementally as the intimacy of our relationship, in which we shared a common history and a current engagement, began to recede. While he was very solicitous about my health and the burdens placed upon me due to his illness, he really had little interest in anything that didn't relate to being in his illness.

Everything we did, and everything we took into consideration, revolved around what was possible for Mark. He didn't want to see anyone but family and a few close friends. I had to diplomatically erect barriers between him and everyone else who wanted to see him or help me or at least demonstrate their concern. To minimize direct contact but maintain some connection I set up a list-serve where I periodically posted e-mails letting folks know how Mark was doing, being careful to supply just the bare facts about the latest results of a CT scan, another trip to the hospital, or the onset of diabetes (once his pancreas was compromised he couldn't produce insulin): a supply of information that didn't invade a privacy that was never explicitly outlined to me but that I implicitly understood. What he thought and felt and experienced with me and the kids was not for public consumption. I had to restrain a friend from setting up a Caring Bridge web site for Mark, something definitely not in sync with who we were and how we wanted to be in the world. I'd seen too many sites that elicited too much tortured comment that perhaps filled the needs of those doing the commenting but would certainly not fill ours.

A couple of weeks before Mark died I sent this e-mail to the list-serve, apologizing for the long time between postings (I reference part of this e-mail in the first Diary of a Bad Year blog): "I find it's increasingly difficult to write these updates. It's almost as if Mark and I are in a separate reality (I use the term 'reality' in all its subjectivity, although as a pragmatist I have to assign some meaning to it). Illness, and cancer in particular, does this to people's lives. Although I am by profession a writer, I haven't really wanted to write about what it's like to face Mark's terminal diagnosis or the day to day details of his decline, partly because it's already been dealt with by so many other writers and partly to protect Mark's privacy." Now, four months later, I am writing, but I hope that what I deem is "for public consumption" means something to my readers and respects the dignity of Mark's life and death.

Saturday, April 16, 2011

Who Are These People?

W̲henever I'm in an upscale community (not a common occurrence), walking around looking at million dollar houses, I find myself asking, "Who are these people and where does all this money come from?" Right now I'm in Del Mar, California, in a house loaned to me by some homies from New Mexico who inherited it from their family. But who are all these other people, in their glass houses with ocean views, manicured landscapes, and shiny BMWs (I swear to God I haven't seen one dirty car since I've been here)?

Who I actually see are the workers: gardeners, plumbers, plasterers, painters, general contractors, and dog walkers, busily keeping all this luxury afloat. The gardeners are all Mexicanos, pruning, planting, and watering all the lush vegetation that has turned these once barren hills (that's when the homies' family bought in) into paradise. In the mornings, as I walk along the windy streets in a circuitous path to the ocean I see some Anglo runners and dog walkers, most of them my age or older. Is this a community of retirees who bought in before the property taxes skyrocketed and who now benefit from Prop 13? Are they second home owners, so wealthy they can afford to hire all these people to maintain their houses for their two or three months' winter stay?

Whoever they are, and whether their money is old money or nouveau riche money, I feel like an alien. Not only am I an alien in Del Mar particularly, but in California generally. Take today for example. I needed to put gas in my hosts' car after driving it down the coast the other day to grocery shop. So I find out where the nearest gas station is and proceed apace. I make sure I know which side of the car the gas tank is on, and whether it has to be popped open from a release inside, and then I venture out. I pull into the gas station and there are all these instructions on the pumps about using your debit card or cash, which I intend to use instead of my credit card, but I'm already envisioning putting the money into the slot and seeing it disappear forever while I try to figure out how it actually connects to gas for the car. Fortunately, it also says I can pay inside, which I do. Then I go back to the car and pull the Regular Unleaded hose out and attempt to put it into my gas tank. But it has this weird accordion end on it, and try as I might I can't get it to stay in the gas tank opening. Whenever I depress the delivery handle it just pops back up. I'm looking around in a panic thinking, maybe I'm trying to put the wrong gas in the tank because the pump says EC Regular Unleaded, whatever that is, but I see that all the pumps say that. So then I start looking around for someone to help me, embarrassing as that's going to be, but remembering that I'll never have to see this person again. But everyone who is working a pump is also working a cell phone and can't hear me. Finally, I see a Mexicano worker put his phone away and I approach: "Habla Ingles?" I ask, and he answers, "Poquito," and I know I'm not going to be able to explain my predicament in Spanish. So then I find another guy, an Anglo this time, and I say, "I'm from New Mexico and I've never seen a pump hose like this and I can't make it work in my gas tank." Now I know I'm perpetuating a stereotype about New Mexicans, who already have enough trouble convincing everyone that we're actually part of the U.S., but I'm desperate here. So he graciously comes over and shows me that you have to shove the hose into the tank until it locks and then dispense your gas. I keep apologizing and he keeps saying don't worry about it but by then I'm completely frazzled and when I get back into my (their) car I pull out into the wrong lane and am forced onto I-5 going south when all I wanted to do was go to a gas station and fill the gas tank. I'm a perfectly competent driver under normal circumstances but now I'm a wailing banshee praying that there is am exit before San Diego where I can get off and find my way home without using up all the gas I just put back into the tank. And there is: Del Mar Heights, which brings me back to Camino Del Mar and the familiar streets leading up to the lovely bungalow that has been so graciously loaned to me by my New Mexico homies. As I've said before, maybe it's best that I don't leave home.

Thursday, April 28, 2011

Elegy for El Valle

It is presumptuous of me to write an elegy for El Valle, my home for the last 20 years, when my neighbors and their parents and grandparents have been here for hundreds. But within the temporal context of my tenure, and the relational nature of my complaint, I'll go ahead anyway.

I've written before about Tomás, the man who was our neighbor for most of those 20 years (he died a year and a half ago). In the eulogy I delivered at his funeral I said: "There is an unspoken law between us that any favor asked will be granted. It is based on an understanding that the favor will not be unreasonable, that it is necessary and not frivolous. Sometimes, because of our cultural differences, there may be a certain shaking of the head, a muttered, "those crazy gringos" or "that loco," but we accede to the other's wishes, and we write it off as what you do for a friend, pure and simple. I loved Tomás unreservedly, despite all the judgments I brought to bear. I hope he loved me the same way."

Tomás was the unofficial mayor of El Valle, the Alpha Male of the village, and when inevitably challenged by some of the younger men who aspired to that role, responded as any benevolent dictator would: he proceeded to try to crush them with every power at his command. But benevolent is the operative word here: he asserted an authority that arose from the surety of what he felt was best for the well being of the community.

Now, as we (I'm an acequia commissioner) begin another acequia spring without his authority it's like we're dealing with an assortment of dysfunctional family members who we somehow have to appease while at the same time circumvent the chaos they threaten to unleash at any given moment. The situation is exacerbated by the loss of Mark, who as a commissioner for fifteen years learned how to balance Tomas's power with his acuity. I long for Tomas to say, "Ya basta!" and lay down the law about who gets the water, when they get the water, who has a legitimate gripe and when they just have to shut-up. As it is, two parciantes are fighting over who is responsible for the capacity of their lateral ditch, which is outside the purview of the acequia commission but has drawn us in anyway because we're trying to promote cooperation; a debate over a water right that is generations old and now divided into percentages that no one knows the genesis of; and payment of contract work for cleaning the ditch, which is something alien to the tradition of each parciante cleaning, or hiring someone to clean, the ditch communally, which we abandoned a year ago because none of the parciantes showed up and neglected to make sure someone would be there to do the work for them. There are now so many divided water rights among absentee landowners and family transfers that I can barely keep track of who I bill for what amount of money.

I got the water yesterday for my orchard and upper field. The first irrigation of the season is brutal; the lateral ditches have filled in with dead grass and debris, the water inevitably flows over the side of the ditch, and you have to run around hoeing and shoveling it free while filling "sackos," or burlap bags with dirt to line the sides of the eroded laterals to keep the water moving toward what it is you're trying to irrigate. It took me all afternoon to guide the run-off orchard water onto my garlic patch, so far the only greenery besides grass that I have in cultivation. Without Tomás, who made sure the manure was neatly shoveled out of the corral and into piles ready for delivery, and Mark, who once the manure was spread could rototill the garden at a moment's notice, I am at the mercy of the current crew who may or may not have the tractor fixed or who may be so overwhelmed with wage labor work they don't have the time or ability to help me. So the rest of my garden waits.

Tomás's son just called and told me that his nephew and wife had a new baby and named him Tomás. That baby has big boots to fill. But it's kinda like the Middle East around here: the days of dictators are over (even the benevolent ones), which is probably a good thing, but the future of acequia democracy may also be in trouble. Meanwhile, I'll continue to take the water and as a commissioner try to channel Tomás as best I can: just irrigate when it's your turn, close your compuerta when it's not, and otherwise, *callete!*

Orlando and Tomás Montoya

Sunday, June 5, 2011

Post-Marxist Humanist Pragmatic

My younger son Max's major in college first was economics, which he now declares a pseudo science, that segued to history, moved on to Spanish, and then reverted back to history only because it was too late to change to continental philosophy, which he discovered in his junior year. Whenever he's home from school for a visit we have these long, complex discussions about how my thinking and being fit into the scheme of all things explored from Aristotle to Jurgen Habermas. While I wish he would sometimes leave the continent and travel to the subaltern, I like being prodded to go back and read a lot of people I either failed to read or didn't read very well, to validate or challenge his assessment of me, which currently is a post-Marxist humanist pragmatic (but subject to change at any moment).

Mark and I, along with some friends, were going to participate in a Marx study group of *Capital* with David Correia, our friend and American Studies professor at UNM, but that fell by the wayside when Mark got sick. So I reread Part I of *Capital*, and then I took up David Harvey's *A Companion to Marx's Capital*. As Harvey emphasizes in his book, Marx was not at all a static thinker, as some would pigeonhole him as pertinent only to a time long eclipsed by global capitalism. Marx's structural analysis of capitalism is conceptual, one that recognizes the transformative nature of its process.

The "post" part of Marxism remains in step with his conceptual thinking as it expands beyond labor power and value in economic terms to the power structures that affect all facets of society: the civil rights movement, women's liberation, gender studies, and the environmental movement. I entered Antioch College in 1969. The black scholarship students moved into a "black" dorm where whites weren't allowed, turning the racial power structure upside down. The second wave of the women's movement was soon to be in full swing, as writers like Susan Brownmiller and Shulamith Firestone moved beyond the call for equal pay for equal work to challenging the very nature of sexuality and patriarchy. Environmental politics was not some nice middle class recycling center but a head-on confrontation with corporate and global exploitation of resources and populations for profit and gain.

One of George Eliot's biographers, Frederick R. Karl, refers to her as a secular humanist, which allowed her to abandon Christianity while retaining its "morality and ethics." While she wasn't very politically involved, per se, her life was a political statement for women's emancipation and a challenge to societal norms. She lived with a married man, George Henry Lewes, for more than 20 years while she wrote her great novels (I've read *Middlemarch* at least three times over the years). I can't come close to her erudition and sophistication, in a life of the drawing room company of Thomas Carlyle and John Stuart Mill, but I like to think my humanism resembles hers: a belief that we, subjectively, as individuals, can strive for both a reflective, and exemplary life, and objectively, as a society, can create the conditions for everyone to flourish. While the stark realities of our unjust and undemocratic world challenge our ability to hold on to personal will, or to refrain from seeing it in nihilistic terms, we can, as Antonio Gramsci put it, maintain a "pessimism of the intellect" and "optimism of the will."

The final component of my label—pragmatist—was the philosophical theory with which I was the least conversant. I read some John Dewey and analyses of other pragmatists, neopragmatists, or neo-classical pragmatists (jeez, it really gets esoteric), but came to the conclusion that I take a little something from a lot of them: an ethics that accepts the notion there are "good" values that can be reasoned out; "informed practice," or recognition that the means are the end; and that there is no disconnect between body and mind, just as there is no disconnect between intellect and environment. As a community organizer around issues of environmental justice, and caretaker of a garden, orchard, and hay fields, over the years I found the only way to keep going was to stay connected and to value what I learned and who I came to love in the process of cultivating, irrigating, organizing, advocating, and resisting authority. When Ike DeVargas and I sometimes fall into a lament over what "could have, would have, should have been," he reminds me that how we worked together was the most important part of what we did— the means, not the end. In the obituary that Jurgen Habermas wrote for the philosopher Richard Rorty (labeled a neopragmatist), who, like Mark, died of pancreatic cancer, he said: "Nothing is sacred to Rorty the ironist. Asked at the end of his life about the 'holy', the strict atheist answered with words reminiscent of the young Hegel: 'My sense of the holy is bound up with the hope that some day my remote descendants will live in a global civilization in which love is pretty much the only law.'"

Tuesday, June 28, 2011

Diary of a Bad Year, Ad infinitum

I'm here in El Valle and it's 90 degrees outside but I've closed all my doors and windows and have every fan I own running full blast (I only have two) so that I can breathe without coughing. The smoke from the Las Conchas fire above Los Alamos has settled over our valley for two days now, so thick it's almost impossible to differentiate between smoke and cloud, except for the orange striations that spread across the plumes along the entire southern horizon. Ash particles so minute that sometimes the only way they are visible is when they are caught in cobwebs (or as my neighbor told me, on her white skirt), rain upon our downwind communities. So here we are, eleven years after the Cerro Grande Fire that burned 47,000 acres in two weeks throughout the Los Alamos area, watching and breathing a fire that has burned 61,000 acres in 36 hours.

The town of Los Alamos has been evacuated as the fire approaches from the south and west towards the mesa canyons full of legacy waste and the active Los Alamos National Laboratory technical areas that store nuclear weapons and waste. I've made an arbitrary decision that if the fire reaches Tech Area G, where waste containers sit in nylon tents waiting shipment to the Waste Isolation Pilot Plant in southern New Mexico, I will load up my dogs and leave for Albuquerque to move in with Jakob and Casey. But really it's just an excuse to stay here in El Valle as long as possible (I pity the poor Los Alamos residents who had to leave their homes as I curse those complicit in this nuclear madness) because I know I've already been contaminated by the radionuclides, PCBs, and other toxins that reside in the ponderosa pine, piñon pine, and mixed conifer forests that are now exploding fire balls, desiccated by years of drought and federal agency mismanagement.

I say "load up my dogs," but this means somehow getting a seventy pound, 14 year old dog who can barely walk and a 10 year old cocker spaniel who is deaf and almost blind into my car and transporting them in 100 degree heat to Albuquerque. I already asked my neighbor, a former Los Alamos construction manager, if he will take my chickens and put them in with his brood. But why should he stick around to take care of my chickens when he should be getting the hell out of Dodge with his parents, of whom he is the caretaker (his dad, Orlando, figures prominently in my blog post Will the Real Mayordomo Please Stand Up.) The only place they might go is Española, where his brother lives, but as we saw in the Cerro Grande Fire, that town will no doubt be a smoke-filled hell hole as well.

When I venture out in the smoke to feed the chickens I see that a little water is coming down the acequia into my orchard, which I'm struggling to keep alive between a long rotation of 22 parciantes in a summer of drought the likes of which I've never before seen. I'd asked the mayordomo to let a little water come down from an irrigator up the valley, and his response was, "Go ask them." I didn't, but for some reason the water is there, so with a wet bandana across my face I manage to at least wet down my trees before the water disappears several hours later. As my former vecino Jacobo Romero said (in William deBuys book, *River of Traps*), "never give holiday to the water," even if the fires are raging and this Diary of a Bad Year has become the Diary of the Bad Year That Never Seems to End.

Wednesday, July 6, 2011

Diary of a Bad Year: Invasion of the Bats

I thought maybe the noise from the air monitoring station that the New Mexico Environment Department put outside my house two days after the Las Conchas fire broke out would scare away the bats, but no such luck. El Valle is one of the LANL downwind communities where the ED has been monitoring the air, soil, and water—largely due to the efforts of Sheri Kotowski of the Embudo Valley Environmental Monitoring Group, which came into existence after the Cerro Grande fire, the first time smoke and ash polluted our agricultural communities.

I was hopeful that besides measuring the potential fallout of Isotopic plutonium, Isotopic uranium, Strontium, Americium, Beryllium, and heavy metals the monitoring station, which sits next to the southwest corner of my house where the bats come every evening to feed, would annoy them enough so they'd vacate the premises. But they're obviously doing more than just feeding because not only didn't they go away, they decided to do some exploring inside my house, just like they did last year around this time. I figure they've got nests in between the tin roof and wood ceiling where they're taking care of the "pups"—what the mammologist at New Mexico Game and Fish, who I phoned in desperation, called them.

Apparently they're getting in through all the little cracks—they only need a half inch—around the beams and stove pipe and ceiling boards up in the loft of my very tall house. When they made their way into the house for the first time last year they met their match in Jake Kosek, our Berkeley friend who's spent a lot of time in el norte. He was here to help bring in the wood supply after Mark was diagnosed with cancer. We were just sitting around in the kids' old bedroom, yakking—Jake, our son Jakob (also part of the wood cutting crew), Mark, and me, when the bats started zooming through the air above our heads. As I recall I ran screaming from the room, but good old Jake just laughed, turned down the lights so the bats would settle down (or settle up, as they hang on walls and beams, they don't perch), whipped off his shirt, threw it over one of the suckers, and tossed it outside. The other bat started up, tried to fly out of the room, knocked itself silly, and landed on the stairs. To redeem myself I threw a T-shirt over the prostrate bat and tossed it outside as well. After Jake left I filled up every crack I could find with expandable foam and nailed lath over that, but there continued to be bats in the bedroom until the pups were fledged: every night I shut the bedroom door while they flew around the room. In the morning they were gone.

Right on schedule they were back again this year. Last night I saw only one flying around the upstairs bedroom but there have been more: two, three, a dozen maybe, after they pushed in the screen on one of the windows where they congregate outside. I quickly slammed the door and by morning they'd flown back out the window, which I closed for good. While I'm not particularly thrilled at having bats flying around my house, I haven't vacated the premises, either. But it has limited who I can invite to spend the night. You can't have the grandmother from Cleveland (the inside joke when referencing someone who has no idea what living la vida loca in northern New Mexico means).

I lucked out that their arrival this year coincided with Jakob and Casey's weekend visit. Jakob is now on a mission to get rid of these "f*#!ing bats." The first night he caught two of them in a shirt, but was a little too zealous and kind of crushed them in the process. They ended up outside, dead. The next day we went over every possible nook and cranny with more foam and lath. Then my neighbor Tony, who comes over most evenings to fill water containers from my well, as the water line to his trailer is busted and they've yet to determine where, told us that he could see where the bats were flying in under one of the beams. So Jakob and I put up the 30-foot ladder, he climbed up with foam and lath and plugged that hole with a vengeance. Then we went inside, crawled into the nethermost regions of the loft with our headlamps and masks, and plugged the same hole from the inside. I'm sure that if we've been successful in stopping the ingress and egress of the bats the animal liberationists who read this blog are going to charge me with animal cruelty (the pups may still be in nests inside somewhere*), but I challenge any of them to share their house with bats, their gardens with gophers, and their chickens with pigeons before they put my handcuffs on.

I'm really ready for both the bats and the incessantly noisy air monitor to be gone. I'm also ready for the day-long buildup of rain clouds to unleash their blessings and salvage what's left of my parched fields (the Temptations' song "Oh how I wish that it would rain, rain, rain" plays over and over inside my head). In my 20 years in El Valle I've never seen it so bad. None of us in the southwest—or at least this generation— have ever seen it so bad. Perhaps the world has never seen it so bad. But that's another story.

---

* I never found any nests. Apparently they were just coming in for fun.

Sunday, July 31, 2011
The Million Dollar Bone Mill

In an issue of the *Santa Fe New Mexican* last week there was an insert published by the National Union of Hospital and Health Care Employees, which is an affiliate of the larger AFSCME/AFL-CIO. The nurses and technicians at Christus St. Vincent Hospital in Santa Fe have been involved in protracted negotiations with hospital management over wages and conditions—safe staffing and experience—and as I write this union members are voting on the proposed contract.

The insert, as part of the union's message to the public regarding the struggles of the nurses and technicians, includes a list of the salaries of "Officers, Directors, Trustees, Key Employees, and Highest Compensated Employees" of Christus. The CEO, Alex Valdez, makes a whopping $457,064 (and $148,122 estimated fringe benefits). But lo and behold, the highest compensation by far on the list belongs to my old friend Dr. Samuel Chun, an orthopedic surgeon, whose makes $935,275. He's not really my friend, but I did see him as often as I see many of my friends when I was referred to him for treatment of a bone spur on the lower part of my thumb. After shooting me up with cortisone a couple of times, which did nothing to alleviate the pain, he proceeded to remove the bone spur, which he did quite well, as he appears to be an excellent surgeon (although he forgot to take a look at a mass on my palm while he was doing the cutting). But then the trouble began, which should have been included in my Diary of a Bad Year, except that it would have made it the Diary of My Two and a Half Bad Years and I wouldn't have been able to use J.M. Coetzee's title.

I wasn't blogging back then but I've always done my best venting by pen so I sent him a letter. He never answered, of course, but now that I'm blogging I'm urging everyone to read my Health Insurance blog post. You never know, maybe someone who is considering orthopedic surgery will read this posting and decide NOT to choose Chun and NOT to contribute to his $935,275 compensation package.

That was the end of my relationship with Chun and his partner, who I suspect makes a six figure compensation as well. I found another orthopedic doc in Española who looked at my medical records and the RSD diagnosis and said to me, let's not go there. So I didn't, and with the help of a good physical therapist and many hours of evaluation by the new doc I eventually healed. In my letter to Chun I suggested that he spend some of the money he was making (at the time I had no idea how much that actually was) on a patient navigator who could follow the progress of everyone who makes his or her way through the maze of his assembly line practice. But that kind of practice works efficiently only when patients are in and out the door. Once it was obvious that I was a malingerer, he wasn't interested.

So that's the story. The solution is simple: Christus St. Vincent can pay Dr. Chun and his cohort a salary just like it pays the nurses and techs who work their butts off to take care of all of us before and after the surgeons stroll in with the scalpels. If they can do it at the Mayo Clinic, they can do it in Fanta Se.

Wednesday, August 17, 2011

Unplugged

Even in El Valle, at 8,000 feet, it's been hot. So I planned to do some big-time weeding in my garden in the early morning when the hoop house throws some shade over my mess of bind weed, mallow, and grass. Instead, I spent that time trying to transfer information from my old laptop to my new used laptop (thank you, Jake Kosek) for all the editing jobs I'm doing, track down a UPS package that I thought was being shipped by the post office (see Marginalization blog), change the bank account on my electronic billing (my community bank got taken over by a multi-national), and answer a bunch of e-mails that needed answering. As I'm doing all this I'm keeping up a steady stream of complaint: I don't want to be doing this, why am I doing this, computers are making my life more complicated (see The Scourge of Computers blog), not less, I can't believe I'm talking to myself like this, I want to go back to my life before I had a computer.

I often think of my pre-computer life. I certainly was just as busy as I am today, but I was busy doing other things like building a house, raising children, fighting the Forest Service (a life's work), gardening, knitting (I actually knit the kids and Mark sweaters and hats), writing stories (on the typewriter), fighting the developers (also a life's work), and taking trips to Mexico and the mountains (see Productivity blog). I was younger, and had more energy, but it was also easier to generate that energy because my efforts produced something other than the busyness required to keep up with the bureaucratic bullshit that has taken over our lives.

Let's take a closer look at the things I was doing that morning. Why in the world do I need two laptop computers? I have a hard drive back-up for all my important papers (two novels, a book of short stories, a memoir of my political activity in northern New Mexico, all unpublished) and other files, but you know how it goes: my old laptop is slow, it won't run any of the constantly upgraded applications that Apple is constantly turning out so people have to spend more money to buy new computers, which means you have to buy one, too, or you can't communicate and everyone tells you you're a Luddite. After two sessions with my computer guru, Robin Collier, there is still stuff that hasn't been transferred off the old to the new, and glitches that I'm still discovering on the new that make me run back to the old (or up to the old, as it's upstairs and the new one is downstairs), cursing all the way.

Then I happen to look at my e-mail and realize that a package that I thought was mailed to me on July 27 and expected to arrive in three to five days was actually UPS'd to me and of course I'd provided the postal mailing address, not the UPS address. So I call the UPS center in Santa Fe (fortunately, the last time I managed to find the number, which is not listed in the phone book because they make you call a centralized number in anywhere U.S.A. that can only help you if you have a tracking number, I had the presence of mind to write it down) and give them the correct physical address (my mailing address is a physical address as well, but neither deliverer will recognize the other's).

Moving on to the next distraction, I find myself once more on the computer trying to pay my credit card bill only to see that my old bank, the one I specifically chose because it was local, is still listed as the payer when it's been taken over by some multi-national bank I've never even heard of because of the mortgage crisis. The new bank sends me about five letters a week explaining how this takeover is being handled and what I have to do and what I don't have to do, which is change any electronic payment information because the new bank is going to take care of that.

But of course it hasn't and I'm worried that my payment won't be correctly processed and the credit card company will charge me interest, which is usury, so I decide to make the change myself, which I can't figure out how to do online, of course, so I have to call the credit card company and have someone walk me through it and then that's done.

Lastly are the e-mails. Normally I don't complain about e-mails. I know that some people get hundreds of them every day and end up throwing most of them in the trash. Of all the technological innovations associated with the computer I appreciate e-mail the most because it means I can impart information or ask a question or have a short chat without getting bogged down on the phone with certain friends who will remain nameless who think that anytime you call it's an excuse to talk for an hour about much more than the purpose of the call. But you still have that nagging feeling that you need to read all those e-mails pertaining to your work or your political awareness and then like everyone else you throw them in the trash.

This posting is full of a lot of "see other blogs," which may indicate that it's redundant, but I think it's more a reaffirmation of the need to chafe and complain and yes, even rant, about the bullshit we, the few and the privileged (see Some Things Are Relative blog) put up with, and really, promote, in this short time we have on earth. I remember a backpack trip long ago, walking the crest trail in the Manzano Mountains, thinking, I wish I could walk this trail forever and never go back. Sometimes it's just all too much.

Monday, August 22, 2011

Diary of a Bad Year: Death or Philip Roth, I Can't Remember Which

I write down ideas, sometimes as titles, as they occur to me in preparation for this blog. What on earth was I thinking when I wrote "Death or Philip Roth, I Can't Decide Which?" Try as I might, I can't remember. So I'm going to wing it and start writing free association about Philip and maybe my original thought will find its way to my frontal lobe and I'll end up writing what I originally intended.

A few years ago Mark and I started a Philip Roth book club with Mark Rudd. He lives in Albuquerque and we live two hours away in El Valle so we conducted our conversation via e-mail. I can't really remember (this is a recurring theme, obviously) what precipitated the formation of our club, but it didn't last very long. We encouraged Mark R. to read the Zuckerman trilogy, Roth's alter ego at his funniest, but before Mark got there he was turned off by the newer novels, like Exit Ghost, and then didn't much like Zuckerman Unbound and The Anatomy Lesson either, so our club fizzled. Mark and I had trouble, too, with Exit Ghost, but I thought Roth's struggle about telling the "truth" in one's fiction, which no longer has much meaning in the postmodern world of relativity, salvaged the book. He apologizes for railing about cell phones and about his audacity to still feel there is a right and wrong way to be in the world, which is certainly something I sympathize with. I guess his alter egos, who constantly struggle to get through all the bullshit to what is "real" (and the way he becomes the women who call him on his own bullshit), allow him to make the attempt while acknowledging that we all come to our analyses with our neuroses, prejudices, and unalterable histories. I went on and reread not only the Zuckerman books but Goodbye Columbus, which I thoroughly enjoyed, and Portnoy's Complaint, but the Monkey bit was too much for me. Roth's obsession with young women is his recurring theme; in the novels when he's preadolescent or a young man himself, or even a middle-aged man who also appreciates middle-aged women, it's OK. But when he's an old man, as in the later novels, it becomes, as Mark R. put it, "embarrassing."

But wait. I just made the obvious connection with death and Philip, whose mortality is staring him in the face (although I still don't know why I said "I can't decide which" in the title of my blog). He must be in his late seventies now (I just Googled him; he's 78). Olympia Dukakis goes around asking all the men she meets in in the movie "Moonstuck" for an explanation of why her husband, Vincent Gardenia, chases women. Finally she gets her answer from Danny Aiello: "Because he fears death?"

Mark died at 62, much too young, at least for those of us in the western world whose life expectancy is somewhere in the late 70s or 80s, to have to face one's mortality. I now think a lot about my own. Even though I'm on life's downhill side, the end of that slide wouldn't be so much on my mind if it weren't for Mark's death and knowing so many others my age who also have cancer and other illnesses. As James Woods points out in his *New Yorker* article "Is That All There Is?", even those who believe in immortality aren't immune to fear and dread of death. He quotes Columbia philosopher Philip Kitcher: "If your life is directed toward nurturing others who need your protection and guidance, and if, unluckily, you die before they are ready to cope without you, the fact that you will be restored—and maybe restored to them in some entirely different state—is immaterial. Your project, on which you have centered your existence, has still been compromised by premature death." I don't think I'm particularly fearful, but I dread leaving my kids behind.

If Mark had lived we would still be publishing *La Jicarita News* (I think), working on books, traveling, gardening, cutting firewood, pretty much everything we've always done, but my life has changed irrevocably. While I don't go around chasing young men, I'm less attached to my work and what my contribution to society has been. I feel that maybe I should be doing some things I haven't been doing seeing as how I, too, could be gone tomorrow. I'm not sure what those things are, but I'm thinking about it.

Thursday, September 15, 2011

Letter to Elizabeth

Instead of posting a comment to your blog, Elizabeth (elizabethtannen.com/blog), I decided to write you a letter via my blog. In the olden days I would have written you on paper and put it in the mailbox, but in those olden days I wouldn't have read what you wrote because there were no blogs. So round and round it goes, but as long as we're still talking, it's OK with me.

I was 28 a long time ago but I remember it well. It was a time of angst and instability, largely precipitated by the pattern set at Antioch College, which I attended for a short but intense time. We went to school for half the year and spent the other half on co-op jobs around the country, in three or six month rotations: rural New Hampshire, Berkeley, and Santa Fe for me. Even after I left, the pattern continued: Colorado Springs (where I was raised and went back to briefly); Cloudcroft, New Mexico; Bend, Oregon; Albuquerque's South Valley; and finally (but not lastly) Placitas. My friends from Antioch were all over the place, set in motion just like me. I had several relationships, both going nowhere from the get go, and many flings. These were the days when Okies (corner of University and Central), Rosa's Cantina (Algodones), and The Golden Inn (on the east side of the Sandias) provided a community of sorts, if drinking, dancing, and having a good old time with a bunch of other students, hippies, and assorted misfits counted as a cohort (I never used that word until Jakob started referring to his PhD class as one).

None of it assuaged my anxiety, which we all seem to share at that age regardless of the time and place. But what I want to say in this letter to you and many others your age who feel disconnected, unsure of where they want to be and with whom, things will settle into place eventually. It may take longer than you'd like it to, particularly now, in the midst of a depression, which our politicians euphemistically call a recession. It's going to be harder for your generation than it was for mine—fewer ways to slip through the cracks with cheap rents, cheap gas, and an appreciation of the second-hand (it's all boutique now).

You may end up someplace you never thought you would, and with "someones" instead of someone. A lot of it will be determined by you—what work you end up doing, where you do that work, or where you to want to be instead of where you find work—but a lot of it will be serendipitous (which is a more elegant way of saying a crap shoot). When I think back on how I ended up where I am, in northern New Mexico, in El Valle, I'm amazed. At 28 I'd never heard of the place. And it happened just like I said: some of it willed, choosing time over money (living in rural New Mexico), bad luck (leaving my home in Placitas because of gentrification), and good luck (knowing someone who lived in El Valle). I ended up with the same partner for 34 years, but he had already been married to his high school sweetheart, divorced, and had somehow found his way from Buffalo to Placitas, a route full of serendipity and dumb luck (finding me). You never know where they'll come from or who they'll turn out to be, these people you'll have relationships with. But it will be VERY interesting.

So, it sounds like you've had a love-hate relationship with the crazy twenties and are ready to leave them behind and make your life a little more stable, which will hopefully make it a lot less anxious. You're right that we tend to think of ourselves "on some sort of ascending path" but that the "better future" may indeed be false, particularly now. But I think, relatively speaking, that it will be better, at least on the personal level. Dan Savage founded the It Gets Better web site to let gays know that the social ostracism they suffer in high school or their early twenties will subside, that they will find the homes and relationships and work that most twenty somethings segue into in their thirties.

There will always be something to worry about, regardless of where you live, what you do, and who your family and/or friends may be (and for many folks friends are family). But you are not going to "revert to an older, lesser version of yourself," regardless of the circumstances (even if it's where you started out). It's what you will be doing, who you choose to do it with, both personally and professionally, and how you go about making a home that determine who you are—even if in the end, none of us quite have a handle on exactly who that is. I often think back on all the stuff I did, the people I did it with, what I built and grew and wrote and thought. Someday you will, too. And it will have been a great ride.

Sunday, September 18, 2011

Guilty Pleasures

For anyone younger than 55 this posting is going to be in a musical foreign language. For those of us older than 55, it's going to be a nostalgic tour of guilty pleasures (not the R&B of my Funky Soul blog).

Mark and I acknowledged our guilty pleasures to each other when certain songs came on the oldies station in Albuquerque that we'd listen to in the car when we couldn't get anything decent on any other stations. I don't know if other people our age also refer to these songs as guilty pleasures, but they know what I mean. (I have to acknowledge here that our son Max, who is 22, knows all these songs, too; from us or the oldies station, or both?)

Terri, my friend from Santa Fe, originally from Philadelphia, does, too. Although five years younger than me she never misses a beat (or title) when it come to pop music. She must have started listening at age eight. We were going to go camping last weekend up above Chama but it poured rain and I couldn't find a housesitter who I could possibly ask to clean up my demented dog Sammy's poop every morning (that's another blog waiting to be written). So she came up to El Valle and we hung out yakking about this and that, watching the U.S. Open (Serena trash talking the umpire over her penalty), and eating. On Sunday we went for a hike up the canyon and then treated ourselves to brunch at the Sugar Nymphs, Peñasco's own gourmet restaurant whose owners I sometimes sell produce to and drink a lot of mojitos with.

I can't remember (my recurring theme) how we got started on guilty pleasures, a term she hadn't used before but a concept she knew well. I started out admitting that I liked a couple of songs that were definitely pop, not rock, but had catchy enough beats that despite the inane lyrics got my toes tapping. Then she asked, "What else," and I thought, I'm really going to be embarrassed to admit another guilty pleasure is Brandi, by a band called Looking Glass (I had no idea who recorded Brandi, I Googled it as I wrote this, but I bet Mark would have known) about this bar waitress named Brandi who's in love with a sailor who's love is the sea, not Brandi. I was just about to admit it when Terri blurted out, "Brandi." I shot out of my chair and jumped up and down with delight.

When we got home we immediately went to YouTube and started playing all our guilty pleasures. We started querying each other about all those questionable pop/rock icons who actually had a good song or two: Rod Stewart with Maggie May, of course. Cat Stevens? (For those of you who don't know who Cat Stevens is he started off as kind of a folk rock singer, then became more known for his writing, and finally became Yusuf Islam when he converted.) I knew there was a song of his I liked, and Terri actually had it on iTunes, but the song, The First Cut is the Deepest, was covered by someone else (Rod Stewart, among others, I just Googled that, too). Anyway, this went on and on and segued into other songs we had that the other one had never heard, like Johnny Cash and Joe Strummer singing Redemption Song.

After Terri left I remembered another guilty pleasure and e-mailed her about this particular embarrassment: Lying Eyes by the Eagles. Everybody has probably heard of the Eagles—they're still out there touring with the same band members they started out with, I think. But Lying Eyes? This doesn't jive with my criteria that a bad lyric song can only be saved by a good beat, or an edge. It goes: "Late at night the big old house gets lonely, I guess every form of refuge has its price. It breaks her heart to think her love is only given to a man with hands as cold as ice." Or something like that. But the chorus picks you up and carries you along: "You can't hide your lying eyes. And your smile is a thin disguise. I thought by now you'd realize, there ain't no way to hide your lying eyes."

Ahhhh. It's just one of those anomalies I have to accept. When I'm in the car, singing "Brandi, you're a fine girl, what a good wife you would be" at the top of my lungs, you just have to let it go and enjoy your guilty pleasures.

Monday, September 26, 2011

Christian Schizophrenia

The state (and I don't mean Georgia) killed Troy Davis last Wednesday, a manifestation of what I call Christian schizophrenia. I could easily be talking about Muslim schizophrenia or Jewish schizophrenia or any number of religious schizophrenias, but right now I'm talking about the good old U.S.A.'s affliction.

People like Jimmy Carter and Reverend Al Sharpton represent one side of the schizophrenic code. They temper the hail and brimstone fervor of an "Eye for an eye, tooth for a tooth" with the "love thy neighbor as thyself." They believe there is redemption in good conduct: society, as well as the individual, are responsible for creating an environment in which the human spirit can flourish and do good deeds. The death penalty allows no redemption. The commutation of Davis' death sentence would have acknowledged his 20 years of self-improvement during his incarceration (or rather his 20 years of torture on death row).

The flip side of the schizophrenic code is represented by folks like Rick Perry, who as governor of Texas has presided over the execution of 235 people. As a fundamentalist Christian he's definitely a "life for a life" kind of guy: no extenuating circumstances such as societal racism, poverty, or misogyny should ever interfere with the state's license to kill. This license to kill is equated with God's will.

Both forms of Christianity conflate justice and religion in their own perverse ways. While I admire many of the liberation theology priests and nuns who have devoted their lives to helping people around the world and who don't want anybody killed in the name of God, they still believe there is a God to whose will we must submit. An NAACP leader outside the prison, right before Davis's execution, said, when she heard of a rumored last minute stay, "We thank God, our prayers have been answered." But then whoops, they decided to execute him after all: God's will again. Within five minutes God had changed from the benevolent, merciful God of the Carters and Sharptons to the vengeful, unforgiving God of the Perrys. How schizophrenic is that?

I don't know whether Davis was guilty or innocent, and the people (jury, lawyers, judge, guards, executioner) who participated in his death certainly didn't know. Only Davis himself knew the truth. That he was put to death by state sanction (something different than the people) is tragic and inhumane. But the really unsettling part of this scenario is that the fundamentalist Christian schizophrenics (and complicity, the "love thy neighbor" schizophrenics) insist that this country was founded on Christian principles (they usually say Judeo-Christian, but that's just a bone for AIPAC) and that these principles should guide every institution, not just the criminal [in]justice system. Its vengeful absolutism already determines the way many institutions are run: No Child Left Behind dictates that you teach kids to take a test and if they fail that test you punish the school by taking away its funding and firing its teachers. Now they want to punish all the old and sick people who don't have IRAs, stock portfolios, or private health insurance because there is something sinful about these folks who haven't achieved the American dream despite what Elizabeth Warren pointed out the other day, "There is nobody in this country who got rich on his own. Nobody."

Fundamentalism has been around forever. But the increased fervor to make it the guiding "light" (darkness) of our combined lives when the Enlightenment is 300 years old, postmodernism permeates culture, and every prejudice the Bible holds dear is being smashed to smithereens is testimony to an even more insidious schizophrenia. It's not endemic to the U.S., but when more than one of our presidential candidates is the face of this affliction it's time to lock up the crazies instead of the criminals.

Monday, October 10, 2011

Diary of a Bad Year: Mark and Steve

As the entire blogosphere knows, Steve Jobs died of complications from pancreatic cancer this past week. Although he lived for almost six years with a rare, "treatable" form of the cancer, it got him in the end. While the doc in the emergency room who treated Mark used Jobs as an example of everything that's wrong with a medical system that provides every option for the rich and bankruptcy for the poor, not even a liver transplant and the best care money can buy could save him (see Diary of a Bad Year, February 13, 2011).

His death has elicited obituaries that run the gamut from the visionary genius "who knew what we wanted before we wanted it" to the capitalist exploiter who produced his slick products on the backs of foreign sweatshop workers. For me, however, his death elicited a resurgence of memories of Mark. It made me think about the disease itself and the differences in their treatment and their prognoses, but in a much more visceral way it made me remember Mark in his corporeality. Steve Jobs and Mark Schiller looked very much alike: tall, thin, close-cropped balding heads, graying beards, and dark brown eyes behind round wire rimmed glasses. When I saw pictures of Jobs in 2009, when the illness had made a thin man gaunt, I was seeing Mark.

I know nothing about the private Steve Jobs. He was seven years younger than Mark, but close enough in age to have experienced many of the same things. I don't know if he loved Mavis Staples and Al Green, or Chet Baker and Thelonious Monk. I don't know what his politics were: many capitalist entrepreneurs consider themselves liberals, especially those who came of age during the sixties and seventies. Mark's politics guided his life from the time he helped organize his high school SDS chapter to his choice of where to live to co-founding *La Jicarita News*. To stir up the mix he'd declare he was the only Stalinist left standing, when in reality what we learned together about race, class, and absolutist positions in northern New Mexican made him a complex, thoughtful activist whose compañeros included loggers, Forest Service rangers, acequia mayordomos, and gasp, even a few environmentalists. His encyclopedic knowledge ranged through poetry, abstract expressionism, jazz, 19th century English literature, rock n' roll (he always knew the names of the most obscure groups played on the oldies station, see Guilty Pleasures blog), the Energy Employees Occupational Illness Compensation Program Act, and Spanish and Mexican land grants. He wrote many, many articles about the history and politics of land grants for *La Jicarita News*, as well as scholarly papers for the New Mexico Historical Advisory Board and the *Natural Resources Journal*. He was working on a book about the tenure of New Mexico Surveyor General George W. Julian, who was responsible for the loss of millions of acres of land to their rightful owners, which he was unable to finish before he died. I've collected the chapters he completed as scholarly papers or articles, and with the help of University of New Mexico professor David Correia, plan to finish that book.

Steve Jobs legacy is unparalleled. I have two Mac laptops and an iPod. My kids have iPhones and iPads. I also have many questions about the value of all that technology and disgust, but not surprise, about its production (see the NYT article about Mike Daisey's one man show "The Agony and the Ecstasy of Steve Jobs" in the Sunday, October 2 issue), but that's not what this blog is about. The Steve Jobs and Mark Schillers of the world who lived creative and intense lives and died before their time is sad, but what they did is what we have, tangibly and in our memories.

My son Jakob called to tell me that he's planning on publishing a photo story about Mark, also triggered by Jobs' death. He took many pictures of his dad over the years, and with Mark's permission, some while he was sick. I started this blog the day before he called. Steve Jobs' death, within a year of Mark's and of the same disease, reminds us of our loss, and being the writers and photographer that we are, the need to express it.

Friday, October 28, 2011

"When You Got Nothing You Got Nothing To Lose"

Bob Dylan's iconic words carry several meanings. To those of us who decided (with the luxury of a middle class background) to live as leanly as possible, the meaning is literal: if you're not part of the system, with a mortgage and credit card debt, when the system collapses you haven't lost much. The other meaning, that when you're poor and struggling and the system offers you nothing in the way of rising out of that poverty, you're already lost.

Some of the folks who started Occupy Wall Street offer a third meaning. Many of them appear to be from recently achieved middle class homes—upward mobility from working class or minority assimilation—and aspire to professional work and home ownership—a piece of the American pie—albeit with a more sophisticated understanding of how that lifestyle is supported both economically and politically. Then they find out there aren't any jobs doing what they've been trained to do, and they can't afford mortgage loans (and no one is building anything affordable anyway) because they're deeply in debt from college loans. So what better way to spend the day than in the street with their cohort.

They are joined by an interesting array of other protesters, from all walks of life, including the working poor, college professors, union organizers, activists, and retirees. But the core group of folks, even with their different spin on "you got nothing to lose," are the direct descendants of the protesters who were in the streets during the Vietnam war: people young enough and unencumbered enough to stay out there in the park day and night while a movement is created. Those of us who were in Washington D.C., Kent State, and every other city across the U.S. in the late sixties and early seventies keep saying to ourselves, "I wish I could be in Liberty Park, too." But there's the mother who requires 24-hour care, the house that needs to be ready for winter, the woodpile that needs to be split, and the animals that need to be fed and cared for.

The anti-war movement addressed all things that sustain a war of occupation: the imperialism of the war mongers, the military industrial complex, and the race and class distinctions that sent a disproportionate number of young men and women of color and low economic status to be killed. These power structures are still with us, and I suspect there's plenty of conversation about them among the Occupy Wall Street protesters. But the overriding focus on the growing economic inequality illuminates Wall Street's free market fetishism, which eludes the control of even the weakest regulatory oversight and defines an even more insidious hegemony than the war mongering political and corporate establishment we've been fighting forever.

I mentioned in a previous blog posting the conversation I had with a young friend who didn't want to hear about what went on in the sixties, that the social network has supplanted the need for organizing in the streets. I'm sure all this twittering and tweeting is a lot less cumbersome than printing fliers on ditto machines, but there's nothing like meeting your compadres face to face in a public space with a common sense of purpose. Maybe this time around, with their general assemblies, their consensus building skills, and the message on the wall "It's the system, stupid," they'll avoid some of the internecine struggles that tore the New Left apart. Maybe not. But I've heard so many of the people interviewed in various Occupies around the country say, "I've been waiting for years for this to happen." It's impossible to keep cynicism at bay without being part of an uprising of consciousness and spirit and action. (Pessimism of the intellect, optimism of the will—Antonio Gramsci.) I may not be there physically, but I'm there, one way or another.

Sunday, November 6, 2011

Diary of a Bad Year: The End

This will be my last installment under the heading Diary of a Bad Year (two bad years, actually). It is signified by the death of Mark's mother, from whom he was estranged when he died last year, on November 27. During this last year of her life we never discussed this estrangement, nor did we discuss anything that would force us into a place I did not want to go.

That being said, as she began to decline I did whatever I could to help, eventually moving her out of her house into a fairly nice residential facility, an "independent living" apartment. But once she made the physical move she essentially gave up: her increased dependency and loss of "control," something she had hoarded all her life to compensate for a bad beginning, shut her down psychologically, emotionally, and physically. Her decline was dramatic: within three weeks of the move she required 24-hour care, and a week later she died.

Dealing first with Mark's death, and now hers, has forced me to face my own mortality, which I've written about previously in other Diary of a Bad Year blog posts. But it has also forced me to think about not just the fact that I will die but how I will die. Not surprisingly, this is a topic that doesn't generate much discussion in our youth obsessed society, but as we continue to live longer, buoyed by miracle drugs and interventions that may extend our life span but render us mentality and physically bereft, we better start doing some serious talking.

The so-called Death Panels that were a part of Obama's health care reform package were quickly scuttled after that nomenclature stuck. In some more enlightened European countries there can at least be a discussion between the patient, family, and physician about "end of life" wishes, which is much more substantive than the health care directives we sign in this country saying we don't want to be resuscitated if we're already dying of cancer or heart disease. They don't say anything about what our choices might be if we're dying of old age and are so infirm that staying alive is cruel and unusual punishment. And the medical interventions that have gotten us to that state are also forms of cruel and unusual punishment. Two years ago I watched my beloved amigo y buen vecino Tomás slowly die of complications from diabetes, a stroke, and finally colon cancer. The last six months of his ordeal were in the hospital, where he was kept alive by extraordinary means, until finally he came home and said, " , I'm tired and I'm not going back."

While he had the wherewithal and presence of mind to refuse more hospitalization, that doesn't really speak to the problem of those who are old and infirm and are ready to die before their bodies actually give out. There was a story in the newspaper the other day about a couple, in their nineties, who decided to stop eating and drinking because, like my neighbor, they'd simply had enough. They were kicked out of their retirement facility for taking this action. Let's penalize those who actually make a decision to exercise choice, as opposed to default, which drains their—and everyone who loves them—physical, emotional, and yes, financial well being (the focus of Medicare on medical intervention rather than long term care is another story).

What about those who suffer from incipient Alzheimer's, who are able to see what the future holds and don't want to go there? What choices do these folks have who want to be the person they are instead of a person who will be unrecognizable to family and friends? Some would argue that as Alzheimer's progresses you are unaware of the loss of identity, that it is those around you who do the losing, so that makes it OK. I don't want my children to lose me. I'm their mother, the person with whom they share their most intimate thoughts, worries, and aspirations (caveat: I know there are tons of things they don't tell me because it's none of my business), but I am also a person they see in a larger context defined by my work, the way I choose to live, and how I treat them. When Mark's mother was dying, what she talked about was not the present, her loss of control, what she suffered, or even those of us who were with her. She talked about her life when she was young, her parents, her brother who died in World War II, her youngest brother who she essentially raised, and her life with her husband, who died five years before her.

The image of the native Inuit putting the old person who can no longer contribute to society out on the ice floe remains very vivid to my generation. That is obviously not an option for today's society (as well as the fact that there may not be many ice floes to put them on). So what are we supposed to do? I don't have the answer, but if we can't even have a conversation about it without a Death Panel label we are, as individuals, and as a society, complicit in what often amounts to torture.

Friday, November 18, 2011

Stuff

For the past three weeks I've been dealing with my mother-in-law's lifetime possessions, the story of her deliberate accumulation of things that become, to the successors, "stuff." It was all acquired during the course of forty years in the same house in Buffalo, then ten in Santa Fe. I've tried to be respectful of what to her were treasures, not stuff, sending the china (I knew her for 34 years and I don't remember ever eating off it), crystal, antique chairs and dresser off to the consignment store, gifts of art or pottery or jewelry back to those who gave them, especially cherished things to friends, books to the library, and much, much more to St. Vincent de Paul.

My mother-in-law, an immigrant from Poland whose family came to New York when she was six, grew up desperately poor in Williamsburg, Brooklyn. She told us stories of getting thrown out of her family's apartment for unpaid rent, carrying their belongings down the street in a wheelbarrow. One of her siblings was killed in World War II; an older half brother became a successful businessman; her younger brother a professor at New York University; and she, after twenty years of secretarial work, went to college and earned a master's degree in social work. She and my father-in-law, also a social worker who headed a United Fund agency in Buffalo, became solidly middle class and enjoyed a fully pensioned retirement—fueled by a booming stock market—of world travel and portfolio security.

They were also of the generation that bought Dalton china settings for twelve on a trip to England, Waterford crystal at the factory in Ireland, Tibetan thangkas in India, gold jewelry from around the world, pueblo pottery and turquoise jewelry in New Mexico, and art from a sophisticated group of Buffalo painters with whom they socialized.

But what really got me, going through the stuff, was the thought of my own children someday going through mine. What do I have that makes me so anxious? A set of red dishes my mother-in-law bought me for my fiftieth birthday? My clothes, mostly acquired at thrift stores? The art gives me pause, but they can give Terri's paintings back to her, if she outlives me (or keep them, of course), and they took some of Mark's work after he died. The John Wengers will probably find their way to those who knew him.

What seems to be upsetting me are the floor to ceiling shelves with books, that, just like the china, nobody wants. James Woods, in a recent *New Yorker* article, wrote about inventorying his father-in-law's library in upstate New York and finding out that "nobody really wants hundreds or thousands of old books." I may not have 400 books on the Byzantine Empire, but I have, due to Mark's love of him, every book ever written by or about Jack Kerouac; every beat poet ever published; every 18th and 19th century English novel ever written (I know that's an exaggeration: let's arrogantly say every "important" English novel ever written); political philosophy from the Greeks through the Enlightenment to Karl Marx and the poststructuralists; and 20th century paperback novels that everyone else has, too. Mark already sold the first editions and collectors' items to folks like Nicholas Potter (secondhand bookstore owner in Santa Fe) of whom there are fewer and fewer in business. My kids will want only a select few, just as I wanted only a select few of my mother-in-law's. Even if the iPad and the Kindle don't destroy the book business altogether, nobody is going to want my "old books."

When I don't have anything of interest borrowed from a friend or checked out from the library, I go to my shelves and find stuff, like this incredible passage from George Elliot's *Mill on the Floss*, which I've owned for 20 years but never before read:

"I will not believe unproved evil of you: my lips shall not utter it; my ears shall be closed against it. I, too, am an erring mortal, liable to stumble, apt to come short of my most earnest efforts. Your lot has been harder than mine, your temptation greater. Let us help each other to stand and walk without more falling—to have done this would have demanded courage, deep pity, self-knowledge, generous trust—would have demanded a mind that tasted no piquancy in evil-speaking that felt no self-exaltation in condemning, that cheated itself with no large words into the belief that life can have any moral end, any high religion, which excludes the striving after perfect truth, justice, and love towards the individual men and women who come across our own path."

How can you not stop and marvel at a passage like that? It speaks directly to my post-Marxist humanist pragmatic self (see eponymous blog post), which is tied directly to all these books on my shelf that no one but me wants. While I'm not quite ready to let them go, not ready to consign them to "stuff," I think it's time to start culling: slowly, carefully, selectively (based on some criteria I've yet to determine). That, instead of an estate, will be my gift to my children: one small shelf of books when it's my time to go.

Monday, December 5, 2011

Letter to Elizabeth, Number Two

I haven't had time to blog much lately, but when I read your piece "On Breaking Two Taboos, Sharing, Playing Games, and Not" (elizabethtannen.com/blog), about a month ago I started composing this letter to you in my head. Now it's in writing.

When I was in my carefree twenties (that's a laugh, carefree maybe, but, as I talked about in Letter Number One, full of existential angst), I remember having a conversation with someone about the "worst part of being alone" and all he could come up with was he didn't like eating by himself. I went into a long discourse about how being alone denied one intimacy, being able to share your most heartfelt feelings with someone who actually cares to listen and respond to those feelings.

I ended up being intimate with Mark for 34 years, and yes, there was a lot of sharing and caring and listening, along with all the silence (comfortable and uncomfortable) that accompany a long relationship. Now, however, I am at the other end of the book shelf, alone again, without the intimacy I complained about not having in my twenties, but aware now of how complicated intimacy can be. I lost the only person in the world who paid constant attention to me, even if it was often critical attention. There will never again be anyone who knew me as Mark did, and in many ways I won't know me as well either because I don't have him around to fill in the gaps: "Who is that person?" or "Did we see that movie?" or "Which kid was it who called big trucks 'hot zooms'?" Neither is he here for me to share the information only he and I were privy to, which makes it hard to validate a feeling or remembrance.

You don't particularly appreciate this when you're living it. Mark and

I, as well as many other couples I know, were constantly jockeying for time alone, to have the house to ourselves so we didn't have to answer to anybody or do anything we didn't want to do, like cook dinner when you wanted to read your book. We're not really wishing for singlehood, as we see our single friends wondering how it happened that they live alone, without the intimacy we're complaining about. We want to have it all, actually: someone around with whom we feel completely comfortable and intimate when we want them around, and when we don't want them around we want them to go away for awhile but know that they'll be back.

When we lived in extended families or tribal groups or all those crazy communes in the sixties we had more than one person paying particular attention to us, which created its own problems, of course: lack of privacy, peer pressure, group think. It's complicated, no matter how you look at it: living alone, living in a nuclear family, living in a group. We fumble along, complaining and compensating, rationalizing and resigning ourselves to circumstances that are both amenable to change and outside our control. I imagine you'll experience it all over the next 30 years, like I have. All I can say is, buena suerte.

Thursday, December 29, 2011

On Not Watching Basketball

It looked like nobody was going to be watching basketball this year until the players and management struck a 50-50 deal (meaning the players and owners will share the billions), and we had a five game bonanza on Christmas Day.

I didn't do any basketball watching last year, either, except for a week—the NBA finals. I'm not a fan of either team (Dallas and Miami), but I'm especially not a fan of Miami. The hype generated by its acquisition of LeBron James as a member of the Three Musketeers (Dwayne Wade and Chris Bosh being the other two), was enough to make even the most die-hard fan jaded. Yes, even Mark, who loved basketball, had already admitted that the spectacle had defeated the substance. But I watched in his memory.

I gave up being a fan, meaning wanting a particular team to win, after the Pistons' and Lakers' great years in the late 1980s: I'll never forget the on-court kiss of Magic Johnson and Isaiah Thomas. We loved Kareem Abdul-Jabbar, Magic, James Worthy, Kurt Rambis, Maurice Lucas, and Michael Cooper (he came from New Mexico), Isaiah, the crazy Dennis Rodman, John Salley, and Bill Laimbeer. Mark stayed a fan through the Laker transition to Shaquille O'Neal and Kobe Bryant. The kids and I gave up after Bryant was accused of rape.

You could make a case for not being a fan of any sports team if you wanted to make criminal activity the criteria: the transition from the ghetto to the "show" (as they call it in that great baseball flick Bull Durham) has littered the playing field with adulterers, wife beaters, rapists, animal abusers, and even a few murderers. To be fair, a lot of them are guilty only of wearing silk suits and driving Mercedes Benz's and Jaguars. I always marveled at Mark's ability to disassociate sports, particularly basketball, from the criteria used to judge just about everything else in life: class structure, economic inequality, corporate greed, media misinformation, etc. While he knew the world of sports was complicit in all these machinations, he didn't care, because he just got too much enjoyment out of watching the ballet of basketball, the gut wrenching physicality of football, and the beauty of the home run. Watching games he became just another fan, yelling in excitement over a great play, groaning with disappointment at a missed opportunity.

Mark and I bonded watching Monday night baseball years ago. These were the last of the Oakland A's days, also the last time I got excited about a baseball team: Catfish Hunter, Rollie Fingers, Vida Blue. Then when the baby came along, one of us would cook dinner while the other one swung Jakob in his Tarahumara swing that a friend had given us. We hung it from a viga and tied a rope to its side so we could sit on the couch and swing it to and fro without it getting in the way of the TV. I sometimes still watch the playoffs and the world series, but once you lose track of who the players are you kind of lose track of the game.

The only football I watch is Friday Night Lights. A friend just told me that the only actor who actually played football is Landry (Jesse Plemons), the Johnny come lately to the team and the ensemble oddball. Mark was a die-hard Buffalo fan (his hometown), which was a kind of torture, even when they were winning (remember, Jim Kelly took them to the Superbowl, what, four times, and lost every time). I never really understood this about his sports nature, either. He knew perfectly well that the Buffalo Bills had nothing to do with Buffalo other than arbitrarily playing there, but he hung with them, and suffered with them, to the bitter end.

But back to basketball. I do appreciate the athleticism, the ballet jumps, and whirlwind speed the players display in every game, but without Mark to remind me, I just don't watch and only tangentially know which team in each division is winning and how it looks for the finals. I'll watch the finals again, just as I did last year, and hope that it's not Miami or Dallas (or the Lakers). I can't really say which teams should be there instead, but hopefully I'll enjoy the spectacle: Marvin Gaye singing the Star Spangled Banner could redeem the show, but alas, that is not to be.

Sunday, January 8, 2012

On Not Being Able to Get a Job

Mark and I used to read the jobs section of *High Country News* to see if there were any that had an element of environmental justice in the description. We would then narrow the list based on location: Helena, Montana sounded pretty good, despite the cold weather, or any place in northern California, but the Dakotas, Idaho (neo-Nazi country), and Arizona (too hot and too racist) were off-limits, which in itself limited the selection of possible jobs to almost none. But it didn't matter, as it was all fantasy, an exercise in futility: Mark and I, and especially I, were essentially unemployable.

Lack of credentials certainly contributed to our dilemma. While Mark had at least earned a BA in English, it was a useless degree, of course, in the traditional job market. But he managed to parlay it into a job at the Living Batch Bookstore in Albuquerque, maybe because the infamous owner, Gus Blaisdell, was impressed by his erudition and liked having people around with whom he could have a conversation, but probably because Mark was competent and willing to work for shit wages. His other job was working on other people's houses in Placitas, where we were living at the time, to acquire the skills needed to build our own house, which we worked on for ten years during the 1980s.

I never even got a BA (when my younger son Max first realized that I didn't have a college degree he said, "Mom, what in the world were you thinking?"). My first real job was with the Forest Service as a fire lookout, no experience necessary. On my first day on the job on top of La Mosca Peak, after a few hours' instructions on how to use the fire finder to locate a smoke and the radio to call it in, I reported the Grants dump. Working for the Forest Service was also my last real job (and not because I was a lousy fire lookout). But I managed to parlay my experience as a hiking patrol in the Sandia Mountain Wilderness into self-employment: I started a publishing company and wrote a guidebook to the Sandias, which was quite a success, and then went on to write guides to cross-country skiing in northern New Mexico, hikes in other wilderness areas, and hikes around Santa Fe and Taos. I also parlayed our "back to the land" life in Placitas—building a house, bartering for services rendered, participating in acequia culture—into a freelance writing career.

So you might say, not so bad, we both managed to find self-employment rather than wage labor jobs, but several things have to be factored into that evaluation. The first being that we made lousy money, had no health insurance, and no retirement. While we didn't have a mortgage, we did have to pay for the birth of two babies born by caesarian section rather than at midwifery centers, as planned (we managed a trade with one of the obstetricians), for Mark's hospital stay when he fell off the house while putting up the roof beams, and for a well that went dry before we'd even moved into our new house.

The other factor that contributed to our dependency on marginal self-employment was what I have to call our incorrigibility. It started in Placitas, when the developers came in with their subdivisions and their covenants (no chickens, no junked cars), and the Forest Service decided to pave roads and develop new ski areas, and we became, well, incorrigible. We demonstrated, connived, monkey-wrenched, wrote editorials and mockeries, and sued all of them. This continued, after giving up on Placitas and moving to El Valle, where threats to the community included not only the Forest Service and developers but lo and behold, environmentalists. This time we parlayed our activist experience, coupled with Mark's degree in English and my book writing skills, into "that radical rag" *La Jicarita News*.

La Jicarita was the beginning of the end of any chance of regular employment. Over the course of 16 years we managed to piss off everyone: certainly the Forest Service; all kinds of other government officials from the county to federal levels; mainstream environmentalists who don't know anything about community-based environmentalism; land grant activists who think only heirs should have a say in the management of land-based communities; many of our Anglo neighbors who worked at Sipapu Ski Area and supported its expansion; some of our Hispano neighbors who regard their water rights as private property and probably think we're Communists; foundations that funded groups at cross purposes; and any number of other people, organizations, and bureaucracies that would never in a million years want either one of us to work for them.

So there you have it. In a couple of weeks I'll be old enough to draw social security and I can jettison forever the fantasy of finding a job. I'm still self-employed as co-editor of *La Jicarita* with David Correia as it transitions to its new life in the American Studies Department at UNM, but as I threatened to do in my Productivity blog post, I'm going to start reading novels during the day to celebrate my new status: it's not quite retirement, and it doesn't mean better behavior, but it's definitely a change, and at this point in my life, change is good.

Tuesday, February 7, 2012

The Swim Team

This post is not really about swim teams, it's about David Sedaris's piece in the *New Yorker* called "Memory Laps," which I read and immediately burst into tears. I already wrote about my lackluster career in competitive swimming in my Olympics blog post. This one is about fathers, in particular, his and mine. Unlike Sedaris's father, who berated him after losing at swim meets, my father never went to my meets. His damage was done at home.

Now that I think about it, he probably never saw me race. Considering all the soccer meets and chess tournaments Mark and I attended over the years, that constitutes really egregious behavior. Not only didn't he attend any "events" of mine, I don't ever remember him stepping foot in any of my schools. My mother was the one who had to go up and bawl out my fifth grade teacher for not letting me retake a standardized test when it was discovered that I'd skipped a line in my answer sheet marking and therefore negated the entire test.

Speaking of test taking, my father claimed that he knew my sisters and my IQ test scores and bragged to his poker playing buddies down at the American Legion about what brainiacs his daughters were. First off, I don't remember taking any IQ tests, and secondly, the only reason he was bragging was to validate his own intelligence through his offspring. He also went around the house quoting Marcus Aurelius and Spinoza, who to this day I've never read because of my aversion to anything he valued (I did relent and read about Spinoza because I was interested in his rejection of religion).

OK, we're headed for a discussion of victimhood here. Why did he need to validate his intelligence through his children? Because he was born in poverty in southern Illinois, coal-mining country just like its southern neighbor Kentucky? Because he never got to go to college, like my mother did, which he used against her in any number of ways, like belittling her looks, her character, her interests? Which he then repeated with my sisters and me when we reached puberty. In "Memory Laps" Sedaris says of his father's constant harassment: "I'd never know if my father did this to hurt me or to spur me on," and he doesn't give us enough information for us to figure it out, either. But Sedaris's focus is on how it made him feel: "My dad was like the Marine Corps, only instead of tearing you to pieces and then putting you back together, he just did the first part and called it a day. Now it seems cruel, abusive even, but this all happened before the invention of self-esteem, which, frankly, I think is a little overrated."

Where is the line between victim and perpetrator? Why do some people transfer their disappointment in themselves to those around them through berating and never going to swim meets? Why are others able to rise above their disadvantage and in so doing bring everyone they love with them? Or, like David Sedaris, create an alternative universe where tragedy is comedy and the theater of the absurd.

I don't know the answers to these questions. The nature/nurture dichotomy—which should be a synthesis, I think—is too complicated for me to jump into here. I only know that as a parent I have tried my absolute best to support, nurture, and educate my children despite my own feelings of inadequacy, my disappointments, my failings. My father was unable to do this, something I don't really dwell on very often or have a need to forgive. I only think about it when I read about David Sedaris's father, and then I feel an overwhelming sadness for the victims and the perpetrators, whomever they may be.

Monday, March 19, 2012

You Can't Go Home Again

Last week I went to Placitas to see my old house. Or rather I went to see what was left of my old house. Actually, all I saw was the *place* of my old house. My neighbors had told me years ago that the folks who bought the house built onto and around it, kind of like folks who build onto or around a trailer to turn it into a more solid construction; but my house, an adobe for god's sake, was nowhere to be found.

Neither were the fruit trees, the cottonwoods, the native grass, the rock gardens, the vegetable and flower gardens Mark and I spent fifteen years cultivating, carefully meting out the precious water that is pumped from hundreds of feet below ground. I guess when they took off the second story, added on rooms (including one at the west end with a turret) and then put on a different second story, the vegetation got in the way. This one now resembles a lot of the houses built over the twenty years I've been away: solar adobe style, boxy, oversized, characterless.

Our handmade houses were something different. In the 1960s, when the back to the land movement stumbled into Placitas, a land grant community at the north end of the Sandia Mountains, some folks emulated the traditional building style of the long time Hispano residents of the village. Others saw homebuilding as venues for their creativity, constrained only by the capacity of their pocket books. Ours was somewhere in between: a two story adobe with a gambrel roof (double pitch) built around second-hand doors and windows that we brought home from wherever we could find them: Coronado Lumber in Albuquerque, the Air Force Academy in Colorado Springs, and Buffalo, New York, where Mark had friends in the antique business. It took five years of building before we moved in, ten years to "finish" (adding the greenhouse, putting in a bathroom upstairs, but you never really finish a handmade house), and one year to sell.

Many of our compadres' creations are still there: Cathy's Dome out on the mesa; Rumaldo's ranchito on lower Las Huertas Creek; the crumbling adobe in the village where Mark and I lived while we built our new house; the triple dome and solar dome (where we fell in love) in Dome Valley; and Daisy's carefully crafted compact house on a windswept hill (thank you for being my companion on this nostalgic trip). But what Placitas mostly is are the thousands of new homes that beginning in the 80s the developers aggressively marketed to attract Albuquerque commuters, retirees, and second homeowners. From I-25 east you pass La Mesa, Tierra Madre, Placitas Homesteads, Ranchos de Placitas, Placitas West, Puesta del Sol, and the Overlook, among others, until a sign on the road tells you you're now entering the Historic Village of Placitas.

Placitas is not unique, of course. Things change (just ask the land grant community). People build houses. Developers build many houses. In El Valle, where I now live, we suddenly have second homes. But Placitas is emblematic of a consumer culture that is the basis of this country's power and wealth. We became the "primary engine of capital accumulation" (David Harvey), which vastly increased the infrastructure necessary to support this kind of massive suburbanization. The housing boom in the 90s exacerbated the overbuilding and created the upper middle class culture that now dominates Placitas. Now, in the 2000s, there must be a slew of foreclosures and some nail-biting developers who won't survive the housing bust, but the damage has been done: loss of the commons, validation of yuppie culture, and the mining of the already limited water resources of a semi-arid environment.

So we left, and it took me 20 years to go back (I've now lived in El Valle

as long as I lived in Placitas). My friends who stayed say they drive up the road alongside the "Homesteads" and "Ranchos" with their eyes pointed straight ahead, following the route home without looking. When they take their morning walk up the hill and see another road bladed through the desert, they look away. They're attached to their homes and their history in the crazy, mixed up place Placitas was and is. I prefer the was.

Tuesday, April 17, 2012

Why I Live in Northern New Mexico

I've been working on a series called "Acequia Stories: The Democracy of Dysfunction, or How Everyone is Equally Crazy," the first installment of which I was getting ready to post after Sunday's typically contentious acequia meeting with all the usual suspects. But then on Monday and Tuesday I was reminded of why I live in this yes, crazy but benevolent, unique place and I decided to write about that instead.

On Monday morning my friend Peter, master woodworker from Chimayó, came up to replace my funky kitchen cabinets with the elegant doors and drawers he'd crafted. Mark and I always wanted new cabinets but never had the discretionary money. But Peter wanted the work and gave me a good deal. He'd already built me a beautiful tongue and groove cabinet for my bathroom in return for my help putting together a book of his oral histories of workers from Los Alamos National Laboratory, an incredible accounting of what went on from the beginning of the Manhattan Project until the year 2000 (we'll let you know when it's ready for purchase).

On Tuesday I loaded up the truck with the old doors to my cabinets, along with the rest of my trash (which included a couple of bales of hay that had been sitting outside for a year or so, turning to mold) and went to the dump. Paco, my year old blue healer, went with me, of course. The cabinet doors were headed for the reuse building at the dump, a recycling project that came to fruition through the efforts of Jean, a local artist who was an original member of the Hog Farm commune. While waiting my turn behind a woman in a car tossing various things into the dumpster I discussed the upcoming Kit Carson Electric Coop election with Jerry, a land grant activist who manages the dump, about which corrupt board members we would be voting against. The folks in the truck who pulled up alongside me when the car moved on were the sister and brother-in-law of my next door neighbor and whose kids went to school with my kids. When they saw the old cabinet doors in my truck they asked if I was going to dump them and when I told them they were headed for the reuse building they said, we'll reuse them, and we transferred them to their truck.

Then Paco and I went to the post office in Chamisal, where Noami the postmistress asked me what I was doing that day. When I told her I planned to rototill my garden she told me about the time her dad was tilling his garden and he said, why don't you give it a try, which she did, and preceded to overturn the tiller and herself at the same time. Many years ago Noami and I hiked to the top of North Truchas Peak in a single day, which she periodically reminds me of when we're complaining about our daily aches and pains.

When I came out of the post office the woman who I had seen at the dump called me over to her car and said, I just wanted you to know that it wasn't me who drank all that beer you saw me throw into the dumpster. Now, I hadn't even noticed that she'd thrown away a bunch of beer bottles, and even if I had I probably wouldn't have thought much of it, but she wanted me to know that she doesn't drink the stuff she only picks up the bottles from the roadside between Chamisal and Las Trampas. This initiated a discussion about why we can't ever seem to get a bottle bill through the legislature to provide a financial incentive to not throw beer bottles on the road. When I told her she was a good Samaritan she gave me a big smile and went off to collect more bottles.

While driving back to El Valle I ran into Albert and his dog Pee Wee, a little terrier mutt who goes everywhere with Albert. He had stopped me on the road a few weeks before and asked if I would write a story about Pee Wee, who he accidentally ran over with his car, popping out one of Pee Wee's eyes. He rushed her to the vet, who couldn't save the eye, and then the second eye developed an infection and the vet couldn't save that one either, so Pee Wee is now blind. Albert takes Pee Wee with him to Peñasco, where he goes to hang out with his buddies, she follows him around the yard when he's at home working, and he keeps her inside with him at night. I'm going to go over to Albert's mother's house later today to sit down and write the story of Pee Wee. Corina, Albert's mother, who is a good friend of mine, will help me communicate with Albert, who is almost completely deaf.

And finally, while I was rototilling the garden my neighbor Nelson came over to bring me some eggs. I gave him the last of my chickens a week ago when I decided that after 34 years I was going to quit keeping them so Paco and I can have a little more mobility, meaning I can leave the house for a few days without having to ask Nelson to come over to feed them, which he always willingly does. I now take him all my compost for the chickens and he gives me as many eggs as I want (he also keeps ducks, geese, and guineas). While he was here he offered to weed whack the rose hips along the ditch that I've been meaning to cut back for the last few years.

Tomorrow Peter will come and finish installing my new cabinets. I'm going to enjoy this aesthetic improvement to my house, work on my story about Pee Wee, start planting my garden, and bask in a good norteño feeling that sometimes slips away from me, especially after I attend an acequia meeting. I'll get back to the Democracy of Dysfunction next week.

Friday, April 27, 2012

Death in the Afternoon—Or So I Thought

It was a blustery, overcast April day in El Valle and recovering from a sore back I decided to get in the hot tub early, before dark.

The hot tub, you may ask? Yes, I have an electric hot tub, which my orthopedically challenged body dearly loves. For many years we had a wood fired hot tub, a Snorkel (a second) that was shipped down to New Mexico from Seattle after a trip there to visit Mark's brother. Every evening around dusk Mark went out and made a fire in the submersible stove, and every night we got in the often 110 degree water (it's hard to regulate the temperature burning pine, piñon, and juniper) with the kids, neighbors, and friends, winter and summer, Orion and the Big Dipper overhead, new moons and full moons, owls hooting and cows lowing, freezing cold and snow, and mild summer evenings with just enough chill to warrant a soak.

After many years the tub deteriorated, the stays warped, the firewood became more precious (meaning the cutting and splitting became more of a chore), and keeping the fires burning on sub-zero nights intimidating. So for a while we did without. Then, as these things happen, we decided it was OK to buy a used hot tub, nothing fancy, no push button settings, no fancy jets, no multi-colored lights, but yes, one that you plugged in and voilá, the water got hot!

And that's where I was yesterday afternoon when the wind whipped the cover, half opened, closed, with just enough room for me to scrunch down without being slapped upside the head and knocked out. At least that's what passed through my mind as I reflexively lifted my arms to catch the impact of the cover, while the water splashed up over my face and hair with the aftertaste of chemicals (albeit a mild dosing, as I'm the only regular customer).

Other thoughts went through my mind as well. One, I was glad I hadn't gotten around to adding water to raise the below-optimal water level, which is always a pain in the butt because I do it with buckets of hot water from the bathtub so I can use gas instead of electricity to make up the temperature difference. I'd somehow hurt my lower back in Albuquerque the weekend before with Jakob and Casey and their grad school friends where I exercised nothing but my brain and vocal cords at a secular seder that was both irreverent and relevant, which is why I hadn't filled the tub and why I was in it before dark.

Two, I wondered how long I could have held the cover up with my arms. If it had been the cover I'd just replaced, I wouldn't have been able to hold it up at all—water soaked, frozen foam is very heavy—so I would have been in there with a pocket of air to breathe between water and cover.

With this thought in mind I managed to get out of the tub and found a rock to put on top of the open cover. I really wanted to be in the tub as the water felt so good on my sore back. But what if the wind blew the rock up off the cover and knocked it onto my head?

That lead to thought number three. I wondered how long it would have taken for someone to find me, dead or barely alive, and if Paco would be OK until that happened. He has a dog door, so he has access to food, and there is plenty of water in the acequia. Would he sit there patiently by the closed hot tub, knowing I was in there, or would he, like Lassie, somehow know enough to run around barking until someone heard him and stopped by?

That someone would be Tony, my neighbor, because he comes over most nights to get water from my outside pump, which is right by the hot tub. He has no water in his trailer—the water line from the pump at his father-in-law's house is broken somewhere—and he would hear me call out "Tony, Tony, I'm stuck in the hot tub" or wonder why Paco was frantically barking. Luckily I had a bathing suit on because if I get in the tub during the day I take that precaution. But he might decide to get water at someone else's house that night, and there I would be, in the hot tub, in the dark.

Well, the wind did indeed pick up the rock and throw it off the cover but it landed on the deck instead of my head and I decided that was enough and got my sorry ass out of the tub and locked down the cover. Then the rain started and it lasted most of the night and this morning everything is lush and green and the wind isn't blowing so I'm now getting back in the hot tub. End of story.

Friday, May 4, 2012

Pee Wee's Story: The Deaf Leading the Blind

Albert, my neighbor, is "severely" deaf and his little terrier mix Pee Wee is "completely" blind: she has no eyes. Albert asked me to write a story about how this happened and suggested the title: "The Deaf Leading the Blind."

Albert and Pee Wee are inseparable. They live together in an immaculate trailer in El Valle. Pee Wee has a solar doghouse but she prefers the trailer. And since she lost her eyes, Albert prefers having her with him inside: "She's my partner."

Albert got Pee Wee about a year ago from a friend in Chamisal. She was supposed to be a present for his granddaughter, who was living with him at the time, but the granddaughter moved to Albuquerque so Albert ended up with Pee Wee. She used to run out onto the village road when I went for walks with my dogs and occasionally accompanied us up the llano. Even then Albert often took her with him when he went to Peñasco to hang out with his friends, or on a quick trip to Taos when she wouldn't have to stay in the car too long, waiting.

One day she was in the car with him when he got out to lock the gate. She must have jumped out the door when he wasn't looking and when he got back in and started up his driveway he felt a bump and then heard her cries. He stopped immediately and found Pee Wee rolling around on the ground with blood pouring out of her face. He picked her up and ran to his mother Corina's house, next door. They washed the blood off Pee Wee's face and tried to insert her eye back into its socket.

This is when the Salazar Clinic vets in Taos and Jeannie Cornelius of the Dixon Animal Protection Society come into the story. Albert rushed

Pee Wee to the clinic where they immediately took her in but were unable to save her eye. Albert doesn't have much discretionary money, but he paid what he could and left Pee Wee with the vet for a couple of days. He then took her home and she seemed to be doing OK, but about 10 days later her other eye swelled up and Albert took her back to the vet. This time he had no money so the clinic contacted Jeannie, the compassionate dog lady who runs an animal rescue service in Dixon, who agreed to pay the bill. The vets kept Pee Wee over the weekend, but the eye got worse, and when they told Albert that they'd have to remove it he broke down and thought, how am I going to take care of a blind dog? He considered euthanizing Pee Wee, but the vets told him how spunky she was and offered to try to find a home for her. One of the vets took the dog home with her and considered keeping Pee Wee herself.

But Albert couldn't let her go. He built a chain link fence around his yard and came back to the clinic and took her home. A week later, which was exactly a month after he accidentally drove over her, he took Pee Wee back for a final exam. The vets' report read: "Looks great—doing well. Eyes look good—pulled stitch from medial aspect of (L) eye. Everything else [they had also spayed her] looks good. Very happy."

So that's how the Deaf Ended Up Leading the Blind. Pee Wee remains "Very happy," at least as far as we humans can tell. She sits on Albert's lap in the car. He feeds her high protein dog food. She follows him everywhere around the yard and occasionally bumps into things but regains her equilibrium after he whistles or claps his hands to let her know where he is. She sleeps in his bed at night. When I went over to get the vet report from Albert for this story Pee Wee and my dog Paco played together in the yard for half an hour, rolling around, first one on top, then the other, nipping, yapping, then running in circles.

Albert also got some medical help recently, a new set of hearing aids. They are outrageously expensive, and he can't afford them, either. There's no deaf person rescue service that we know of, so he'll have to make payments for a long time to come. But now he can better hear Pee Wee's bark when she wants to alert him that she needs help or someone is coming. He wants to thank everyone who helped him, financially, physically, and emotionally, through his ordeal with Pee Wee—an ordeal that in the end became a blessing.

Albert and Pee Wee

Sunday, May 20, 2012

Acequia Stories: The Democracy of Dysfunction, or How Everyone is Equally Crazy

OK, I've heard enough about the romance of acequia democracy. As I wrote in my posting "Elegy for El Valle," acequia meetings are often forums for long-standing feuds or a recent offense that's easier to duke out in the acequia playing fields than court. Not that we're not litigious: "Take him to court!" is the common command even before mediation is given a chance. While it's often just bluster, I can't count the number of times private lawyers, judges, district attorneys, and the State Engineer's Office (a really bad idea) have gotten involved in acequia issues they should never have known about.

So instead of going to court I'm going to tell some stories about the Democracy of Dysfunction as I have seen them played out in my norteño lifetime. It may be dysfunction, but it's still democracy—kind of.

Story Number One: How the Commission Tried to Give Us An Additional Water Right and We Refused

Mark and I got taken under the wing of Tomás soon after we moved to El Valle. He was the commissioner on one of the three acequias in the village and he was also the de facto mayor of the village, the one with the tallest woodpile, the most tractors, all the connections—basically, the Alpha Male benevolent dictator. What that meant to the guys in the village challenging his position was that whoever was friends with the enemy was their enemy as well. Tomás didn't bother to attend the acequia meeting where these guys were commissioners, but Mark and I went because we had water rights on two ditches—the "dark" side and the Tomás side—

and we figured someone needed to know what they were up to.

So we show up at the meeting. The only attendees are the three commissioners, one of their mothers, and two parciantes. When they get to the agenda item about whether there have been any transfers of water rights they inform us that instead of owning a half a water right we now own a full water right. Actually, they only present this information to me, although Mark is sitting there right next to me, because the land is in my name and we're not married. I can't really remember why we put the land in my name, but there it is. Tomás used to own the land and when he sold it to the young man we bought it from—a kid from Santa Fe who had big ambitions to be a farmer but then kind of burnt out—Tomás divided the water right and kept half for his house and field and half for the land he sold. So when we bought it from the kid we had half a water right, meaning we got to irrigate for 12 hours each rotation.

We bought the land in 1992. It is now 2000 and these guys are just now telling us we have one water right instead of half a water right. Or telling me, that is. I have a printout of the minutes of the meeting (which for some reason the commissioners actually tape recorded), which reveals much better than I ever could just how crazy these meetings get.

• David tells Kay that her property historically had one water right.

• Kay [jokingly] says that one right for her property was fine with her but that Tomás would raise hell over that.

• Mark asked why the Commission suddenly has a problem with the issue since in recent history the Commission had recognized that Kay's property had ½ water right and Tomas had ½ water right. Mark said he had no problem with ½ a water right on Kay's property.

• Ruben asked Kay if she had a problem with owning only ½ water right.

- Kay said she had no problem with it.
- Ruben told Kay that if she didn't have a problem with the transfer Tomás should just get the permit at the State Engineer's Office. We can't just let individuals move water rights around without following procedure.
- David said as an individual he would have a problem with it.
- Mark said that he and Kay were objecting to the way the discussion had proceeded and would have to speak with a lawyer before continuing.
- Mark and Kay leave the building.
- Mark and Kay return to the building. (We didn't have time to talk to a lawyer but we talked to Tomás and he said *he* was going to talk to a lawyer.)
- Kay said she felt the meeting was not legal because we were counting a quorum by majority of water rights and not on one-person-one vote majority. She said she wanted it on record that she was objecting to the meeting.
- Mark and Kay leave the meeting again.

Tomás ended up having to get a lawyer to write a letter stating it is perfectly legal for parciantes under community acequias to transfer a ditch right to other lands served by the same ditch, and that the State Engineer's Office doesn't want to hear about it, much less issue a permit for it.

So they backed off. For the time being. And only on this issue. There would be plenty more to come.

Tuesday, June 26, 2012

Butchie

In George Eliot's *Mill on the Floss* (Eliot is a reference for many of my blog posts) the main protagonist Maggie Tulliver dies tragically, hounded by Rousseau's "society," which he believed makes man (or woman) a "tyrant both over himself and over nature." Is the "evil-speaking" and "self-exaltation" of the society matrons who hound Maggie the only way we know to feel better about ourselves?

The bullies I encounter here in the hood, northern New Mexico, carry the weight of post colonialism, but with their "political shenanigans, bullying, abuse of power" (Orlando Romero, *The Santa Fe New Mexican*) they speak evilly about those who could actually be their partners in arms and exalt themselves by embracing patronage. This was recently played out at the county level when a group of politicos came to trash the land use plan the county staff had worked hard for several years to write (starting with neighborhood associations and working up) with their usual complaints: "Nobody is going to tell me what to do with my land"; "How come I didn't know about this?"; and "Are we going to let these newcomers tell us what to do?"

The meeting was the last straw for Butchie Denver, the Taoseña activist (she actually lived in Lama). As she reported to me on the phone when she got home (this is probably a mix of Butchie's and my own sentiments, but seeing as how often they were the same, I'm not going to worry about it): "Well, to begin with, without a land use plan the developers are certainly going to have a say so in what happens as agricultural land gets bought up and water resources are transferred to urban use. Like hell they didn't know about the plan, they just want an excuse to trash it because it wasn't their idea and they don't care about contributing to the common good. And these 'newcomers' they're referring to are the staff that their all-Hispanic county commission hired to implement their vision of planning in the county. But trash it they did—the commissioners rolled right over, and now the county has no land use plan in place and a disconnected staff and commission."

Butchie, aka one of Las Brujas (the other two being Trudy Valerio Healy and Fabi Romero), so dubbed by her longtime partner Tony Trujillo, was instrumental in wresting power out of the hands of the Democratic machine in Taos County through hard work, some intimidation, and knowing everything there was to know about everyone. Butchie also served for years on committees to revise the county land use plan, which is why she was so pissed off about the meeting that trashed it.

Yesterday Butchie died of cancer. She'd only been ill for a short time, and it was a shock to all of us. Tony took her out to the Bay Area two weeks ago for better medical care and to be with her daughter and granddaughter. While she was in hospice care Tony and I often talked on the phone and I heard a great many stories: her adventures at Woodstock; her husbands (there were more than one: Tony told me, "I never married her so she couldn't divorce me"); her daughters, step-children, grandchildren, and great grandchildren; her move to Questa with a chimpanzee, a tiger, and a mountain lion (an explanation of this would take another blog post); and her career as an artist of retablos.

As an activist Butchie brooked no nonsense. She'd show up in anyone's office—county commissioner, planner, attorney, town mayor—track them down at home, or confront them in public to express her displeasure when they failed to contribute to the common good. If she thought you were basically trying to do the right thing but got off track her approach was usually, "You know I love you but you're really being an asshole." She knew everything there was to know about water and how it was being used and abused and was an invaluable resource for me in my position as chair of the Taos County Advisory Board on Public Welfare, which reviews all proposed water transfers within and from Taos County to ascertain if they're in the best interest of the citizens of Taos County. She fought like hell alongside me to get the county to approve the advisory board after the regional water planning committee was hijacked by the powers that be. I don't know what I'll do without her.

But Tony told me not to worry, that Butchie will still be there watching my back, and the backs of all the others to whom she was a loyal and trusted compañera. Rest in peace, Butchie. You deserve some.

Butchie with the Taos County Commission in 2012 (and Bill Whaley, second from right)

Monday, July 9, 2012

"A sense of liberation"

In her book *Memoir of a Debulked Woman: Enduring Ovarian Cancer*, Susan Gubar says than when she found out she had this cancer in her early 60s she felt almost "euphoric" because it meant that instead of a prolonged death enduring pain or dementia—what she envisioned—she was going to leave this world at a time in her life when she was still successful in her career, was in a good marriage, and her daughters were grown and on their own.

I'm the same age as the author and I've been around a lot of death lately. Mark, my partner of 34 years, died of cancer in his early 60s (described in my Diary of a Bad Year series of blog posts). Butchie, eulogized in my previous blog, died less than a month ago of cancer. Last Sunday I went to a wake for Sebia Hawkins, a longtime anti-nuclear activist who also died of cancer having just survived an aneurysm that set her back for more than a year. Ed Quillen, publisher and editor of *Colorado Central* and longtime columnist for the *Denver Post*, dropped dead of a heart attack in early June. So it's not surprising that I've been thinking about "the right time to die." Susan Gubar described her situation as a time between a life cut short— certainly how I felt about Mark's death—and debilitating age, which I've seen far too often in my parents' generation.

While my kids are also grown and on their own they just experienced the death of their father and they're still quite young; one just out of college and the other starting a family. We've been lucky enough—and privileged enough—to make it this far together, so I'd like to see them through a few more years.

The critical component to this "through" is that "I" see "them" through a few more years. I distinctly remember the day I realized that my own mother and I were reversing roles: I needed to be the one upon whom she could always depend instead of the other way around. It was a gradual process, but my feelings that day were stark: I felt the loss of the person she had always been in my life, and I wasn't ready for it, although I was already a mother myself.

Now I'm that person in my kids' lives, and I don't want to be the one who will depend on them. I want to keep editing their papers and articles; keep counseling them on life choices; discuss Habermas and the "Orientalist" gaze; and spend money on them. Neither do I want to be the person who can't weed whack the grass in the orchard; irrigate the hay fields; fix the lose pipe under the sink or replace the gasket in the faucet; split my kindling, or any of the other daily tasks I'm confronted with in my house and on my ten acres.

What these things contribute to, of course, is my sense of who I am, which is constructed from what I do in the world, how I am related to others, and how I take care of myself. On NPR the other day I heard an interview with a woman from Japan who was discussing the cultural impacts of growing old in her country. Historically, when one got older than one's usefulness, grandpa or grandma was thrown off a cliff or left out on the mountain to starve—literally. Now, with 21 percent of the population 65 or older, that's not going to happen, but the idea of usefulness continues to resonate, and several of the people interviewed on the program expressed their terror at becoming a burden on their families and society and vowed to end their lives before that occurred.

Nora Ephron died last week at 71. She had no illusions about what it meant to get old, even in the good old USA. As Susan Gubar hopes for herself, Ephron left this world still writing the articles, books, and screenplays she'd been producing for most of her adult life, despite her complaints about loss of short term memory and the elasticity of her neck (she also left two grown kids, oddly enough named the same as mine: Jac[k]ob and Max). I doubt if she felt Gubar's initial "euphoria"—Ephron had the same illness my mother had, a form of leukemia that makes one susceptible to infection, hers being pneumonia—but it seems she left at a time when she felt she was still who she had been for most of her life: a successful writer, a mother, a wife, a warm and funny person.

When I read back through this piece I realize I give rather short shrift to the "what I do in the world," or the "legacy" part of the equation. That's a function of the ephemeral nature of the effect one has in a dynamic world, the disappointment that elicits, and the fact that I was so often implicated—happily so—by the day-by-day demands of the life I chose. I had the luxury of making choices about how to live, but choosing "the right time to die," if it's allowed at all, is going to be a daunting task.

Wednesday, August 15, 2012

Good Samaritans

How many times did I break down over the years without a cell phone and AAA insurance (and usually no money, either)? Let me count the ways. Pud hauled Mark and me into Blue Springs, Missouri, where he worked on our car all day at his house while we whittled away our time in a 1950s motel room before paying him about what he probably had to pay for the parts. The eighteen wheel truck driver with track marks up and down his arms, hauling lumber from Mendocino to LA, picked Jordan and me up after our VW bug died on Highway 1 and drove us across the Golden Gate Bridge, down Van Ness Avenue to Mission, and down Mission to Nineteenth Street, where our friends lived. "Wouldn't want you girls to get picked up by just anyone, you know." I was parked on the side of I-25 one night trying to figure out why my rear wheel was loose, when this nice man pulled over behind me and tried to figure it out with me. The next thing we knew we were both lying in the ditch and our cars were down the road ahead of us, totaled. Another man, drunk, had plowed into both our cars, the force of which knocked us head over heels. After the cop drove the helpful man and me to his trailer in Bernalillo—he kept saying, "I never liked that car anyway"—he got his wife's car—she kept saying, "You're so lucky, you both could have been killed"—and drove me home to Placitas. Good Samaritans all, no?

So it's thirty years later and Paco, my dog and I are driving down to Albuquerque, via the Jemez Mountains after covering the protest at Los Alamos National Laboratory on Nagasaki Day, and my trusty Subaru (the nicest car I've ever owned) suddenly tells me it's overheated, via the temperature gauge and a written exclamation on the dashboard where the odometer reading usually is. This time I have both a cell phone and AAA. Except that when I dial my son Jakob's number to tell him I'm broken down and won't make it to dinner, a voice comes on my phone and tells me my service has been "deactivated." I have over 1,000 unused minutes on this phone because there is no cell phone reception where I live, in El Valle, so the only time I use my phone is when I'm in my car, like now, and I need to call someone and tell them why I'm in my car instead of where I'm supposed to be.

After the voice tells me that my phone has been "deactivated" it gives me some options, one of which is to "reactivate" it. So I press that number, and after a few false starts I actually get someone from India on the line. I explain that even though I have all these minutes on my phone it's been deactivated and I need to reactivate it so I can call AAA and get rescued. He tells me that he will gladly reactivate my phone but he can only do that if I call him from a different phone than the one I need to reactivate. It's only a matter of seconds before I'm yelling, how in the hell am I supposed to call you from a different phone when I'm stuck out in the middle of nowhere (actually, I'm about 22 miles from Bernalillo) with an overheated car and no phone? And he's calmly answering, I'm sorry ma'am, but you have to call me from a different phone before I can reactivate your account.

But I have one more option. After I hang up on the man from India my service informs me that if this is an emergency I can call 911. I decide that the situation now qualifies as an emergency—my hood is up and I'm obviously stranded, but no one has stopped—and I reach the 911 operator. I explain what the situation is, describe where I am, and she says she'll send someone out within 45 minutes.

So I wait. And wait. I decide to get out of the car, even if it means standing in the hot sun. Thank god the backseat is in the shade so Paco has some protection. I wait some more. Then, after dozens of cars have passed by, one stops. It has a missing backseat window covered by a flapping shade, and a young girl gets out and asks if I need help. I ask her if she has a cell phone, and she does, but it doesn't have a signal here by the side of the road. Then the driver gets out, and I know right away he's a Mexican national. He speaks no English, but the young girl translates, and I tell him, you can't check the radiator, it's too hot, and thanks, but if you don't have a cell phone there's not much you can do.

Later, when I'm telling my son Max about what happened I tell him to guess, by category, who was the first person to stop and help me, and without hesitation he says, a Mexican. That's because years ago when he broke down coming up La Bajada hill in his funky Subaru the only ones who stopped to help were Mexican nationals who put him in their van, gave him something to eat, and took him to his grandmother's house in Santa Fe.

But there's another category to come. I wait another half hour (no sign of whoever the 911 operator supposedly called to come help me) and a Mercedes Benz passes me, pulls a U-turn, and comes up behind me. A black man and woman both get out of the car and she immediately says, honey, do you need help? Don't worry, we're pastors, this is what we do. She has a Bluetooth in her ear, he has an iPhone, so soon I'm on the line with AAA and after a lot of explaining through a garbled connection, the operator tells me she's sending a tow truck (but it's up to the driver whether Paco will be allowed to ride in the truck with me and the driver). When I tell the woman pastor that it's been about an hour since I called 911, she says, this is unacceptable, how can they leave a single woman out here on the road by herself, you need to call them up and give them a piece of your mind.

Meantime, the man has retrieved a jug of water and a partially filled container of antifreeze from his car and says, I'm going to fill up your overflow and maybe it will flow back into your radiator reservoir, maybe it's low and that's why you overheated. This is the first time I've ever heard that there can be a reverse flow back into the radiator, but what do I know? Then we wait a little while and he tells me to turn on the car and let's see what happens. The temperature gauge is where it's supposed to be, so he says, we're going to follow you into Bernalillo. Keep the windows open and if the temperature gauge starts to go up stick your arm out the window and raise it with your hand up. Then we'll all pull over.

So they follow me most of the way into Bernalillo. My car does not overheat. Just on the outskirts of town they pass me and pull over in front. He sticks his arm straight out the window for a minute or so, then turns it up, then lowers it back to straight. I stick my arm straight out the window, they gaily wave at me out their windows, he turns onto the Albuquerque bypass, and they're off to do some more pastoring.

Max, and the others I query, are a little slower to guess my second Samaritans were black; it's not a large profile in New Mexico. But like the "others" (as Hank Williams sang it, "just a picture from life's other side"), those who stop to render aid are the ones who have been stranded themselves: the poor, marginalized, or discriminated against. Someone driving a Mercedes Benz may give you pause for thought, but like the Okie who once picked me up in a Cadillac, the car or where it's going doesn't much matter: it's where they've been.

Wednesday, September 26, 2012

Existential Thrill—or Fear and Loathing—on the LA Freeways

My son Max picked me up at LAX around 5:30 in the afternoon. He'd warned me that it was the worst time of day for traffic, but the 4:00 p.m. flight from Albuquerque was the only nonstop flight of the day and I really did not want to change planes on such a short flight. Little did I know that the car trip from LAX, to Pasadena, where Max was staying, would take longer than the plane trip from Albuquerque to LA—and with more existential angst and near death experience than any number of take off and landings on a mode of transportation with which I have never come to terms.

Max already had an hour's worth of bumper-to-bumper traffic under his belt when I got in the car so we decided to take an hour off and have dinner near the airport. He asked his smart phone where the nearest Thai restaurant was and then the GPS app showed us how to get there. While the GPS map was correct this time, it was only seducing us (or Max; I'll never trust a GPS device even if I can figure out how to use it) into a much more sinister relationship as the night progressed.

I have an aside here. The first time I visited Max in California was on my trip to Del Mar (see Who Are These People blog post). He picked me up at the Ontario Airport and we headed south. I innocently asked him, "So where are we now," and he answered, "I have no idea," and I said, "Well then how do you know how to get where we're going?" and he answered, "I just go where the GPS tells me." And he meant it literally: she told us which highways to follow, which exit to take, and what streets led to the house. Her voice was very confident and directive: do what I say or you are lost forever on the LA freeways (as opposed to "beneath the streets of Boston").

I have another aside. In California when people discuss freeways they are always prefaced by the word "the": the 10, the 405, the 110, the 5. Nobody had ever been able to explain this to me until Max suggested it's because everyone spends so much time in their cars on the freeways that they develop a very close relationship and "the" expresses that intimacy. They are not just some amorphous highways but something they share, "the" highways that get them home. And speaking of getting home; on the LA freeways between 5 and 7:30 p.m., in the thousands of cars that are trying to get there is one person, by him or her self, spending that hour or two every day in the car by him or her self. I suppose this only increases the intimacy: you, your car, your highway.

Back to the story. After dinner we got in the car and headed to Pasadena, this time following the GPS map that led us right into downtown LA because you have to go there to get to Pasadena. First, the guy in the pickup didn't want to let Max into the right lane where the GPS was telling him he needed to be to get on another freeway, so after Max nudged in anyway the guy pulled up beside us on the left and gave us the finger. We made it onto the freeway only to discover it was the wrong freeway (Max sometimes actually knows where he's supposed to be going). So we had to get off and drive around a few blocks to get back on the freeway going the other direction. We were trying to turn left at a light; the turn light was red but there was nowhere for the oncoming cars to go as traffic was blocked up on the other side of the intersection. The two cars in front of us turned left, traffic still hadn't moved, so we started to turn as well when one of the oncoming drivers decided he didn't really like the situation and decided to drive right into the side of our car—almost. I didn't actually see what happened as my head was in my hands, but obviously he stopped. Max was more than a little rattled at this point, but we got back on the freeway and suddenly the exit onto the correct freeway was on the opposite side than what the GPS indicated and he crossed five lanes of traffic at the last minute to make the turn.

By this time I was saying my mea culpas—I'll never fly into LA during rush hour again—and my hail Mary's—please god get us to Pasadena, Max is too young to die. I was aghast thinking about how he had been doing this while I was at home in New Mexico where I see maybe five cars driving down the hill from Truchas to Chimayó on any given day. But he's not doing it anymore; we drove to Scottsdale, a sanitized component of a sprawling megalopolis, but one with few freeways, many wide streets, retirees who don't go anywhere, and yes, many of whom belong to the Tea Party ((don't ask me why Max is living there, even temporarily). I just know that if it's your kid in a car on freeways sometimes sanitation is good.

Tuesday, November 6, 2012

A Dog's Life

I was in Albuquerque the other day with my two dogs, Paco and Star, who know nothing about being in town, so I took them to the dog park as a facsimile of country life. You'll notice that I use the pronoun "who" when referring to them: considering how often the word "that" is used instead of "who" when referring to people, I think it's OK to extend the little used "who" to pets "that" we treat as humans.

While I was at the dog park I met up with this lovely Mexicana, a volunteer at the local animal shelter, who was there with six little dogs, all damaged goods. Four of them were hers, the ones she had rehabilitated at the shelter and adopted, and two were "unadoptables:" one who bit other dogs (she had trained him to keep a ball in his mouth so if he opened it to bite he'd lose his pacifier) and the other whose cast had recently been removed but he continued act as if it hadn't (no one wanted to adopt a cripple who was actually mental).

She told me in vivid detail each dog's abuse history. I won't go into it here, but suffice it to say it illustrated the Hobbesian interpretation of human nature. It also elicited a conversation of how the cultural differences in both Mexico, her home, and northern New Mexico, my home, are revealed in the way humans relate to animals. She didn't accede to political correctness when discussing a dog's life in Mexico, but I tried to explain it in more utilitarian terms: a dog is supposed to protect the property or round up the cows while a cat catches mice and "rattas" (gophers).

I cop to the bourgeoisfication of owning animals. Sometimes I go so far as to think there must be something wrong with anyone (of my class) who doesn't own at least one: Mark brought home more strays than I did;

both my sons are smitten; my mother adored the two kittens I dumped on her in college; and my two closest friends have four dogs each. My father, who I've already written about (see the Swim Team blog), claimed he was allergic to animal hair, so we had to make do with a parakeet.

After I dumped the kittens on my mother I also dumped college and acquired my first dog, Chani, whom I dragged across the country several times, including a trip on the subway from the East Village to the Bronx (the subway police made me get off at Times Square and find a box to put her in; today they would have just kicked us off). I found Judge, a huge Husky-type mix, in the woods of eastern Oregon where I was working as a seasonal employee for the Forest Service. It took me many tries to get near him, but when I finally got him in the car he collapsed and had to be carried in and out of my cabin for a week because his paws were rubbed raw. I brought him back to New Mexico and had him until the infamous dog poisoning in Placitas, in 1981, when some deranged person set out meat laced with poison and killed hundred of dogs over the course of a couple of days.

Waldo, who looked like the movie personality Benji, also succumbed to the poisoning, but he wasn't strictly my dog. He lived with three families in the village and took turns gracing us with his presence. We tried to tame him—let him sleep inside, took him in the car to go for hikes—but he bought into the philosophy that "it takes a village."

We also rescued Dutch, an Australian shepherd, from somebody's bathroom in a trailer park (they left him there all day while they were at work), and adopted a dog named Pooper, from friends with too many other dogs, and renamed him Scooter. Our El Valle dogs were all rescued, too: Luther, after being hit by a car in Taos, and Django, who someone dumped in a culvert on our road. Mark picked up Sammy, a cocker spaniel, running down the streets of Chimayó after folks at one of the stores near the Santuario told him, "You better take him before the dog lady gets him," the implication being that while the dog lady meant to be kind by rescuing dogs, when you end up with 20 of them all living in the same yard, it's still a dog's life.

The summer after Mark died I had to put Django down, as she couldn't walk anymore, and Sammy went in December, blind, deaf, and incontinent. Before Django and Sammy died I vowed that I would wait awhile before I got another dog. I gave away my chickens, too, thinking that for the first time in 40 years I could go away on a trip without having to get a housesitter or persuade someone to babysit my dogs or cats (there were 15 cats through the years, but I'll save that for another story). And this time I was going to choose the dog, not have it choose me.

Or have them choose me, which they of course did. I rescued Paco up in La Junta Canyon when I was there with a bunch of folks looking at the diversion dams that carry water from the Rio Pueblo watershed to the Rio

Star and Paco

Mora watershed (this is another story as well). He looked like a blue heeler puppy (maybe he jumped out of a rancher's pickup; heelers are definitely the dog of choice in northern New Mexico) but he turned out tall and lean and has no interest in cows. Star, who, like Waldo, isn't strictly my dog, is also a heeler mix. She actually belongs to my across-the-road neighbor who got her to keep his other dog company, but she prefers Paco's company and basically lives here. The deal was sealed when I started letting her sleep in the house (she'd already made herself at home in the house via the dog door, which I close at night). And while I sometimes take her to Albuquerque and the dog park, she really prefers El Valle, so I don't take offense when she decides to stay home and check in with the neighbor.

So there you have it. I figure animal pets are like children: you take what you get and love them all.

Wednesday, November 28, 2012

"If I Can't Dance I Don't Want to be Part of Your Revolution."

That's Emma Goldman speaking. I came of age at the time in history, the 60s and 70s, when we thought we were going to make our revolution and that dancing was going to be a very big part of it. We didn't make the revolution but we did achieve the democratization of dancing, freeing everyone to dance any way they wanted or with (or without) any one they wanted. When you're out on the dance floor jumping around to "Respect" who can tell who's dancing with whom? We danced in cavernous halls to local garage bands, in dorm common rooms, at keg parties out in the woods, and in our bedrooms, in front of the mirror, practicing the moves.

Dancing is my life's signifier. I experienced my first real kiss while dancing with a juvenile delinquent in the hall of the Unitarian Church in Colorado Springs, where I grew up. Our youth group, Liberal Religious Youth (LRY), which provided me with entrance into the world of sex and drugs and rock 'n roll, was sponsoring a dance for "disadvantaged" kids who had ended up at the youth detention center in town. I remember going home that night and lying in bed savoring the taste and texture of that incredibly sensuous thing that had happened to me. I never saw the bestower of that gift again.

LRY groups sponsored "conferences," a euphemism for all that sex and drugs and rock 'n roll, at all the churches on the Colorado Front Range—Boulder to Pueblo. I got to dance with—and kiss as well—Denver bluesman Otis Taylor (excuse my name dropping) at one of these affairs. This was before he was actually known as a bluesman, as he must have been about 17 at the time. We danced up a storm, with a kiss here and there, but I refrained from any further activity, being only 15 myself and intimidated by this tall, handsome man who was a lot more worldly than I. I never saw him again, either, until Mark and I went to his concert many years later in Albuquerque. I didn't go up to remind him who I was; I'm sure it was a memory on my part, not his.

After high school, at Antioch, we danced all the time in the C shop, the late night café where you could eat burgers and fries to the sounds of the Stones (Let It Bleed came out in the fall of my second year; I'll never forget following the sound of "Gimme Shelter" down the hall to the common room wondering, what is that song?), Paul Butterfield Blues Band, Janis Joplin, and all that great Detroit, Philly, and Memphis R&B. When I was 20, during Christmas vacation, my mother, sisters, and I took a trip to Mazatlan, Mexico. On New Year's Eve we found ourselves in a discothèque across the street from the beach that was crammed full of Anglo and Mexican tourists as well as locals of all ages, from grandmothers to babies. My sisters and I soon hooked up with some vacationing students from Guadalajara and danced the night away. A grandmother came up and asked my mother to dance, so she got some action as well. We ended up reconnecting with the students after we took the train to Guadalajara, and we danced another night away on the shore of Lake Chapala drinking sangria with tequila shots.

I dropped out of Antioch after a couple of years and in my subsequent drifting I ended up in Cloudcroft, New Mexico, where I went to work for the Forest Service for a summer. There were a lot of cowboys in Cloudcroft, and I met one named Emory who taught me to how two-step and play pool at the Lodge, the famous hotel on the hill. This cowboy taught me how to ride a horse as well, so I acquired two skills highly valued in northern New Mexico where I eventually ended up.

The trip from Cloudcroft to Santa Fe was a long one, in more than just miles. At the Central Clearing House I found myself working with all the twenty-something activists fighting the coal mines in the four corners region and the subdivisions surrounding Santa Fe and Albuquerque. We threw a fund raising dance party at the Mine Shaft bar in Madrid where the Family Lotus, Liza Gilkyson's first band, played for all the Santa Fe elite, hippie entrepreneurs, and assorted desert misfits that comprised tthe Anglo community in the 1970s.

From Santa Fe I moseyed down to Albuquerque and the University of New Mexico, where the dance scene revolved around Okie Joe's, the student bar on the corner of University and Central. There, every Tuesday and Friday nights during happy hour (ten cent beer, dollar shots) the backroom blared "Brown Sugar" on the sound system or Cadillac Bob performed live. Everyone I knew went there, and Mark and I made it there as well on our first date. I discovered that he loved to dance, too, which was a prerequisite for any serious relationship between the two of us.

We lived for 20 years in Placitas, the former land grant community just north of Albuquerque that morphed into yuppiedom (see You Can't Go Home Again blog post) before our very eyes. Before that happened, though, there was plenty of dancing. A couple from New Orleans had regular dance parties where they turned us on to that city's R&B/funk of the Meters, Allen Toussaint, the Wild Tchoupitoulas, and the Subdudes. At our house one New Year's Eve we danced until two in the morning and finally had to let the fire go out to get everyone to leave. There were dancehalls everywhere: Placitas's own Thunderbird Bar, where Tracey Nelson and Mother Earth, Cadillac Bob, and Sonny Terry and Brownie Mcghee played; Rosa's Cantina in Algodones; the Golden Inn, where I heard Toots and the Maytals (it was so crowded you couldn't dance but just moved as part of the group pulse); and the Line Camp up north where Buddy Guy and Junior Wells tore it up.

Once we made the move to El Valle we had to incorporate ranchera dancing into our repertoire, which wasn't very hard as it's basically a polka move with a little salsa thrown in. And Mark learned how to two-step. We went to dances at the Indian gaming casinos, weddings, graduations, and Santa Fe concerts (the best was when Joe King Carrasco came up from Puerto Vallarta and played the Santa Fe Brewing Company to a crowd of dancing fools). What made it even more fun, though, was the fact that our neighbor and village patrón, Tomás, loved to dance, so when it was his turn to be mayordomo of the church he celebrated the village feast day with a dance in his barn and took us on Sunday afternoons to Las Vegas where we danced at the local bar.

Then there was El Grupo, our radical compadres who were fighting both the Forest Service and urban environmentalists over community access to forest resources: the environmentalists were promoting Zero Logging on public lands, regardless of who was doing the logging and to what extent, while the Forest Service was imploding from ineptitude and institutional paralysis. El Grupo—activist community loggers, grazers, acequia parciantes, journalists, lawyers, and academics both brown and white—used to go dancing at the Chamisa Lounge in Española to let off steam and enjoy each others' company amidst the lowriders, ex-convicts, and regular working class blokes who patronized the bar.

Mark had an extensive 45 record collection—rock, R&B, blues, Motown, pop—and when we still had a turntable that could play them, and before they warped, we'd put them on and dance around the house. Later we danced to albums, then tapes, then CDs. He died before I got Wifi and began playing Pandora on my iPod. I have a favorite dance station, "What Becomes of the Broken Hearted," that plays all the great R&B and Motown hits that we loved to dance to. I miss Mark the most when I find myself dancing around the house to "It's Too Late To Turn Back Now" or "Be My Baby." They say that couples who are together for many years start to look like each other. Mark and I, together for 34 years, only looked like each other when we danced, a synchronized dance team that will never be replicated. On this second anniversary of his death I can still dance by myself, to all the music that evokes these memories, and while it is soothing to my soul, it also breaks my heart.

Friday, January 11, 2013

The Phenomenon that is Scottsdale/Phoenix

This time I went to visit Max in Scottsdale, where he moved after living in Los Angeles, where I also visited him and described in my Existential/Fear and Loathing blog post. The impression ones gets of Scottsdale is distinctly suburban, with wide, tree lined streets bordered by meticulously manicured lawns of grass—green grass in the middle of the Sonoran desert—cacti, ornamental cedar, pine and palm trees, and bougainvillea.

Yes, there was bougainvillea in bloom in December, along with green-leafed deciduous trees and poinsettias lining driveways and porches in the Christmas spirit. There were also trees full of green and yellow parrots, jumping around and cackling to their hearts' content. I assume that, just like in the movie "The Wild Parrots of Telegraph Hill," which tells the story of the quirky man who fed the San Francisco flock of parrots generated from a few stray birds that escaped their cages, these Scottsdale parrots share the same origin story. Except there didn't seem to be anyone around to feed these birds; the only people I saw outside were the gardeners and plumbers and electricians who were working on the ranch style houses in their manicured settings.

All I could think about while walking these streets was what it must be like five months of the year when the temperature is at least 100 degrees, and sometimes 115, and how much water it takes to maintain the grass and flowers and hundred-foot tall palm trees and backyard swimming pools (I saw those from the window of the airplane when I flew in). The water comes from the Salt River Project, an enormous system of dams and canals that first brought water to this former farming valley. Starting in the mid 19th century farmers built canals to redirect water from the Salt

River; in the early part of the 20th century they used their land as collateral on loans that resulted in the construction of Roosevelt Dam, 76 miles northeast of Phoenix.

Back in the 1970s water irrigated 80,000 acres of citrus orchards: that landscape is now reduced to about 20,000 acres. The remainder is filled with the sprawl that is greater Phoenix: Scottsdale, Mesa, Tempe (location of Arizona State University), Glendale. You only know you've passed from one community to the next when the sign on the side of the road tells you so.

So actually, the amount of water necessary for lawns instead of lemons, oranges, and grapefruit is already available. But I want to know what, besides cows, can live on green grass? I can assure you there are no cows grazing the Scottsdale suburbs to supply the local restaurants with grass fed beef. There are only people and palm trees and the occasional parrot, which until the Salt River goes dry can enjoy their aberrant existence in this Sonoran oasis.

But while we wait for the inevitable drying out, it seems the area is losing some of its oasis status for people, especially visitors. Since the passage of the 2010 immigration enforcement law (SB10170), which allows the police to determine the immigration status of anyone "stopped, detained, or arrested," if there is "reasonable suspicion," convention bookings have dropped by 30 percent. In a recent *Arizona Republic* article the mayor of Phoenix was quoted as saying, "What you may have read about our Legislature, don't hold against the rest of us. The rest of us, we're normal. We like diversity."

Max and I decided not to spend any more time checking out how normal the Phoenix folks are and we drove to Albuquerque, another town that certainly appears to like diversity, although the New Mexico governor, like her Arizona counterpart, is doing her best to make it appear otherwise: at the top of her agenda is overturning the law that allows undocumented immigrants to get drivers licenses. Albuquerque is also another sprawling western city, like Phoenix, dependent upon imported water to sustain its population.

But the good thing is that it's situated in the high desert instead of the low desert and shortly after we got there, nighttime temperatures dropped into the teens. Which means there aren't that many tourists who require resort hotels and golf courses and conventions centers like those of Scottsdale and Phoenix, which also means that Albuquerque has managed to retain some funky soul. Just ask Brian Cranston.

Monday, February 18, 2013

Reflections on the Super-duper Bowl

Let's talk Beyoncé. Was it singing? (and I'm not talking about whether she was lip syncing); was it dancing? (in thigh-high boots with 5 inch heels I'd call it stomping); was it an excuse for pyrotechnics?; was it spectacle? Was it . . . 75,000 tweets for CRAP?

I didn't know until recently that she can really sing because I always dismissed her as a entertainment package, not an R & B singer in the tradition of Aretha, Etta, and Laura Nyro (who was finally inducted into the Rock 'n' Roll Hall of Fame) who stood up on the stage or sat at the piano and sang with their souls. Now we have Beyoncé and Lady Gaga and Destiny's Child (with Whitney Houston, RIP, kind of in the middle) who prance around the stage in a little bit of satin or leather and it's really hard to know what they're doing.

Michael Jackson and Prince, our androgynous links from the Detroit, Philly, and Memphis R & B days, also crossed over to pop but they made it clear they could actually sing and dance and play guitar. In his new book *Telegraph Avenue* Michael Chabon, in the voice of one of his characters, also laments the loss of R & B talent, not to pop but to rap: "But face it, a lot has been lost. A whole lot. Ellington, Sly Stone, Stevie Wonder, Curtis Mayfield, we got nobody of that caliber even hinted at in black music today. I'm talking about genius, composers . . . knowing how to play the fuck out your instrument."

I think it was Madonna, though, who really fucked things up. When I went to Wikipedia to peruse her profile—one of the longest I've ever seen on that site—she's quoted as saying she wanted to grow up as a "black kid;" Prince was one of her idols. Apparently she also wanted to be a gay one: my friend Terri says she thinks Madonna's early style derived from the New York gay bars before AIDS. So the lack of her talent as a singer/dancer/actress converged with desires of who she wanted to be and voilá, crossover R & B as pop spectacle via MTV was born: shake your booty and you can be whoever or whatever you want.

Some academic feminists (and men) would be aghast at my assessment. Many have found that Madonna is the perfect political icon talked about by the famous Judith Butler in her book *Gender Trouble* because of her reconstruction of identity. The infamous Camille Paglia wrote that Madonna liberated sexuality from its Puritanical roots. That is, until she also wrote about how old and plastic Madonna was looking and how unseemly it was that she was still shaking her booty. And then there was the critic who asked the question, "Is Madonna a glamorized fuckdoll or the queen of parodic critique?"

But really, what the whole thing reminds me of is Elvis, minus a few pounds. We watched him rise from a rockabilly white boy to a soulful crooner of love songs to an icon of Las Vegas glitter. Only now the glitter isn't confined to Las Vegas; it's at the Grammy's, the Emmy's, the Oscars, and, of course, the Super Bowl. I wonder if it all could have gone anywhere else, what with MTV, rap producers who have shoved aside the likes of Jerry Wexler, and the fact that making millions of dollars is the common denominator of 21st century modernity.

I thought about watching the Grammy's to see if they could prove me wrong until I got my Sundays mixed up. If I'd known Amy Winehouse would have been there . . . maybe I would have remembered.

Friday, March 22, 2013

Jamaica Kincaid

I had one of those days recently when I really missed Mark. I'd just read a review of the new Jamaica Kincaid novel, a scathing, sometimes fantastical recounting of her marriage to William Shawn's son Allen Shawn and how he left her for a younger woman. I somehow had forgotten this interesting fact, that the two of them were married, amidst all the other lore I'd accumulated about the rather strange but intriguing Shawn family: that the seemingly staid William Shawn, longtime editor of the *New Yorker*, had secretly conducted an affair with his colleague Lillian Ross for many years; that Allen's twin sister Mary, who was autistic, had been "put away" by the family; and that Wallace Shawn, the funny looking younger brother had turned into a consummate stage and screen actor and playwright. In fact, "My Dinner With Andre," in which Wallace stars with Andre Gregory, was one of Mark's all time favorite movies. Boy, did I really want to talk about all this with him and run right out and buy Kincaid's book.

But I was spending the weekend with my kids and neither one of them had ever heard of William Shawn or ever seen "My Dinner With Andre," so my story lost its punch. At least Max, who graduated last year from Claremont McKenna College, where Jamaica Kincaid now teaches, had some interesting gossip to relay about her, but which I will refrain from retelling.

Mark's and my accumulated knowledge, born of 34 years of accumulated experience, is now reduced by half. Without access to the full percent, the compartmentalization of my other relationships becomes more obvious. While this doesn't diminish their value, it intensifies my loss.

With my neighbors in El Valle I share our sense of place, our desire to be buen vecinos, our delight in the mitote and craziness that gets played out in this tiny village. My political relationships, born of thirty years of activism and community organizing, extend to concentric circles of concern that rarely intersect with my personal circles of engagement. I maintain intimate relationships with a few friends and family members who come close to being with me in that holistic world: music, books, movies, art, politics, personal revelation. But they're an effort, a phone call or e-mail away; they're not sitting across the room from me as I'm reading the *New Yorker*: "Listen to this!"

A lot of this has to do with age, of course. Who still gets off listening to Steely Dan? Who wants to read *Middlemarch* every year? Who wants to talk about the Vietnam War, Watergate, the fall of Allende, and the Iran-Contra scandal? Who wants to hear Mark's story about how he got out of the draft by crying? Who wants to hear my story about hitchhiking north out of Albuquerque and sleeping on the floor of Ulysses S. Grant's commune in Placitas? At the end of 34 years Mark and I didn't want to hear each other's stories either (listen to This American Life podcast, #226 Reruns, March 10 for the very funny stories of the way couples listen and don't listen to each other) but we knew the details, the context, and the meaning without the words, as no one else ever would.

So I'm still looking for someone to talk to about Jamaica Kincaid's novel. But I'm also glad I don't have to participate in one of our hackneyed routines: his lament about the UNM Lobos (they just lost in the first game of the NCAA tournament) and my refrain, I told you so!

Thursday, April 4, 2013

Only in France

In the *New York Times* Style section there was an article about the French debating gay marriage in "Their Fashion." The kind of conversation they are having hasn't taken place in this country since the 1970s. Only the French would still be objecting to gay marriage "because they [gays] want a bourgeois life." That sententious statement was made by fashion designer Karl Lagerfeld, who dresses the bourgeoisie (and whose punk couture is featured in a new show at the Metropolitan Museum in New York). His comrade Frédéric Montel explained that marriage is "a conservative movement, about stability in society . . . and becoming rather ordinary."

The article also quoted a feminist historian who thinks the movement for same-sex marriage is "a project for gay men, not lesbians." Back in the 1960s Julia Kristeva, also French, described the institution of marriage as "identification by women with the very power structures previously considered as frustrating, oppressive or inaccessible." (*Women's Time*)

When conservatives in this country get behind gay marriage as a family value it's time to get back to the conversation (not about the bourgeoisie, heaven forbid, a term absolutely censored in American discourse) about why we're doing all this work to prop up an institution because we can't be part of it. It's like the Don't Ask Don't Tell solution to gays wanting to serve in the military: why in the world should we be fighting for the right for anyone to serve in the military? Why in the world are we fighting for the institution of marriage when half of them (the heterosexual ones; since the other kind exist only in a few states, we can't get statistics) end in divorce? Why are we letting this issue distract us from far more important issues not only in the lives of women but to all of us?

Last week the call in show on KUNM (the University of New Mexico radio station) was about gay marriage, specifically the ACLU's lawsuit against the Bernalillo County Clerk for refusing to issue marriage licenses to two lesbian couples. The lawsuit claims that the New Mexico marriage statutes and the New Mexico Constitution do not bar same-sex couples from marrying, and therefore the state should issue civil marriage licenses to any same-sex couple that applies for one.

The KUNM producers, in their knee jerk attempt at "objectivity" had fundamentalist preacher Glen Strock on the telephone as their token reactionary. He spewed his venom about homosexuals as an "abomination" and how they need the rest of society's help because of their "mental illness, promiscuity, and drug addiction." While no one brought up the divorce rate and the havoc that brings to Strock's society, several people at least tiptoed into a conversation about the institution by making the distinction between civil unions and marriage: the first, sanctioned by the state to everyone who applies for a license; the second in a church or private ceremony to reflect the individuals' beliefs or need for some sort of public recognition or rite of passage. It doesn't do much to enhance the conversation about monogamy, the nuclear family, the impossible expectations, all the questions the institution raises, but at least it would protect the legal rights of those who wish to form a union.

But as Yasmin Nair questions in her blog (thanks, Terri, for turning me on to this, (http://www.yasminnair.net/content/gay-marriage-conservative-cause), what legal rights are we talking about? The right to heath care benefits? As Nair points out, there should be universal health care for everyone, regardless of marital status. The gay-marriage-as-legal-right argument buys into a neoliberal agenda that requires state sanction of what should be our inalienable rights. Again, Nair: "Let us, queers who understand the problems with gay marriage as an economically and socially conservative issue and our straight allies, begin to dispense with the silly idea that there has ever been anything about gay marriage that could even vaguely be described as left/liberal/progressive. Rather, progressives, liberals, and self-described lefties would do well to echo Republican Jon Hunstman, and speak the truth plainly, that gay marriage is a conservative cause."

And so it comes full circle: Karl Lagerfeld, maven of the fashion industry, who disdains gay marriage because it's a conservative movement, and Jon Huntsman, a Republican presidential hopeful, who embraces gay marriage because it's conservative. Only in France, but maybe in America, too.

Thursday, April 11, 2013

In Memory of Shulamith Firestone

Over the years I occasionally Googled (shame on my laziness, depending solely on Google) Shulamith Firestone, wondering what became of this second wave feminist who wrote the *Dialectic of Sex*, a brilliant, ground breaking, and sometimes wrongheaded (in my humble opinion) book that profoundly affected me, only a few years younger than she. I found nothing beyond the mention of the book: no other publications, no political activities, no personal statistics about where she lived, who she lived with, how she spent her time.

Yesterday, in the *New Yorker*, I found out. Firestone died last August, alone, suffering from mental illness, in the 10th Street apartment she'd lived in since the 1970s. I cried as I read Susan Faludi's account of Firestone's life: stifled and expelled by an Orthodox Jewish father; abandoned by a mother who failed to defend her; and betrayed by a sisterhood that descended into chaos and power struggles unable, as Faludi describes it, "to thrive in the world they had done so much to create."

I've often written of the internecine fighting that ruins movements and demoralizes its movents, but the radical feminism of the 1960s and 70s was so powerful and so necessary that despite its failures and destroyed lives so many of us would not be who we are today without it. That's what makes Firestone's story, and others like her, all the more tragic. Faludi quotes from feminist Kate Millet's essay, "The Feminist Time Forgot," about those who had "disappeared to struggle alone in makeshift oblivion or vanished into asylums and have yet to return to tell the tale." Firestone was one of those who "vanished into asylums," many times, diagnosed as schizophrenic. Several times support groups were organized by one of her sisters and women friends, but in the end she died alone and poverty stricken in her tenement.

As I said in my Marriage blog, I recently reread the *Dialectic of Sex*. The idea of cyber babies she posits as the means to free women "from the tyranny of their reproductive biology" makes me laugh. Other readers will object to any number of other views that "take on the world," as Millett thought her book did. That's what a revolutionary book does, and Shulamith Firestone was indeed a revolutionary. I suppose I'm glad that I finally found out what happened to her, but I'm also profoundly sad. Rest in peace, "Shulie."

Saturday, May 11, 2013

Springtime in New Mexico

It's been a lousy spring in northern New Mexico: freezing cold (except for a few days when we were tantalized with 70 degrees); incessant wind; and negligible rain. I lost all my fruit except for a few plums and sour cherries; the sweet cherry blooms were starting to form and then disappeared after three nights of 15 to 20 degree temperatures. The apples never formed blossoms at all. I know the folks down in Albuquerque are thankful that the ninety-degree days have yet to begin, but unless it's hot in Albuquerque it's still winter up here.

Right now I'm experiencing the juxtaposition of sitting by the fire before going out to check the irrigation water in my fruitless orchard. While the run-off from the high country snow has yet to come (Jakob was up skiing the chutes and measured five feet of snow) my first-in-line village is using the mid to low level run-off to jumpstart the hay fields and orchards that will all too soon be thirsty. The dismal monthly predictions issued by the Natural Resources Conservation Service have most watersheds at less than 50 per cent of normal snowpack, and the farmers in southern New Mexico are pumping the aquifer to keep their crops alive because there isn't enough water in Elephant Butte Reservoir to release for irrigation. Texas is suing New Mexico claiming non-delivery of Rio Grande Compact water because, as we all know, groundwater and surface water are inextricably entwined. Looks like dismal spring will segue into dismal summer, especially for those whose livelihoods are threatened by this terrible drought exacerbated by climate change.

I can still grow some vegetables in my garden and hoop house and go to the grocery store for the rest. Living off the land is more an idea than a reality for me (much less a necessity, of course). That's not to say, however, that my attachment to, and appreciation of, this place where I live isn't foremost in mind even as I complain. I have a warm, homemade adobe house, small courtyard of grass and flowers, orchard, garden, hoop house, fields of hay, two acequias, and one river as my "place." I can't imagine who I might be in a different place. Half my time is spent dealing with it: irrigating the hay fields; pruning the trees; rototilling, planting, and then weeding the garden; weed whacking the orchard grass; waging war against the burdock down in the bosque; trying to figure out why Jack the horse has lost hair on two patches of his back; cutting firewood for winter. Speaking of winter; that's when I have to split the firewood and kindling, bring it to the house, make and sustain a fire every day, shovel the driveway and deck, and feed the horse.

What else would I be doing? Writing novels? I've written two of them plus a collection of short stories (all in the bottom drawer of my desk, as we used to say before computers). Working at a real job? The only ones I ever had were as a seasonal employee of the Forest Service in a fire lookout or patrolling the mountains by truck or on foot. Now my job is to harangue the Forest Service in the pages (actually, on the web) of *La Jicarita*, which I can do without ever leaving my "place."

How long I can keep doing this remains to be seen. I figure if I'm lucky I've got ten more years here by myself, with a little help from my friends (like cutting the wood) and mother nature, with a little more rain and snow. Then what? I haven't lived in a town for 40 years. Albuquerque? Too hot, in water crisis mode, and there's no guarantee Jakob and Casey will still be there. Santa Fe? Unaffordable, bourgeois, also running out of water (although busily importing agricultural water to make up for it). Wherever Max ends up? Doubtful; we may talk on the phone all the time and have fun together, but does he want to live with his mother? Nah.

So back to just being here, day by day, until I can't be here. Then I'll be there, wherever there might be. I'll worry about where is there tomorrow.

Sunday, May 26, 2013

"I'll Take You There"

Mavis Staples "took us there" last Friday night at a benefit for the Outpost Performance Center in Albuquerque. The "us" were the folks over 50 who grew up listening to Pops, Mavis, and sisters, known as the Staples Singers; the "there" was the place that only live music by one of the great R & B singers of all time can take you. We're talking Aretha Franklin, Etta James, Laura Nero, Patti LaBelle, and potentially Beyoncé, who now says she wants to get back to her "roots" and be a "real" soul sister instead of an MTV playdoll (see Reflections on the Super-Duper Bowl blog post).

Mavis came out with a cane, having "blown out" her knee, with an amazing band that's been with her as she's resurrected a career that got a little off track through the eighties and nineties. Even though I could count on one hand the 20, 30, or 40 somethings at the concert, there are a few in the know who helped in her new career: "Have a Little Faith" was produced by Jim Tulio and "You Are Not Alone" by Wilco's Jeff Tweedy.

These guys know their R & B history. And there must be others out there who know their jazz, but they don't come to the concerts at the Outpost, either. When I go there to hear Ravi Coltrane or Bill Frisell or Oliver Lake, gray hair and wrinkles predominate.

What's going on? In the May 27 *New Yorker* George Packer quotes a Silicon Valley start-up engineer talking about his techie cohort: "They're ignorant, because many of them don't feel the need to educate themselves outside their little world, and they're not rewarded for doing so. . . . People with whom I used to talk about politics or policy or the arts, they're just not into it anymore. They don't read the *Wall Street Journal* or the *New York Times*. They read *TechCrunch* and *VentureBeat*, and maybe they happen to see something from the *Times* on somebody's Facebook news feed."

Notice we're not even talking about reading the *New Yorker* or Andrew Solomon or Zadie Smith currently on the newsstands and best seller lists at Amazon. Ever heard of Edmund Wilson or Twyla Tharp? Janet Frame or Rainer Werner Fassbinder? An entrepreneur Packer interviewed told him he went a few years without reading a single book. Yet these are the guys (and it's mostly guys, and they're mostly white) who call themselves the "Best and the Brightest." Do they even know that's the title of David Halberstam's book? Do they really want to be identified with the academic policy wonks in the Kennedy administration who were responsible for the Vietnam War?

But according to Packer's article, they have no interest in politics or the history that contextualizes it. When they do decide that for whatever reason—good PR? bad conscience?—it might be a good idea to give some of their billions to non-profits and charitable foundations, Bill Gates ends up supporting the educational policies of Michelle Rhee, teaching to bad tests, and Mark Zuckerberg wants to reform immigration by bringing in more educated foreigners to work as engineers and designers.

It's not just the techies, of course, who have no interest in politics, art, literature . . . . but I'm beginning to sound like a broken record (see Jamaica Kincaid blog post). It seems a generation of people who knew at least a little about a lot of things is fading away while a generation that knows about nothing but one thing is the future. But hey, the one thing they do know about, social media, is how they're going to "entertain each other and interact with each other and do things for each other much more efficiently" (as one of Packer's interviewees waxes poetic). That what they're doing so efficiently has no content doesn't seem to matter.

Tuesday, June 4, 2013

Role Reversal

For reasons unknown I have a free subscription to *Backpacker Magazine*. I usually don't read it, although I've been a backpacker all my life: don't need anymore gear and don't want to feel bad about all the beautiful places I've never been.

But I happened to flip to a short article the other day that starts out: "Mom wanted to turn back." So, being a mom, and being 63, a year older than the mom in question, I continued reading. The family had canoed into Canyonlands National Park but were out hiking up one of the side canyons when they encountered a "van sized rock" that was blocking passage through the canyon slot. No problem; the sister hoisted mom onto the shoulders of one of the brothers while the other brother pulled her up from the top of the rock.

This role reversal made a big impression on her, as it did on me the first time Jakob had to finagle the safety strap off my telemark skies because I couldn't stay on my knees long enough to do it myself. This was at the same ski area where years ago he and I climbed up the slopes in the deep powder—before it opened for the season—and I was the one on my knees struggling to get his skis on him in four feet of snow. He remembered, and casually commented, wasn't it funny, him helping me with equipment.

Then there was Saturday before last, in four feet of snow again, only this time it was sloppy spring snow and our snowshoes were busting through the crust every few steps as we slogged our way up the trail in the Pecos Wilderness. We were doing this because he needed to take photographs of ski clothes in the snow for one of the magazines he reviews for, and the only snow to be found was above 10,000 feet.

He also thought it would be a great way to celebrate a belated Mother's Day, so the role reversal that day made even more of an impression on me. On one of the steepest sections of the trail, as I followed behind, my snowshoe fell into the depression his shoe had made but continued downward until it was wedged under a log and I was up to my thigh in snow. I pulled and tugged and tried to reach my binding with my hand, to no avail. Resigned, I had to call for help. Laughing, he quickly dug me out with my pole and pointed out, once again, how funny the situation was.

I'm not sure what I'd call it: funny is better than sad, which was an element of my emotional palette. But I also felt proud of both of us, actually: he, who was obviously delighted to be of help; and me, for being out there skiing and snowshoeing with diminished strength and skill but at least still out there.

Exhausted before we made it to the lakes we took off our snowshoes and Jakob spent two hours taking pictures: jackets on, with the dogs, (who also hated the post holing), without the dogs, with the ridgeline as backdrop, without the ridgeline, with trees, without trees, on the rock, in front of the rock; jackets off, lying in the snow, in the sun, in the shade, until the whole damn camera card was full. It was all rather ridiculous, but that made the role reversal a little easier to take: not all the laughter was at my expense.

Friday, August 2, 2013

Waiting for Lucia

While waiting for my grandchild Lucia to be born doesn't bear the absurdist burden of waiting for Godot—who never shows up—it does require distraction. How this distraction fits into daily life is where the anxiety comes in. Do I start a new article because I know I need something for next week's *La Jicarita* or because it's going to make the time pass until the phone rings and Jakob tells me, "Casey's in labor"? Do I need to make time to water the houseplants and hoop house and flower garden RIGHT NOW in case the phone rings and I have to get in the car and go to Albuquerque (my bag is already packed)? Do I dare take a hike? Should I write a blog post because I can't really focus on anything else? Obviously, the latter possibility prevailed.

I went to the neighbors' house for dinner last night—Jakob knows the number (no cell phones in El Valle)—and with several generations of mothers present the talk naturally turned to birth stories. When we were younger, having our kids, we told our birth stories over and over again, partly to delight in our shared experience and partly to reaffirm in our own minds that we actually did this, we birthed these little creatures who would go on to consume our lives forever.

Now that we're grandmothers, or impending grandmothers, we get to tell our stories all over again. And what a diversity of experience they reveal: a home birth where the midwife had to walk up the impassable muddy road because of the spring mud; 12 hour home births with older kids in attendance; first births that came in two hours; induced labor births that ended in C-sections. When the discussion turned to the option of epidurals when complications or extended labors demand relief, the dad who was listening in said something about difficulties that may result from an epidural. He was quickly put in his place when his wife said if she'd have had access to an epidural during her long labor—she delivered at home—she'd have taken it in a heartbeat. Casey will soon have her own story to tell, and it will be fascinating.

I'm reading a book of essays by Elinor Lipman, who is mostly known for her novels of "Austen-like wit." In one essay she writes that her son "is the best idea we ever had." That bold claim seems absurd when put in context. I worry about Lucia being born in a time of NSA surveillance, climate change, unquestioned technological change, increasing income disparity, and on and on. Of course, my kids were born during the Reagan administration, which set the course for the neoliberal agenda that is the cause of much of what I'm worrying about for Lucia. I was worried then, too, but I still had my babies. Maybe we keep having them because they help allay these fears through both their need and their gift: parenthood. I'm very glad I didn't miss it.

The fact that they're now having babies—or one of them is—is mind boggling. It won't really register until I'm in the delivery room holding my granddaughter. So I'm waiting, Lucia, as are your mom and dad. Please let them know it's time for the phone call.

Saturday, September 28, 2013

Having Babies

My daughter-in-law Casey recently posted an article on Facebook "The Unnatural Mom" by Krista Infante, who reflects back on the birth of her son and the guilt and inadequacy she felt when the experience didn't replicate the "birth plan" she formulated. It's a common story, but one that needs to be repeated to remind mothers, and fathers, that every birth story is different and is only one chapter in the longer story of being a parent and loving a child.

As a member of second wave feminism my own opinions about childbirth were a reaction against its co-option by the male ob-gyn industry that developed post World War II, confining our mothers to hospital beds, replacing breasts with bottles, and raising the percentage of caesarian sections to levels beyond the need to save lives to the desire for "efficiency" and to insulate against lawsuits. We wanted to make the decisions about home versus hospital, midwife versus doctor, drugs versus no drugs, which were really options, not clear-cut choices, in a world of few certainties except the overriding need do whatever is necessary to have a healthy baby.

As pendulums often do, this one swung quite far in the so-called quest for a "natural" birth that over the years grew to include birth plans, birthing classes (which replaced Lamaze classes whose "hee-hee-hoos" breathing techniques proved to be largely useless, to which I will attest), bath tubs, birthing balls, doulas, and every conceivable consumer product the baby industrial complex could invent.

In recent years some Google and Yahoo post-feminists have declared war on "natural" and are rallying to swing the pendulum back to their version of the days of ob-gyn supremacy, C-sections, and formula, all

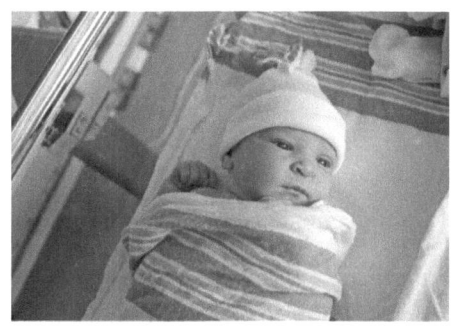
with the goal of paying as little attention to that bothersome work of "producing" a baby so they can get back to the all important work of producing cell phones and surveillance.

So what's a mom to do? I can only tell you that Casey, who fell into the "natural" category in preparing for baby Lucia, magnificently proved, over the course of four days, that we do whatever we have to do to safely birth a baby, and everything else flies out the window. After three days of labor at home, bad enough to deprive her (and Jakob and me, to a lesser extent), of sleep but not bad enough to enter the hospital, where the midwives waited, she was exhausted. Then, over the course of the next 24 hours, so many decisions had to be made during so many unexpected events that at one point I found myself saying (to myself), I can't do this, I don't think I can do this, and I wasn't having the baby. But Casey focused and persevered as labor periodically stalled, as the epidural that was supposed to relieve the pain didn't work, as her blood pressure rose and the baby's heart rate dropped trying to get the epidural to work. When someone raised the option of a C-section, she announced to all of us that she did not want one, and despite the exhaustion and pain she would continue to labor. When the midwife finally said it was time to push, Casey did so for four hours with every ounce of strength she possessed, and finally, at the end of four days, there was little Lucia, who, as I said in my previous post Waiting for Lucia, will now consume our lives forever. You did good, Casey, and now you have a birth story that is all yours. Have fun telling it.

Sunday, October 6, 2013

I'm in love. With Alabama Shakes. With Brittany Howard.

I was completely depressed by my fight with the politicos in Taos County over water rights and needed some relief. So I put on Alabama Shakes, turned up the volume, and fell in love. How could I not, listening to Brittany sing, "Bless my heart, bless my soul, I didn't think I'd make it to 22 years old." And then she sings, "I'm not who I used to be."

Who is this Alabama child? All I know from the Internet sites is that she started playing guitar in high school, went to another guitar player in high school and said, hey, want to play guitar together in high school and write some songs? Add a drummer, a lead guitarist (although Brittany is lead any time she wants) and somehow, these twenty something southern post high school band mates are the bomb.

It's kind of R&B, kind of blues, kind of white southern rock, with a twist of female angst that takes it someplace else. She's soulful, she's sassy, she's big, she's beautiful, "she's black, she's white" (as one fellow Alabaman described her), she's rock 'n roll!

Some in the media have been comparing her to Janis Joplin, but she defers from this and rightly so. While they both have that raspy voice, Brittany rocks out with something equally primal but with more cool than angst. In one interview she talks about singing at the Grammy's with Mavis Staples (see I'll Take You There blog post) and how unique Staples' phrasing is in any genre: gospel or blues or R&B. Maybe we'll be saying that about Brittany, too, as she starts off on a career that will hopefully take her wherever she wants to go.

And along with the voice she can play that guitar. I carry many guitar riffs around in my head—the opening strain of "Gimme Shelter," Mark

Knopfler on "Sultans of Swing," Eric Clapton on "Layla"—and now I've got the driving garage band guitar on "Hang Loose" and "I'm Not the Same." And it's a woman doing the driving! Keep hanging in there, Brittany, we'll be with you every step of the way.

Sunday, December 8, 2013

Entering the Affordable Care Act

"There are eight million stories in the naked city" . . . or there are 20 million stories about trying to sign up for the Affordable Care Act. (OK, you have to be 50 or older to think this is clever.)

I got a letter yesterday from the New Mexico Income Support Division telling me I've been approved for Family Planning Medicaid, which covers only "medical services for family planning: to prevent or delay pregnancy or to manage family size."

I'm really glad to hear that this service is being provided through Medicaid. But seeing as how I'm 63 years old, I have two children aged 32 and 25, and a 4-month old grandchild, it's unlikely—impossible—I'm going to need these services. Every time I look to buy anything on the Internet there's an immediate ad on Facebook trying to sell me the same thing from a different company, but the Income Support Division doesn't know how old I am?

I already know I won't qualify for regular Medicaid under the ACA. But I had incredible luck—right time, right place—when several years ago an insurance program in New Mexico called State Coverage Insurance (SCI) rose from the ashes to provide coverage for folks like Mark and me. We'd never had any health insurance, ever: we traded various products and services for bills—pot for one of the kid's birth, ski lessons for Mark's hernia—or we paid $50 a month for 10 years. Miraculously, the SCI program that targeted those who made too much money to qualify for Medicaid but too little to possibly afford private insurance saved my sorry 55 year-old butt. That's the age when it seems our baby boomer bodies start to fall apart: knee replacements, hip replacements, autoimmune disease, high blood pressure, the dreaded cancer . . . .

Now I have to buy a private insurance company policy that without the tax credit subsidy from the federal government would bankrupt anybody: five, six, seven hundred dollars a month for health insurance? Do I gamble and hope I won't end up in the hospital this one year I have to buy insurance—before I'm of Medicare age—and go for the high deductible, low co-pay plan? Do I play it safe and take the low deductible, high co-pay for those doctors I unfortunately have to see fairly often knowing that like many others my age hospitalization is probably on the horizon? Maybe I'll just close my eyes and wherever I click is what I'll get.

I'm far better off than younger folks who will be faced with high premiums for many years to come. We all know this is a paean to the insurance companies, an extension of the already privatized health care business with some concessions for coverage. Even Mexico, for Christ's sake, implemented universal, single payer health insurance last year. While we continue to send junk food and subsidized corn their way maybe they'll export some health insurance al norte.

So, my friends, LOL, in all its ambiguity: lots of luck (or lust), laugh out loud, laugh on lipitor, or lean on levity but don't spend too much time trying to figure out why this country is so fucked up.

Monday, January 20, 2014

Total Noise

I write much better than I speak. In her book *What to Look for in Winter: A Memoir in Blindness* Candia McWilliams describes this attribute as "What comes down my arm and not out of my mouth." I'm not sure how it does this—comes down my arm—but I'm very thankful it does, because otherwise I'd appear a blithering idiot.

I always marveled at writers who would say their books just "wrote themselves," which I never believed, but it does seem there is a connection between your arm and your creativity that sometimes eludes your consciousness. Somehow, the act of writing distills a jumble of information that lacks any coherent structure and comes out valuable.

David Foster Wallace, in his introduction to *The Best American Essays, 2007*, calls this jumble "Total Noise: the sound of our U.S. culture right now, a culture and volume of info and spin and rhetoric and context that I know I'm not alone in finding too much to even absorb, much less to try to make sense of or organize into any kind of triage of saliency or value." He goes on to say that the essays he's chosen for this anthology respond to the "tsunami of available, fact, context, and perspective that constitutes Total Noise by serving as models and guides for how large or complex sets of facts can be sifted, culled, and arranged in meaningful ways—ways that yield and illuminate truth instead of just adding more noise to the over all roar."

I'm not putting myself in that category, the "illuminating truth," and besides, it sounds like way too much work. What comes down my arm is more serendipitous and at the same time more rote: all those words and their arrangements in all those novels, essays, biographies, treatises, magazines, and newspapers I've read over the years have provided a pattern for my own. I'm also trying to find a way, like Wallace, through the "tsunami," but how successful I am is where the serendipity comes into play.

Every few months someone writes in *The New York Times* or some magazine that you can't really teach someone how to write. You can help them make outlines, critique their word choice, or laud their imagination, but you can't identify, much less offer, that secret ingredient—intelligence, creativity, sheer fortitude?—that creates value.

Christopher Hitchens said that if you can talk you can write. Although I'm a little embarrassed to admit it, Max and I listened to Christopher (he hated being called Chris, so I keep referring to him as "Christopher" in the voice Adrianna used when speaking to Christopher Moltisanti in the "Sopranos") read his memoir on CD on our long car trip to Chicago to deposit Max at grad school. Christopher, or "Hitch" as he became with the literati, certainly could talk and proved he could write as well.

Max tells me that I write like people talk, which is a twist on what Christopher says. I guess that means I use the pen/computer to have a conversation, which although one-sided, has at least the time on my part to be prepared, edited, rewritten, and finally flung out into the world. It may leave me somewhat removed, but at least it doesn't leave me blithering.

Saturday, March 29, 2014

Orwell Lives

Not surprisingly, there has been a resurgence of interest in George Orwell. But actually it began long before the release of the NSA documents. My favorite provocateur Christopher Hitchens, who never really lost interest in George, wrote a book, *Why Orwell Matters*, in which he sets up Orwell as the bulwark against postmodern relativism. Adam Hochschild wrote a homage to *Homage to Catalonia* in the *New York Review of Books*, reexamining Orwell's participation in the Spanish Civil War and his commitment to the social revolution in Catalonia, crushed by the Soviet Union.

And then there's Edward Snowden. In a Christmas message recorded in Russia he says the massive spying by the NSA was far beyond the thought police described in Orwell's 1984: "The types of collection in the book—microphones and video cameras, TVs that watch us—are nothing compared to what we have available today. . . . A child born today will grow up with no conception of privacy at all. They'll never know what it means to have a private moment to themselves, an unrecorded, unanalyzed thought. And that's a problem because privacy matters, privacy is what allows us to determine who we are and who we want to be."

Coincidentally, I was rereading *1984* and the day after I heard Snowden on the Internet I read this passage in the book:

"By comparison with that existing today, all the tyrannies of the past were half-hearted and inefficient. The ruling groups were always infected to some extent by liberal ideas, and were content to leave loose ends everywhere, to regard only the overt act, and to be uninterested in what their subjects were thinking. Even the Catholic Church of the Middle Ages was tolerant by modern standards. Part of the reason for this was that in the past no government had the power to keep its citizens under constant surveillance. The invention of print, however, made it easier to manipulate public opinion, and the film and the radio carried the process further. With the development of television, and the technical advance which made it possible to receive and transmit simultaneously on the same instrument, private life came to an end. Every citizen, or at least every citizen important enough to be worth watching, could be kept for twenty-four hours a day under the eyes of the police and in the sound of official propaganda, with all other channels of communication closed. The possibility of enforcing not only complete obedience to the will of the State, but complete uniformity of opinion on all subjects, now existed for the first time."

While the methods have become more efficient, both Orwell and Snowden decry the "watching," which translates into the loss of privacy and the manipulation of public opinion. But who exactly is doing the watching? Is Orwell's Big Brother the same as the NSA? According to the French philosopher Saint-Simon, any differences are negligible as they're both members of the technocratic elite who must govern the rest of the masses (there's some Nietzsche here, too), the low class illiterates, incapable of improving their lot. This "double morality" of Utopian socialism is the only way to progress, to be well governed. While Orwell's rendering of this kind of governing in *1984* is truly chilling, the NSA's gross surveillance is also Saint-Simon's philosophy in action, just other forms: corporations, the military industrial complex, and the state using technology to protect us, not from terrorists, but from ourselves.

Knowing what happens to Winston when he rebels against the Party in *1984* it's no wonder Snowden fled the U.S. once he released the documents revealing the extent of the NSA surveillance. Ironically sequestered in

Russia, Snowden asserted individual liberty in defense of the "greater good," addressing the age-old dilemma of personal freedom versus the "social contract," as Rousseau named it. Obama and cohort, who have prosecuted more whistleblowers than all previous administrations, profess belief that the American definition of the "greater good" justifies unrestricted access to our personal lives and retribution against those like Snowden who question how that greater good is achieved.

Institutionally defined, then, it doesn't allow much room for individual interpretation. Big Brother knows best.

Sunday, May 18, 2014

Play That Rock Guitar

I was walking down the corridor to the common room in North Hall at Antioch College when I first heard the opening guitar strain of "Gimme Shelter" and I thought, "Oh my god, what is this music?" Years later, Mark and I were driving down the highway in northern California when "Sultans of Swing" came on the radio and we said to each other, "Who is this, is this Dylan?" and then we heard Mark Knopfler's guitar riff and we said, "This is not Dylan."

At the Sunshine Theater in Albuquerque we danced in our seats as Buddy Guy danced down the aisle with his guitar. And there was the sad day when we came out of San Pedro Parks Wilderness and heard on the truck radio—over and over—the soulful licks of Stevie Ray Vaughn. We turned to each other and said: "Oh, no, he's dead."

A couple of weeks ago in the *New York Times Magazine* Saul Austertliz wrote about the current phenomenon in music criticism called "poptimism," the term used to counterpoint "rockism": "disco, not punk; pop, not rock; synthesizers, not guitars; the music video, not the live show. It is to privilege the deliriously artificial over the artificially genuine." Austerliz, a music critic himself, explains that other critics have bought into poptimism to not only be in touch with "the taste of average music fans" but to atone for their past mistakes of buying into white male rockers who basically stole their licks from black blues and soul music.

But I have to say, bless you, Saul Austerlitz. I'm a child of the sixties who is guilty as charged: I love punk; rock; guitars; live shows. But I also love Marvin Gaye, Martha Reeves and the Vandellas, and Little Richard as much as I love Bob Dylan, Janice Joplin, and the Rolling Stones (not such a fan of the Boss, who he places in this cohort). There weren't just "white" guitars, remember: we had B.B., Buddy, and Jimi.

Austerliz describes a music critic retracting his initial disappointment with Beyoncé's new album saying, "If you don't like the new Beyoncé album, re-evaluate what you want out of music." I think Beyoncé could be an Aretha or Patti LaBelle in another time and space but I'm not going to reevaluate the lousy records she makes now.

Indie rock, jazz, regional American music—not part of a "poptimism" that Austerliz suspects is actually an attempt to "resurrect a unified cultural mainstream" that those of us who are, need I say, old, once shared. I still listen to jazz (Charles Lloyd and Bill Frisell live in Santa Fe–wow!), Texas blues, and world beat along with my compadres and comadres, my "shared musical mainstream" who remain open to anything else we deem good (how about Amy Winehouse and Alabama Shakes?).

Finally, though, I have to disagree with Austerliz's contention that "poptimism" only applies to the world of music, not that of literature and movies. A recent article in the *New Yorker* reminds us that techies are too busy making money to read books or magazines other than *TechCrunch*. And in a *New York Times* "Vision of the Future" graphic one of the interviewees lists the Professions of the Past: "Higher education" and "Diamond mining." Jeez, we get to liberate both body and mind in the pursuit of our highest calling: capitalism.

Sunday, July 20, 2014

Fun and Fear at the Baseball Stadium

My son Max and I went to the Isotopes game on Saturday night of the 4th of July weekend; the stadium was packed. Unfortunately, there was a game delay because of rain in the 4th inning and we left; fortunately, our tickets were a gift.

It's the story of what happened while we were leaving that I want to tell. First, let me set the stage. When we entered the stadium, a little after the game started, we had to walk around a group of about eight Albuquerque Police Department cops who were standing in a line a few yards in from the gate, doing nothing except talking and laughing with each other. Max and I figured they were there for "crowd control," which will become a very ironic supposition as this story progresses.

I was feeling like an ice cream so we walked along the mezzanine where all the food booths sell every kind of fast food—and beer—you can imagine: hot dogs, pizza, cotton candy, etc. When I finally spotted what I thought was ice cream I saw that it was made up of some weird kind of colored dots that looked like sprinkles, dubbed "Dippin' Dots." I declined. Just imagine if those food booths had been in India or Palestine or Mexico: tandoori chicken or curried rice; lamb kebobs or humus; tacos al pastor or guacamole. You know, tasty, healthy (in my humble opinion), real food.

In our seats, ice-cream-less, the view of the Sandias was spectacular but I couldn't help reflecting on what the stadium was like 25 years ago when we went to see the Albuquerque Dukes. All the parents with little kids sat up in the bleachers and looked down on the seats with backs where the leisured class paid a whopping ten bucks to sit; we paid three or four. The kids ran around the bleachers playing and tracking down the snow cone man while we drank the beer we brought to the game in our backpacks before Homeland Security invaded our privacy. When the Dukes came off the field after the game the kids were there hanging over the railing next to the dugout waiting for autographs, which the Dodger farm team players, many of whom later became famous, graciously supplied.

Back to 2014. We had just settled into the flow of the game when the rain began. The officials quickly called a rain delay and the workers laid out the plastic rain tarp over the field. Max and I got up, along with just about everyone else in our section, and climbed the stairs to the covered mezzanine where we all stood around trying to decide, as The Clash put it, "should we stay or should we go." After a few minutes of this indecision we realized we'd better start heading for the stadium exit in case we decided on the "we should go" part of the equation. But then we realized that getting to that gate was not going to be easy, partly because everyone else was milling around, undecided as well. And the crush of people kept swelling with more undecideds coming up from their seats as the rain intensified.

Suddenly we snapped: this scenario could be a set up for the ones you always hear about in soccer stadiums when suddenly people trample each other to get out the gate. Already, a woman came pushing through the crowd, followed by her children, saying "I'm going to be sick" and we went right after her, Max leading the way (he's a big guy from all his weight lifting), me holding on, saying, "If I die I bequeath everything I own to you and Jakob. Sell the house and split the proceeds."

There wasn't a cop in sight, either in the crush of humanity or at the exit gate, doing "crowd control." We finally burst out the gate into the rain. As we walked toward the parking lot several ambulances came careening down the street. I never found out if they were there for injuries people may have sustained in that crush, but what I'd really like to know is just what the fuck those cops were doing during that scary time. Or then again, maybe their absence was a blessing; we're all more afraid of what they're capable of doing—lasers, batons, guns—than we are of the scary situations.

Tuesday, August 12, 2014

Rocky Mountain High, Colorado

I just spent a week in Colorado driving around, visiting friends, experiencing the Rocky Mountain high. My impression? Too much of everything: water (I'll explain this in a minute); traffic; bikers; hikers; rafters; ATVers; tourists; pot (there's a glut). Welcome to the capital of eco-entertainment bourgeois consumerism.

I started out in Cañon City, which may be best known for its prison fortresses, state and federal, where both New Mexico's Manny Aragon did his time and the Unibomber is still doing his. But it's the mighty Arkansas River that is the real distinguisher. The river's irrigation system, which winds throughout the entire area, used to water fields of alfalfa and grains, orchards and vegetables, but now flows in little canals along the streets in front of houses, and everyone who lives in those houses has a water right and an irrigation pump. I've never seen so many green lawns in my life. When I arrived the temperature was 99 degrees and it hadn't rained much all summer, but the river was still running high from winter snow melt and the pumps were busily delivering it to the grass.

The other ubiquitous water use in Cañon City is recreational: running rivers in large inflatable rafts, plastic kayaks, fiberglass kayaks, inflatable kayaks, inner tubes, etc. From its headwaters in Leadville, Colorado through Buena Vista (which the locals pronounce "Bew-na" Vista), Salida, the Royal Gorge, to Cañon City these rafters infuse money into the economy, traffic onto the highways, and bodies in the river: there have been 10 deaths so far this year on the Arkansas.

The Arkansas Valley through Cañon City would be the perfect place to create George Sibley's "post-urban" culture or "basin-centric cultures capable of watering and feeding themselves" that I wrote about in *La Jicarita* on July 17. It's not too late for Cañon City folks to replace their lawns with vegetable gardens and berry bushes; fortunately, the real estate developers are not knocking down the door and the rural nature of the community remains intact. Coupled with the money generated from rafting and tourism, maybe the economic base is there. Beware the real estate developers in the front range cities, however; I suspect they will always see water as commodity for sale to the highest bidder.

In Leadville, the rafting business, along with four-wheel drive tours, bike competitions, and mountain climbing have transformed the old mining town into a tourist haven of renovated buildings full of restaurants, bars, and boutiques. A lot has changed since my El Valle neighbors lived there many years ago to work in the silver, lead, and molybdenum mines in the mid-1900s. There is also a large Hispano population in the area, immigrants who commute to Vail, over two mountain passes, to work in the ski and summer resort industry. When I stopped to gas up in Leadville, which I passed through at the end of my trip, I heard Spanish being spoken for the first time since I'd left New Mexico.

After visiting my sister in Colorado Springs, that bastion of family values, I drove north on I-25 towards Denver to visit a friend. This friend, who lives up Boulder Canyon in Rollinsville, told me about a bypass around Denver. But that didn't save me. From the Springs north to Castle Rock, which is located in Douglas County (I recall that it was the fastest growing county in the U.S. for awhile), traffic was bumper to bumper on a Saturday—no accidents, no road work, both sides of the highway. What were all these people from the Springs and Denver doing out there? Escaping their urban confines to recreate . . . in Castle Rock? Shopping at Ikea, one friend suggested.

I finally made it to Rollinsville, which sits right in the middle of Rocky Mountain high country; Rocky Mountain National Park is just a few miles away and the Indian Peak Wilderness and Eldora Ski area are 15 minutes down the road. Some new recreationists have recently joined the bicyclists, skiers, runners, and mountain climbers: Black Hawk and Central City, former mining towns half an hour away, are now home to gambling casinos.

Rollinsville also sits right in the middle of a lodge pole pine forest that is being ravaged by the pine beetle. The previous decade's forest fires caused last year's floods to wipe out entire mountainsides and houses in Lyons, Ward, Estes Park, and Jamestown. These communities are mostly home to urban commuters who work in Boulder and Denver (the hippies are still there, though, in Ward and Nederland) but recreate at home. The commuter traffic up and down Boulder Canyon is phenomenal, particularly in the winter. When the floods hit the canyon last year and caused its shutdown, commuters had to find alternative routes through other dangerous, beetle infested canyons that may be the next to flood.

The recreational traffic is also phenomenal. When we went out to hike in the Indian Peaks Wilderness area we had to navigate entrances guarded by officials in orange vests with notebooks issuing permits and directing us to a parking area that would have added a mile to our hike. My savvy hiking friend lied and told the guards she was only dropping me off and drove through the barrier. We found a parking space someone had just vacated.

When I complained to her that I hated all the regulation and permitting required to go for a simple hike in the woods, she remarked that if they didn't control the traffic the place would be overrun with cars trying, just like us, to get to where they want to go. There are hundreds of thousands of recreationists from Boulder and Denver, as well as locals, using these

trails every weekend.

In part three of his series on the politics of sustainability, *La Jicarita* editor David Correia explored what he calls "bourgeois primitivism," a "magic act . . . to fashion forms of consumption that appear to reduce environmental impact without requiring any sacrifice of class-based luxuries." Or, "environmentalism as self-improvement via an urban lifestyle." In the world of recreation, this translates to driving many miles over paved roads to participate in a bike ride over mountain passes, raft a river, or run the Leadville ultra-marathon. It also translates into an enormous amount of money spent on high tech bikes, kayaks, skis, jeeps, and ATVs.

In a recent *High Country News* article, "The Death of Backpacking," Christopher Ketchem talks about finding it increasingly difficult to find anyone to go backpacking with him. There's no one under 40, which is his own age, willing to join him in that "wretched fun." Instead, what he finds are "gearheads," or those who are out there trying out the latest technological toys—daypacks, bikes, carabiners, rafts—on day trips that have comfortable beds and beer instead of tents and freeze dried food at the end of the day. That's where the money is: lots of mechanical stuff to purchase and maintain, apps to guide you to that equipment, paid professionals to guide you on the actual adventure, and motels and resorts to rest your body.

So, my final assessment? I'm glad to be back in New Mexico where there are fewer people, no 14,000-foot peaks, more funky soul. But we're headed in the same direction as Colorado: water brokers keep trying to move water to Santa Fe and Albuquerque to underwrite growth; city fathers want to expand the Taos airport to shuttle in more people to Taos Ski Valley (recently bought by billionaire Colorado hedge fund and real estate developer Louis Bacon), and Santa Fe's eco-bourgeoisie are just the latest manifestation of colonialism. Fortunately, however, by the time the B and Bs reach El Valle, I'll be dead.

Saturday, September 6, 2014

"Get out of the new one [road] if you can't lend a hand for the times they are a changin' . . . ."

I'm bombarded daily by e-mails from the Democrats—Tom Udall, Barbara Lee, Barack Obama, Nancy Pelosi—asking me for 5, 10, or 25 dollars to fund their "Paint the South Blue Program" or fend off the Republicans who are targeting Udall as "one of the most vulnerable senators," although I suspect a majority of New Mexicans don't even know the name of his Republican opponent (Allen Weh). The e-mails convey a sense of desperation—I'm scared of a Tea Party takeover myself—but there's also a strong component of righteousness: we're the good guys and we're going to do the right thing.

But Udall has come under some heavy criticism lately for his position on Israel—uncritical support—and his promotion of nuclear weapons production at Los Alamos and Sandia national laboratories. Not surprisingly, the *La Jicarita* article I wrote on the Santa Fe protest at Senator Udall's new office on August 2 generated more comments than any other posting on our website. All of the commenters are appalled by the devastation of the Israeli attack on Gaza; most of them also agreed that protesting the assault is a moral imperative (Zionists either don't read *La Jicarita* or don't want to waste their breath). What they don't agree on, however, is what kind of protests they should be, what kind of strategies and tactics are most effective, and what constitutes private property or open meetings.

At the Santa Fe protest Udall's staff, in reaction to the morning's protest at his office in Albuquerque during which some folks inside loudly voiced their disgust with Israel, was on high alert at the union building that houses the office. They asked everyone to sign in and at first told activists that they couldn't distribute any literature regarding the assault on Gaza. That limitation then morphed into telling demonstrators that they couldn't come in the building at all, that it was "private property." Jeff Haas, one of the organizers, was allowed to read a statement from the podium but only before Udall and Senator Al Franken, a well-known Israeli supporter who I assume was either chosen as a fund raising partner before the anti-Israeli demonstrations heated up or, more cynically, because of his Zionism, showed up. Democratic solidarity must reign in the presence of the senators. However, the jeering and booing that emanated from the audience when demonstrators tried to interrupt Udall and Franken during their speeches revealed how tenuous that solidarity is between progressives and party stalwarts over Israel.

I've always had a cordial relationship with Udall—Mark and I interviewed him several times for *La Jicarita* and worked with his New Mexico staff on land grant and acequia issues. But at the protest I felt compelled to get his attention and confront him about the complicity of the senate in arming Israel. I had no desire to be "polite," as some commenters believe the protesters should have been. I finally pushed my way to the front where he was shaking hands with constituents—and listening to a few others who also wanted to talk about Gaza—and got his attention:

Tom: Hi, Kay, how are you doing?

Me: Why won't you have a dialogue about what's happening in Gaza?

Tom: We are talking about it.

Me: When?

Tom: With our constituents who we meet around the state and who come to the office.

Me: We've come to your office. Why aren't you having a conversation here, with us?

He moved on to the next person.

I've also been after him about his calculated support of the nuclear mission at LANL and Sandia. In an August 25 e-mail his office sent me there's a picture of him sitting at Sandia with Senator Richard Durbin, who chairs the Defense Appropriation Subcommittee, talking about their support of the B61 Life Extension Project, a GPS guided 50-kiloton mini-nuke bomb that is, as he calls it, "important for our national security." They also talked about the great "tech transfer" programs at the labs that will supposedly create businesses and high tech jobs in New Mexico.

An article in the *Santa Fe New Mexican* during the same week talked about the push to increase the production of plutonium pits, the triggers for our stockpile of nuclear bombs, from 30 to 80 by 2030. After Rocky Flats near Denver, Colorado was shut down in 1989 the National Nuclear Security Administration (NNSA), which runs the nuclear labs for the Department of Energy, has looked to LANL as the only possible site to produce the pits, even though its primary function has been research and development and it lacks a facility large enough—and more importantly, safe enough—to manufacture such an increase in pits (between 2007 and now 30 pits have been produced). *La Jicarita* has covered the abysmal history of the Chemistry and Metallurgy Research Replacement Nuclear Facility, originally intended to house the production, which was finally put on hold after a cost overrun of billions of dollars and concerns about the seismic potential of the Pajarito Plateau, where LANL is situated. The NNSA now wants to use an unnamed modern pit facility that consists of tunnels from the plutonium facility (PF4) to the Radiation Lab (RULAB), from which six or eight small labs and workrooms will branch off.

Greg Mello of the Los Alamos Study Group (LASG) wasn't "polite" in his pointed debunking of the longstanding claim of politicos that without LANL's economic engine New Mexico would grind to a halt. We've been stalled for years even with the billions of federal pork flowing into the labs:

"As lab spending rose over three decades, the state's relative income rank fell dramatically. Over seven decades, there has been no major 'tech transfer' from the labs here, especially from Los Alamos National Laboratory. Our economic potential is now limited by our human development policy failures, exemplified by Udall's choice to promote nuclear weapons at the expense of human and environmental needs. Unless we change those priorities, why would any (non-exploitative) business locate here?" (See LASG's July 2006 analysis "Does Los Alamos National Lab Help or Hurt the New Mexico Economy?".)

While most of Congress is hopeless on the issues of Palestine and nuclear weapons production, that doesn't mean we shouldn't be out there confronting politicians like Udall, whose reelection is a given. He could step out from under the cudgel of the American Israel Public Affairs Committee (AIPAC), whose formally bi-partisan flow of money on Capital Hill now flows to the right as it allies with the Likud Party in Israel, and as the senior senator from New Mexico he could push mission change at the labs.

Let's not spend any more time arguing over "being polite," "not pissing people off," "not creating a backlash." Night after night the protesters in Ferguson, Missouri stayed in the streets to vent their anger and frustration at the killing of the unarmed teenager Michael Brown and night after night the police department met them in camouflage with tanks and assault rifles and tear gas and rubber bullets. Protesters in Albuquerque faced off against the same militarized police force on the streets and their administrative enablers in the city's offices to decry the use of unnecessary force on the citizen population (for those of you who haven't heard, the bogus felony battery charge against protester David Correia, my co-editor at *La Jicarita*, has been dismissed). Other acts of police violence have been protested and posted on Internet sites across the county. Finally, a conversation has begun about the American militarization of the police that began in the 1970s and has escalated today to epic proportions: millions of dollars worth of surplus military equipment from the wars in Iraq and Afghanistan given to police departments; soldiers trained to use this equipment to shoot and kill a foreign enemy are now police officers who see American citizens as the enemy.

It's extremely hard to maintain the momentum these kinds of movements require to remain effective. If you're not prepared to join in the struggles—in the multitude of forms they may take—don't sabotage them with internecine bickering. To paraphrase Bob Dylan, just get out of the way.

Friday, October 31, 2014

New York, New York, It Used to be a Wonderful Town . . .

Every few days there's an article or essay in the media about why someone is thinking about leaving New York City, why they've already left, or why they think their friends should leave. This is nothing new: the complaining has been going on for years, but at first, when the wealthy pushed out the poor, people said, well, maybe it's not so bad, now there won't be as much crime and I won't have to feel guilty about all the homeless sleeping on the streets. Now that the wealthy have succeeded in pushing out the middle class, the complaining has gotten louder.

I decided to go see the city for myself on what I figured would be my last visit. Mark's uncle Bernie, the "favorite" uncle, died at the end of the summer after suffering many years with Alzheimer's. His daughter, Marian, who lives in Los Angeles, and his son Jamie, who still lives in Greenwich Village, asked the family to meet in NYC for an informal memorial: spread Bernie's ashes, talk about our relationships with him, and have a party with some of his former colleagues and students (he was a professor of psychology at New York University).

The last time Mark and I had been in New York was to see Marian and Jamie's mother Lorrie, who was dying of lung cancer. Bernie had already been diagnosed with Alzheimer's, and Lorrie was heroically trying to get him into an assisted living facility before she died. If that wasn't depressing enough for Mark, just walking from 22th Street, where Bernie and Lorrie lived, down to Jamie's condo on 10th street, was more than he could handle. (Bernie and Lorrie had only recently moved to their overpriced apartment on 22th Street after he retired and they were forced to vacate their NYU apartment on Bleecker Street.) None of the ethnic restaurants Mark used to frequent were still there. None of the record stores or bookstores were still there (not that they're anywhere). New dorms and office buildings owned by NYU towered over the apartments where lower and middle class people used to live.

Mark was born in Brooklyn, in Williamsburg. While his family moved out of the city when he was very young, he came back often to visit his grandmother, who remained in Williamsburg, to visit Bernie and Lorrie in the Village, and to briefly live on 2nd Street between Avenue A and B, the Lower East Side. Those were the days when bathtubs were still in the kitchen and Thompson Square Park was the center of the heroin trade. How he ended up in rural New Mexico is a story unto itself, but he observed the changes to the city on his forays back and joined the chorus of complainers lamenting its lost soul.

So I knew my visit was going to be a bag of mixed emotions, and it was. Getting there set the tone: my early morning flight out of Albuquerque was canceled and while running to get on another flight I left my cell phone on the TSA conveyor belt. Ten or twenty years ago, flying all over the country or to Mexico or Europe, I managed to do just fine with no cell phone. This time, I panicked. The phone numbers of everyone I was meeting in NYC were in my phone and I knew none of them by heart. Fortunately, I do know my kids' phone numbers so when I got to Phoenix (I know, I was going the wrong direction) the airline let me use a courtesy phone and I called Jakob, who called Max, and they called and e-mailed Marian and my brother-in-law Mike to let them know I was going to be late.

It took me two hours to get from JFK airport via bus and cab, to Spring Street, in Soho, where we had rented an AirBnB. If you had asked me what an AirBnB was a year ago, I might have guessed it was some kind of gun that shoots air instead of BBs? (Which would have been a nice switch for the Florida State University football players who've been running around shooting real BBs at people and property.) But now I know it's an apartment that Marian had rented online, to house Mike, his partner Betty, Marian and me during our stay in the city. It was actually quite lovely, just below street level, fully furnished with two bedrooms, large living room, kitchen, and bathroom, except that the toilet didn't flush all that well, there was no hot water in the kitchen, and on Friday and Saturday nights, our first two there, every hipster in Soho was out partying. Marian and I, trying to sleep in the rooms closest to the street, ended up wearing our iPod ear buds with pillows over our heads (after dropping a few Valium as well).

Was it really that long ago that the streets of Soho or Noho or Lodo—I have no idea what distinguishes these neighborhoods from one another—were lined with factory warehouses sheltering a few galleries and lofts where struggling painters set up shop? People were already starting to complain of gentrification back then, but my friend Lucy Lippard got a great deal on a loft that, if I recall correctly, cost under $10,000.

There was a real estate office a couple of doors down from our apartment. As out-of-towners are wont to do, we looked at the prices of places listed in the window. Now, I remember being flabbergasted by prices in Telluride, Colorado, and Point Reyes, California, but let me tell you that in the Spring Street window there was no listing for anything less than a million dollars. Actually, the lowest price there was $1.4 million for a 450 square-foot condo. Four hundred and fifty square feet. That's the size of my living room in El Valle.

Onward to Brooklyn.

Bernie grew up in an apartment on Driggs Avenue, in Williamsburg. On Saturday we took the subway into Brooklyn and found the apartment, still there although no doubt renovated, at the juncture of what appeared to be

a Latino neighborhood and the beginnings of gentrified Williamsburg. As we walked further along we entered a re-creation of Soho: bars, restaurants, twenty and thirty somethings out on the street partying down. At a bar we bought cocktails for $13 and small, finger foods for significantly more. It all tasted great, which it better, in what must be a cutthroat market.

    Bernie and Lorrie first lived together in Crown Heights, on the far side of Prospect Park from Park Slope, headquarters of the baby industrial complex and the authorial Jonathans. That's where we headed on Sunday, to scatter Bernie's ashes comingled with some of Lorrie's that their kids had held onto. The scene in the park could have been anywhere USA: ducks begging for handouts from kids on shore; couples holding hands; joggers with kids and dogs. When I'm in these environments, though, full of people who obviously have lots of money, I wonder who they are, how they got there, and what they have to do to stay there. One of the complainers who wrote an editorial in the *Daily News* had a different take, however: The ones jogging in the park and feeding the ducks are probably doing the only fun things they can afford instead of going to Yankee Stadium or Madison Square Garden or the Met or out to eat because all their money goes towards paying their rent and buying food.

We ended the day at a lovely Italian restaurant that Bernie and Lorrie used to frequent, around the corner from their apartment on Bleecker. There, colleagues and former students told stories and shared memories, and the family sat around afterwards with our own stories. The trip home wasn't much easier than the one going, but the cab driver who took me to Grand Central Station to catch the bus to JFK found out I was from a rural village in New Mexico and asked me all kinds of questions about what it was like: did I grow things, did I have animals, how many people lived in my village, etc. And every time I answered he sighed and said, "Oh, that's so nice," or "Oh, I wish I could live there." I asked him how long he'd been in New York: 40 years, he said.

I had to wait until the next day to get my phone back from the TSA people who had it at their headquarters in Albuquerque. Then I drove home, and as the cab driver had put it so simply, it's so nice—damn nice—to be in El Valle.

Friday, November 21, 2014

Is That Supposed to be Funny?

It's time to take on the *New Yorker* cartoon contest (and I don't mean with alliteration). I'm certainly not the first—or last—person to do this. When I Googled "New Yorker cartoon caption," the second entry, under the *New Yorker* website itself, was this: "Every week, the New Yorker has a caption contest. Every week, it would be way funnier if they just talked about sucking dick. By Nate Heller & Emily Heller."

For example:

"I made this wall so we have a place to hang those artsy photos we took of you sucking my dick."

On the other hand, the caption my son Max and I came up with was this:

"I couldn't find an iron curtain."

Succinct, subtle, allusively political, brilliant, no? The three finalists: "Which kid do you want?"; "I think we should stop seeing each other"; and "Happy anniversary!" Pedestrian, trite, unimaginative, yes?

Film critic Roger Ebert once complained that he submitted approximately 2,000 (or some such outrageous number) captions before one of his was chosen. I'm sure there are many Roger Eberts out there who ask themselves, on a weekly basis when their cartoon isn't chosen, "What the f*#! do they want" and "Who the f*#! chooses the winner??!!"

I was going to ask the *New York Times* a similar questions last year about the couples who appear in Weddings in the Sunday Styles section but someone else beat me to it. This is what she/he asked the Public Editor: "How do editors select which announcements to publish, and why don't editors make a sustained effort to include different types of couples?"

The editor answered that essentially those who are profiled are the ones who manage to make their way out of the herd and end up at the "top of their medical school class at Yale or Stanford." That's when I wrote the Best and the Brightest blog about a couple who defined a different kind of achievement, and thoroughly enjoyed my endeavor.

I'm assuming most of us who submit these "succinct, subtle, allusively political, brilliant" captions think that the opposite criterion, i.e, "in the herd," applies to the *New Yorker* contest. So I'm inviting all of you who want to express a different kind of achievement than what gets chosen for the cartoon caption to submit your "succinct, subtle, allusively political, brilliant"—or whatever— caption to my blog. Send it to kmatthews1018@gmail.com and if it's fit to print—and funnier than "suck my dick"—I'll post it on my blog for my many (not!) loyal readers to enjoy.

Friday, February 6, 2015

Russell Brand Tells it Like it Is

I watched Russell Brand on Democracy Now! not long ago. Despite several stupid questions from Amy—"would you run for London mayor" or "would you run for parliament" when he's sitting there telling her that the elected power elite don't represent the interests of the people—it was a very entertaining 45 minutes. Humor always makes radical political pontificating more digestible. (And all us 'Mericans love his accent.)

One thing in particular that Brand said struck me. He called the class of people who used to work in manufacturing the "throwaway class." Because of the outsourcing of these jobs and the changing nature of manufacturing itself, these people are now seen as the dregs of society, sapping the welfare system because they can't get jobs, holding back the economy and those who engineer it.

Does this "throwaway" language sound familiar? How about the Facebook page of the Albuquerque cop who described his job as "human waste disposal." Or one of the cops who shot homeless James Boyd in the Sandia foothills, talking to a state cop before the shooting: "For this fucking lunatic? I'm going to shoot him with [unintelligible] shotgun here in a second." The homeless, the mentally ill, the PTSD vets who are in and out of treatment are fair game, it seems, for those in APD who think we'd all be better off without them, but picking them off one by one is not very efficient.

Benjamin Netanyahu is much more efficient. He bombs the Palestinians he wants to be rid of in Gaza and smashes the houses and destroys the crops of the ones in the West Bank. He's been documented saying he'll never agree to an Israeli state for anyone other than the Jews, and his foreign minister is quoted saying, "I want to get rid of these people [the Palestinians] through transfer, or exchange."

What they are all getting at is eugenics, of course. The man who coined the term was another Brit like Brand, albeit of the ruling class, very much unlike Brand. According to Francis Galton, his ruling class was "genetically superior" and should therefore rule the world. Across the ocean, this translated into American policies to protect the Puritan gene pool from inferior "stock" through immigration laws. And while people of color have felt the brunt of this discrimination profoundly over last few centuries, it doesn't mean that the ruling class is opposed to throwing away other white people.

Orwell brought the conception to its nadir in *1984*, where the Proles, the rabble that lives outside the brotherhood, are left to their own ignorant devices. Except that the tables are turned: the Proles appear to be the only ones who have the capacity to enjoy themselves, even in their abject conditions and exclusion from power. The carefully conditioned Inner Party can't remember what a good time might be.

Our "Proles" may end up spoiling the elites' party, in a different way. With all those good manufacturing jobs gone that raised so many from working class to middle class, who's going to be buying and consuming the goods—all those iPhones and video games and flat screen TVs rather than cars and washing machines and lawn mowers—that keep the American economy afloat? And when folks can't pay for healthcare or home mortgages they'll end up sapping the welfare system even more. Aha! Remember the industrial revolution when workers couldn't afford to buy any of the things they made?

One could argue that the solution to alienated labor is no labor at all. There is enough wealth in the world to provide every human being enough money to meet our basic material needs. I can just hear the reactionaries screaming that would be the end to civilization as we know it, but a lot of us would be screaming back—thank god! Feed and clothe and house all of us and see what we're capable of.

Sunday, June 7, 2015

Pilgrim and Waldo on the Appalachian Trail

On the one hand, you have Bill Bryson, the out of shape middle-aged journalist (and his even more out of shape friend Stephen Katz) failing, over many months, to hike the entire 2,100 miles of the Appalachian Trail but giving us a marvelously funny book full of historical, naturalist, and intellectual ruminations in *A Walk in the Woods*. On the other hand, you have ultrarunner Scott Jurek's Instagram postings of an ultra fit man running up and down the trail in his attempt to speed through the entire route in 42 days.

In the middle, you have the 2015 hikers who started out in Georgia in April and are in fine form at the beginning of June in Virginia. That's where I saw almost 50 of them on the Appalachian Trail near Roanoke, day hiking my measly 9 miles. I wonder what form they'll be in when they reach Maine in September.

They're called "thru hikers," but they also give themselves trail names. The first one we met (I was visiting my friends Elaine and Richard, former Taoseños, now Roanoke residents) was Pilgrim. A German, he looked like he'd just stepped out of an outdoor catalog: polypropylene matching shorts and shirt; Osprey mid-weight backpack; state of the art accordion pad for sitting and sleeping; telescoping hiking poles; mid-weight boots. He told us his basic pack weighted just 20 pounds and he carried 10 pounds of food. A slim, trim, hiking machine.

A young woman—the vast majority of them are millennials—soon came up and bumped him with a "What up?" They weren't exactly friends—both started out alone and only occasionally hiked together—but as thru hikers they were bonded. They all are, I guess. It helps that they have to share the shelters and campsites spread out over the course of the trail, but affinities are found or formed over the endless days of 10 to 20 mile hikes.

When we reached the overlook at lunch, there were about 10 of them resting on the rocks eating their high energy fare. Soon the sweet smell of pot wafted over us as they broke out the dope. I think I'd be tempted to bring along some stronger stimulants as well, but they seemed very happy with weed as they chatted away during their brief respite.

We met many more coming up the trail as we headed down after lunch. While the gear was identical—Osprey packs with rain covers, hiking poles, etc.—the bodies and apparel weren't. There was the man with the full Paul Bunyan beard with his tank top/short shorts partner. There was the shirtless man with the wraparound headdress. There was the woman with the umbrella and her backpack-carrying dog (it started to rain but no one wore a raincoat as it was too hot). When we stopped to chat with Waldo, the young man who informed us that he usually hiked 19 or so miles a day but stopped when his body told him to, I asked him why everyone carried the same brand backpack, figuring there was an online promotion of said Osprey. But no, he said, everyone shops at REI where brand Osprey rules.

To someone from the west—me—it was all a bit claustrophobic. The ubiquitous deciduous forests (full of blooming rhododendron) were lush and thick, but without the diversity of terrain and ancient feel of the mixed conifer western forests I'm used to, and with the crowd of thru hikers (albeit they were congregated in Virginia because of the season), it felt a little redundant. Here's Bryson's description of the same forest I walked in Virginia:

"So the forest through which Katz and I now passed was nothing like the forest that was known even to people of my father's generation, but

at least it was a forest. It was splendid in any case to be enveloped once more in our familiar surroundings. It was in every detectable respect the same forest we had left in North Carolina—same violently slanted trees, same narrow brown path, same expansive silence, broken only by our tiny grunts and labored breaths as we struggled up hills that proved to be as steep, if not quite as lofty, as those we had left behind."

The word that is often used to describe the Appalachian Trail environment is pastoral. There's nothing wrong with pastoral: in other essays I've quoted Bryson in his eloquent defense of the mix of wild/domestic terrain that characterizes the trail, as one leaves and enters civilization along the route. I don't buy into the lament that to have wilderness one must exclude people, the cry of the deep ecologist.

I guess it's just what you're used to. The operative words in Bryson's quote are "at least it was a forest." During our conversation with Pilgrim, he mentioned he'd hiked the Camino de Santiago from the French border through the Pyrenees Mountains of Spain (everyone is Pilgrim there). We questioned him about details: one only has to carry a daypack, with hostels, hotels, and cafes at every night stop along the way. He called it a "cultural hike." So take your pick: a pastoral hike along the Appalachian Trail (but with plenty of hard work); a wild hike along the Continental Divide Trail; or a cultural hike along the Camino de Santiago. I'll take them all—as long as I'm not trying to do any of them in 42 days.

Friday, June 26, 2015

Tree Story

M̲y cottonwood tree has transitioned from male to female. For twenty years it was happy to be a male, as were we with it being a male, as female cottonwoods drop that eponymous stuff every June all over everything, like snow falling in January.

We were OK with the cottonwoods down by the river doing their thing, far enough away to be kind of pretty rather than annoying. But our transgendered cottonwood sits in our front yard, where we planted it 22 years ago as a cotton-less cottonwood, or male, to shade what would become our beautiful courtyard full of flowers, bushes, and grass. It quickly grew to enormous size, as tall as our two-story, 30-foot tall house. And never once did it shed cotton, because, after all it is/was a male.

When it began raining down its cotton this year I of course went to the Internet to try to figure this out. I found out that nurseries sometimes make mistakes in their gender classification, but the fact that our tree never released cotton for 20 years seems to negate that possibility. Sometimes, female trees take a few years to produce cotton, leading you to believe you have a male instead. A "few years" does not translate to 20 years.

Like so many other places across the world, New Mexico has had an unusual spring and early summer: it's been raining. Ordinarily, after a few April showers things dry up, warm weather descends, and by the beginning of June it often reaches 100 degrees in Albuquerque. This year, in typically 10 degree cooler El Valle, I was dressed in wool socks, long pants, and a jacket until about two weeks ago, when temperatures finally reached near normal and the rains abated, at least a little (this is not a complaint, but a celebration). So one could surmise that maybe all the rain and cool temperatures caused the cotton release. Except that MALE COTTONWOODS DO NOT PRODUCE COTTON.

What has my transgendered tree wrought? Well, the largest, most beautiful columbines I've ever grown—definitely the product of rain and cool temperatures—are coated with cotton that makes them droop and moan. My green grass is blotted white. Cobwebs of cotton fill every nook and cranny of window casings and doorways. Every time I open a door, cotton blows in to cling to anything soft, particularly the rugs. My dogs make sure it gets distributed upstairs where they join me at night.

Yesterday a quick rainstorm, with lots of wind, blew through El Valle dropping what I fervently hope is the last of the cotton. I raked up as much as I could from the yard but the columbines took a beating. It kind of reminds me of what's happening in the transgender world of people. Seems to me that all that fury and disdain dumped on the feminists who created beauty out of hard work and growth, much like my columbines, just clogs the relational paths that we all share.

Friday, September 25, 2015

Babysitting

I wrote this piece in January of this year, when my granddaughter Lucia was 18 months old, but neglected to post it until today.

Max called me the first time at 6:30 pm.

"Hi, I don't have time to talk right now, I'm eating, I'll call you in a half hour," I told him.

"I'm with the baby," he said.

"Oh, I didn't know you guys had agreed on tonight. How's it going?"

"OK, but what if she poops. How will I know if she poops?"

The she in question is my granddaughter, Lucia, aka Lulu, and Max's niece. Lulu's parents, Jakob and Casey, had asked Max to babysit for the first time a few weeks before so they could go out to dinner, but Lulu had come down with a cold and they canceled. But now, here we were, and Max was babysitting.

I'd already shown him how to change a poopy diaper the last time I'd been down to Albuquerque, where they all live. There were a lot of "Oh god's" and "I really hope she doesn't poop while I have her" but he said he thought he could do it.

"So how's it going so far?" I asked.

"It's OK. She had more macaroni and cheese than I've ever seen her eat. Do you think that might make her poop?"

"You never know, but she usually poops earlier in the day. Try not to worry about it."

"Back to my original question. How will I know if she poops?"

"You'll know."

I heard Lulu cry out in the background.

"What happened?"

"She just sat down pretty hard. I'm going to give her a pretzel. She really likes pretzels."

"OK, just play with her like you always do and she'll be fine. Jakob and Casey will be home soon if they just went out to dinner."

"OK."

"Call me if you need me."

"OK."

Lulu loves Max. When he goes over to visit he sits on the floor with her and talks to her like she's a twenty something (what he is), cracking jokes and discussing political economy. She likes the words and appreciates his tone. He follows her around so she doesn't hurt herself. She calls him "Maa!" as she can't quite get the "x" out.

Max calls me again at 8:15.

"She pooped."

"OK, did you change her?"

"Yeah, and I cleaned her up like you showed me but I'm not sure I really got her clean enough."

"Was it kind of solid? Then you don't have to worry that you got it all cleaned up."

"Yeah, but I don't know. Maybe I should give her a bath. Then I'd know she's clean."

"That's a great idea. She loves to take baths."

"How hot should I make the water?"

"Not too hot that she would react negatively to it, but hot enough so that it's comfortable for her to spend some time in it. She loves to play in the tub."

"OK, I'm going to put her in the bath."

"Make sure you never take your eye off her while she's in there."

I thought for sure my comment would elicit a sarcastic response, but his anxiety negated that.

"Jakob and Casey will probably be home soon. Call me if you need me."

The next time he called it was a quarter to nine. He was in the car on his way home.

"Jakob and Casey got there while she was still in the bath, so that was good."

"So you did fine. Did you have fun?"

"Yeah, if you consider following a little thing around trying to keep her from falling down and cracking her head open fun, then I guess I had a really good time."

"It'll be much easier next time."

"I really don't think I'm a good babysitter.

"I bet they think you're an excellent babysitter. Believe me, they'll be back for you."

When I spoke with Jakob the next day and told him about the phone calls he laughed and said the bath water was completely tepid but Lulu was having a great time in it anyway. All she could say the rest of the night was "Maa!" "Maa!"

Postscript: He came back, many times.

Thursday, October 22, 2015

Insomnia

At the ripe old age of 65 I've become an insomniac. I go to sleep every night around 10 but bang, between the witching hours of two and four I'm awake and I stay awake for at least a couple of hours until I fall back asleep or give up and get up.

Not that my usual sleep patterns are all that great. They were permanently interrupted upon the birth of my children, especially the second one, Max, who didn't sleep through the night until he was past two years old. I can't remember the last time I slept through the night. But at least when I would wake up I'd get up and pee, go back to bed, turn over a few times, push a few thoughts out of my brain, and go back to sleep.

Now when I wake up there are a number of things going on that keep me awake despite all my attempts to breathe deep. One is there's always a song playing over and over in my head. A couple of nights ago it was the Eagle's "Witchy Woman." I don't like the Eagles (except for my Guilty Pleasure "Cryin' Eyes") and I certainly don't like "Witchy Woman." Sometimes it's a much better song running through my head, like "It's Too Late to Turn Back Now," which is on my best of rhythm and blues compilation playlist. But then there'll be a night of "Build Me Up Buttercup" —not a guilty pleasure.

Of course, it's the inner dialogue stuff that's the worst. It's bemoaning the fact that I had to pay a lot more money to the crew stuccoing my house because I fucked up and chose a color that was way too orange instead of the reddish brown I thought it was going to be and made the crew redo the wall with the right color. It's worrying about the release of my new book and wondering if anyone will actually read it and if they do they'll think it's no good. It's worrying about my teeth, which need some work. It's worrying about my kids, who are mostly fine but each facing some decisions and life changing events (like a second grandkid in December). It's wondering what I'm going to do with the rest of my life now that *La Jicarita* is no longer demanding all my time and I'm not forced to go to meetings unless I really want to.

I can't turn off the inner dialogue so I resort to drugs. About five years ago, after I'd had orthopedic surgery for a bone spur that caused untold secondary pain and misery (see Health Insurance blog post), I became addicted to ambien. That's the sleep drug of choice prescribed by doctors who seem oblivious to its addictive tendencies and ability to elicit nightmares of epic proportions that cause some people to get up in the middle of the night and create havoc, like driving their cars and smashing into other cars they happen to encounter on the road.

The much better sleep drug is Valium, which I've had intermittent access to over the years from sympathetic doctors who don't cop to its bad rap as "Mother's little helper." That began in the '50s, I believe, when American housewives were supposedly taking it to enhance the drudgery of their banal lives (and immortalized in the Rolling Stones song "Mother's Little Helper"). The fact that it helped take the edge off real anxiety—and helped one to sleep—got lost in the myth, and the pharma industry was able to make lots more money coming up with sleep aids like Ambien that have much more dastardly side affects.

Mark always used pot as his sedative of choice. He suffered from insomnia as long as I knew him, and while smoking marijuana couldn't prevent it's onset in the middle of the night, it did help him to eventually get back to sleep. Since I'm out of Valium at the moment I've decided I'm going to give it a try. Although I smoked a lot as a teenager and young adult, it hasn't been my drug of choice for many years. I'm one of the ones whose experience with pot morphed from "taking the edge off" to paranoia. I use alcohol to take the edge off, and it works very well, thank you. But it doesn't prevent me from waking up in the middle of the night in insomnia mode.

I actually got a medical marijuana card at the urging of my primary care doctor, who urges all his patients with chronic pain to give it a try so he can wean them off opiates. I don't really need the card to access pot, which is as pervasive in our culture as Coca-cola. All I needed to do was mention my idea about using it for sleep and voilá, everyone was offering me some. Now I have a little stash that will last me awhile, if it's as strong as everyone says it is and all I need partake is one puff.

I smoked a little last night and woke up at four a.m. with the Hall and Oates song "Rich Girl" playing in my head. No surprise there; I'd watched part of their live concert in Dublin on TV before going to bed. Coincidentally, Max and I had just had a conversation about them and he told me they were the best selling duo of all time, but according to Wikipedia, they were only second to the Carpenters—also not a guilty pleasure. I sat up and smoked a little more pot, but I really don't know if I went back to sleep or not: I was either dreaming or remembering dreams in some vague space and time. Was this the result of being too stoned or not stoned enough?

So I'll give it another try tonight and see what happens. Or, as I was just reading in the *New York Times* Book Review, the "By the Book" writer of the week, whom I've never heard of, recommended listening to a talking book to help one fall asleep. Not that I give much credence to someone who includes Ayaan Hirsi Ali, Richard Dawkins, and Sam Harris (these last two have given atheism a bad name) in his list of most admired writers. I guess I could download something suitable on my iPod, but in the meantime I'm going to take a nap. If you only sleep for an hour you don't suffer from insomnia.

Tuesday, November 3, 2015

Berkeley Breathed is Back!

I just found out that Berkeley Breathed is back—on Facebook. He's the creator of Bloom County, graced by the character of Opus, an adorable, guileless, and brilliant penguin. The daily comic strip was syndicated in 1,200 newspapers from 1980 to 1989, then morphed into a Sunday only Opus in 2003, which ran until 2008. Breathed then retired Opus and friends, although I'm pleased to hear Breathed himself had plenty of work, just not in a newspaper in Bloom County.

I have an Opus comic strip from 2007 on my refrigerator called Dial-a-Mom, which appeared again, in a new iteration, in 2017. I can only fit one panel here that's legible:

After I "liked" Bloom County on Facebook and got to see all his recent strips (and all the wonderful one liner comments full of puns and quips that accompany each posting) I also found out Breathed was interviewed on Fresh Air, and there I found out a lot of other stuff. One, that he had been miserable when he originally wrote his weekly comic strip (he never said why) but that now he was having the time of his life and couldn't wait to get up each morning to write his daily strip. Two, that he was awarded the Pulitzer Prize for editorial cartoons and was shunned by all the other editorial cartoon writers who appeared on the editorial pages of our newspapers, not on the comics page.

But for me, the most interesting thing he said was about how age had mellowed him in terms of the pointedness of his ridicule of certain people. He used the singer Barry Manilow as an example. Manilow ("Can't Smile Without You") is the '70s singer in the same category as Neil Diamond, who was immortalized in the movie "What About Bob?" when Bill Murray, playing the barely functional neurotic Bob, reveals that it was he who left his wife, not she who left him, because she liked Neil Diamond.

Back to Barry Manilow. Breathed pilloried Manilow, along with many other deserving public figures like Donald Trump, but years later, he's out on the street in Santa Barbara (I think that's where they were) with his son and he sees Manilow walking down the street. He stops, and with his son in tow, goes up to the singer and Manilow tells Breathed's son that his dad is one of the best cartoonists of all time and Breathed tells his son that Manilow is one of the best pop singers of all time.

This made me stop and think about how I feel about pissing people off now that I'm older. And I've pissed a lot of people off over the years even though I'm fairly well known as a nice person (just ask anyone I haven't pissed off). Like Breathed, it's my job to investigate, and in the process make people uncomfortable (hopefully), although I wish it were with the genius of his humor rather than the journalistic sarcasm I often employ.

Breathed's remorse seems to emanate from life experience: maybe it's not as important as you once thought that you get everyone to acknowledge the schmaltz of Barry Manilow's pop. Did he deserve being the foil of Breathed's rapier wit? In the larger scheme of things, probably not.

Mine seems to emanate from the fact that just as my skin has literally thinned with age so too has it thinned in the metaphorical sense: I'm not as stoic about criticism as I used to be. Sometimes I don't interpret a take down as proof of a job well done but as an arrow that stings. Actually, maybe that's where Breathed's comes from as well. If he and I are capable of feeling the pain, maybe all those other folks out there are as well. Does that mean we're less judgmental? Not really; in fact I'm more judgmental than ever as my half empty jar continues to diminish in these days of absurdity. It just means that I've lived long enough to know that life is tough for everyone, even the ones I think are idiots.

While I haven't reconciled with many who became the enemy, I've walked past the animosity with some to a space that allows a little wiggle room for working together on whatever we can. And now that *La Jicarita* is mostly retired, I probably won't be involved in nearly as many situations where the possibility of making enemies is endless. There is the fact that the book I wrote about all the enemies I made has just been released—*Culture Clash: Environmental Politics in New Mexico Forest Communities*—but it's old hat: anything I say about anybody in the book was already said to their faces—or in *La Jicarita*—at some time or another.

I'll watch Bloom County closely, however, to see if Breathed treats "the Donald" et al. a little more kindly, even though the times, if anything, scream out for pillage. Fortunately, he hasn't lost a beat when dealing with the representational: see the woman in the crocheted halter top. So I don't think we need worry that a little bit of kindness here and there will encumber the fun. Berkeley Breathed is indeed back.

Monday, January 18, 2016

At the Malheur National Wildlife Refuge: There's More Than a Little Irony Here

The takeover of the Malheur National Wildlife Refuge in Oregon by the armed ranchers, led by Ammon Bundy, has elicited comment and analysis from just about everyone, be they metropolitan reporters for the *New York Times*, members of the Wildlife Federation, writers for the radical journal CounterPunch, PETA activists, and the congressional representative from that corner of Oregon. Even with that much commentary it's hard to say that anyone has "nailed" it, but the few who have focused on the historical context of the conflict seem to have come the closest to explicating a complicated situation.

The metropolitan *New York Times* reporter Alan Feuer published his article in the January 10 issue of the paper titled "The Ideological Roots of the Oregon Standoff." He traced these roots to what is called the Wise Use movement (see also the lengthy *CouterPunch*, article "Rancher Rebels: The Rise of the Wise Use Movement"), that surfaced in the 1980s and which I described in *La Jicarita News* as a politically reactionary movement that advocates a balance between environmental protection and economic need but has essentially been a smokescreen for corporate attacks on environmental laws. Ranchers like the Bundy's figure into the movement in their push for the privatization of lands currently owned by the federal government, precluding environmental regulation and opening the door to extractive resource development.

The Wise Use movement was very successful in infiltrating small, western communities that were already frustrated with federal government bureaucracies like the U.S. Forest Service and Bureau of Land Management, agencies they saw as a threat to their livelihoods. In reality, during those same years, both agencies were essentially in the pocket of the extractive industries; timber dollars funded most of the Forest Service's "multiple use" management. But the Wise Use movement was able to capitalize on the economic frustrations of local communities to create a very strong anti-government sentiment that opened the door to the more radical militia movement that the Bundys represent.

The ideology of the Wise Use movement has been resurrected by the American Lands Council, a Utah-based organization that promotes the agenda of transferring federally owned lands to the states. Ken Ivory, a Republican state representative from Utah and president of the American Lands Council, travels around the county "educating" states about their "jurisdictional rights to manage, protect, and care for the lands within our borders," as described on the Council's website. He's backed by a board of directors of other white Republican men from Utah, as well as Americans for Prosperity, the conservative group backed by Koch brother money.

Unfortunately, several counties in New Mexico, Otero and Sierra, have been persuaded by the Council's offer of a "seat at the table" with a $1,000 contribution. The Wise Use movement has long been extant in rural areas like Otero and Sierra counties, but was also a player—albeit with a weird twist—in the 1990s conflicts in northern New Mexico between the land grant communities, the U.S. Forest Service, and urban environmentalists. These forest communities, like other rural western communities, had long fought over Forest Service management of public lands that burdened them with bureaucracy and impacted their economic viability. Unlike other rural communities, however, these communities are inhabited by the heirs and extended families of Native and Hispano land grants deeded by the Spanish and Mexican governments, whose common lands had been stolen by colonial and corporate interests and eventually placed in the hands of the federal government. It was quite a shock, then, when the environmentalists showed up with agendas to shut down access to these public lands and labeled the community and environmental justice activists who fought back Wise Use. *La Jicarita News* was called such innumerable times. The founders of the Quivira Coalition, which sought to establish dialogue between the environmental and ranching community, were also called Wise Use. As were members of the Santa Fe Group of the Sierra Club who refused to endorse the "Zero Cut" (no logging on public lands) initiative.

While the ranchers and farmers in the Malhuer area have some legitimate grievances, they are mostly the descendants of white settlers who benefited from the removal of the Indigenous people (Paiutes) who originally inhabited the area as well as from governmental largess in the form of homesteads and settler protection. Some of them continue to benefit from federal largess in the form of low grazing fees and farm subsidies. I don't know how many folks readily acknowledge this, but many of them do not support the militia tactics that the Bundy cohort is perpetrating.

It remains to be seen if the community wants to disengage—and can figure out how to do so— from a seemingly forced alliance with the militia. The militia, on the other hand, seems to want to claim an alliance with everyone. In one of the most bizarre statements yet to come out of the occupation, one of the group's leaders had this to say when asked about Paiute claims that they are destroying Native sites: "We're here for the natives," he said. "The federal government has been their biggest oppressor."

What an illustrious group we so-called Wise Users make: Natives, Hispano land grant heirs, environmental justice advocates, rural communities, and right wing white militia nuts. Who would have thunk?

March 22, 2016

Being Invisible

One of my favorite authors, Thomas Berger, wrote a book about a man who suddenly has the ability to make himself invisible at will (*Being Invisible*). He anticipates all the advantages that might provide: being the proverbial fly on the wall; listening into conversations of famous people or people whom you hate; being able to take things and not pay for them; getting into concerts and museums for free; avoiding someone on the street or in the office whom you find annoying. During the course of the novel, he of course learns than "character, not circumstance" is the issue: being literally invisible isn't much different than feeling invisible even if you aren't. Just read Ellison's *Invisible Man* or Nora Zeale Hurston's *Their Eyes Were Watching God*.

All of us women over a certain age are also very familiar with that feeling (except if you're a woman over a certain age who is a member of the power elite who the rest of us wish were invisible). I remember one of the first times it really struck home, that because of my graying hair and wrinkles the younger people (and most of them, sadly, were women: sexism is a given, ageism cuts to the bone) to whom I was being introduced just thought of me as some anomalous old woman. They knew nothing about me and showed absolutely no interest in finding out if there was something they might want to know about me. They were all young and in the flush of finding out about themselves: no room for old women, to paraphrase Cormac McCarthy. It happened again the other day in a more intimate setting with friends of family: I was just a grandma, not a person like them who had a personality, a job, a role, a life.

While I'm not in a position of power, I am in people's faces occasionally and therefore quite visible. How many times have I appeared before the county commission to argue against capitalism and for the commons? How many times have I stood up before the Forest Service and berated them for policies that disenfranchise landbased people? When did I get in Tom Udall's face and chastise him on his support of the Israeli assault on Gaza? How many times did I raise the ire of the environmentalists by decrying their policies that are in effect racist?

Visibility in real time is even more ephemeral than in social media. Being out there in the public eye is a lot more difficult than being out there on Facebook and Instagram. One of my journalist friends, who's working on a book about his tenure as the editor of an alternative newspaper, recently wrote me: "We're both anachronistic activist/journalists. It's like what we've done is 'quaint' or something."

In a *Huffington Post* article blogger Erica Jagger complained about our complaining: "I loathe the power that stale older-women-are-invisible narrative wields." I would say back to her, it's not a "narrative," that overused bullshit word that belongs in novels, it's a fact, borne out by daily experience.

After all this rolled around in my mind today I put on the "Essential Bob Dylan" without even remembering which songs were on volume two. But there it was, "May your heart always be joyful and your soul always be sung and may you stay forever young," and his plaintive cry broke my heart.

Saturday, May 14, 2016

Sojourn to the Urban Landscape

There I was, the country girl (old woman), from El Valle, New Mexico (echoes of Danny Lyon's vato declaring "I'm from Bernalillo, New Mexico") riding a rented bike among a whirlwind of riders, Lake Michigan to the east, the Trump Tower and Chicago skyline to the west. They came in all shapes and sizes: shorts and T-shirts; hot pants and tank tops; flip flops and helmets; babies in bike seats; dogs in baskets; man buns and beards; fat tired mountain bikes; and blessedly little full bike gear regalia. I could hardly watch the scenery as I dodged and passed, slowed and zoomed around other bikers, joggers (the older man shirtless and in flip flops particularly impressive), inline skaters, walkers, and dogs on a crisp, Sunday afternoon with Kimiko, Alan, and Naomi, former New Mexicans, now part of the urban community that scares, intimidates, and fascinates this country girl (old woman).

There'd been a lot of talk among us about the infamous Mayor Rahm, who was supposed to attend the 150th anniversary celebration of the School of the Art Institute of Chicago (where Alan works) but pulled a no show, as has been his wont since the release of the Laquan McDonald video. So when we met up with a Chicago police officer at the Navy Pier and needed to know where to renew the time on our rented bikes (a totally screwed up system that's too complicated to explain here), Naomi kiddingly (brazenly) asked him, "How much do you want to tell us where the nearest bike rack is—five dollars, 10, 20?" With a straight face he answered, "Are you implying that the entire Chicago police force takes bribes? Let me tell you, we get paid way too well to threaten our salary by taking a $20 bribe for a speeding ticket. On the other hand, vice, corruption, fraud . . . ."

Then he smiled and asked us where we were from. I said, "New Mexico" and he said, "So am I" and I said, "Wow" and he said, "Just kidding" and turned, pointed out the bike racks and said, "Have a nice day."

To get to Lake Michigan we had to ride our bikes through residential streets from Kimiko and Alan's house on a route that took us past Wrigley Stadium, where the Cubs were playing a game that went 13 innings (they won). Street hawkers and vendors were everywhere, the bars were full of fans drinking and watching the game on big screen TVs, and the streets were lined with cars that search for parking for miles around this stadium smack dab in the middle of a huge urban environment. Regular neighborhood residents have to plan their car trips around the Cubs' playing schedule or the traffic will whittle away your patience until your blood pressure boils.

Getting stuck in various traffic jams on this nine day trip to Minneapolis and Chicago reminded me that the only time my son Jakob ever used to call me from grad school in Berkeley was when he was stuck in traffic. It eventually contributed to his departure from the Bay Area back to New Mexico, where often I can drive the entire eight miles from Chimayó to Truchas and see maybe five other cars. In Minneapolis, my friend Catherine and I got stuck in traffic on some freeway coming back to the city from Paisley Park, where we paid our respects to Prince. Why he chose to live in a bunker-like complex off a busy street in a tacky Minneapolis suburb remains a mystery, much like everything else about his life, but it didn't stop thousands of fans from trekking out to stuff flowers, purple balloons, photos, messages, stuffed animals, records, guitars, and Doritos (he must have been a Dorito man) onto the chain link fence that surrounds the compound. While the autopsy report is still not out, the best guess is that he got hooked on pain meds after his two hip surgeries and died of an overdose of percocet.

Fence surrounding Paisley Park

So it was an interesting sojourn to the urban/suburban landscape and reminded me that I'm way too old to ever live anyplace larger than Santa Fe (and even the thought of that gives me pause), and that I never want to own a smart phone (not a single soul who I spent more than five minutes with didn't use a phone at some point in the encounter). As I look out my window today, the grosbeaks are feeding in my yard, the apple trees are in full bloom, and the green, green grass in the fields is already a foot tall. I'll be hitting the weed whacker first thing tomorrow morning.

Monday, August 29, 2016

You know, like, I just can't take it anymore!

They're dropping like flies. First it appeared as Valley Girl speech. Then it burst into the language of everyone I know under the age of 40. Then I heard famous people, over the age of 40, saying it in *New York Time's* interviews. Now I hear it from Ira Glass on "This American Life." And Terri Gross on "Fresh Air." And finally, it's there in a 65 year old acquaintance who I thought was a generation removed and inured to such linguistic drivel. But, "you know, like" this is how we talk now and if you think it's weird and perverse and grating and a bastardization of the English language then go get a life.

I went online to see what other folks are saying about this phenomenon. There's a ridiculous article in the *Huffington Post* that tries to defend the usage as a "discourse marker" used by thoughtful people. Countering that are the researchers at Michigan State University who claim people who use the word "Like" to start a sentence are not only perceived as less intelligent but as less friendly to boot! The website WikiHow provides ten steps to stop saying it.

I listened to a show on Fresh Air where a linguist from Stanford defended both the use of "vocal fry"—saying words in a creaky, low-pitched way—and "up-speak," where you end a declarative sentence by raising your voice like you are asking a question (the use of "like" in this sentence is legit, by the way, meaning "as if") as part of the evolution of language. When I first noticed "up-speak" quite a few years ago I thought it had something to do with living in California because the only people I know who speak that way live there. I suppose this California linguist would also defend "You know, like," as another step in this evolutionary pattern. A lot of folks in California also think there is no evolutionary progress, only relativity, so I guess you could say, relatively speaking, like, what does it matter?

One of my sons lets me call him on it. The other one tells me, "Get over it." But when someone starts in with the "you know, like" or "like, you know" I get so distracted by the so-called "discourse markers" that I can't pay attention to what they're actually trying to say. But maybe this is just another step in the evolutionary process of replacing direct communication with virtual, so it's like, all good. Except that it isn't.

Tuesday, October 25, 2016

It's Obscene

I turned on the 2016 World Series tonight anticipating, in theory, the excitement of two teams that haven't made it this far in many, many years, and particularly, the anticipation of Chicago Cubs fans, who I saw in action this spring when I visited the Wrigley Field hood. Then the reality of the Cleveland Indians logo hit me, right there on their caps. It's obscene. The TV is off.

I grew up in the 1950s when the Yankees dominated baseball and I learned to love the underdog by betting against my father's assured smirk when the Pirates or White Sox lost. During the tumultuous 60s I was too busy trying to save the world to follow sports—and didn't own a TV—but in the mid 70s, when I settled in one place—and bought a TV—I was delighted to discover the Oakland A's and their rebellious players—Catfish Hunter, Rollie Fingers, Vida Blue—flaunt baseball decorum with their long hair and mustaches. We watched Monday night baseball in the 80s, swinging babies in cradles hanging from the beams of our handmade house. I knew most of the players on the teams we followed into the nineties, and as life got more complicated, at least always watched the playoffs and the series. I loved Giants pitcher Tim Lincecum with his flowing locks and witnessed the deplorable end of Barry Bond's career at the Giants Stadium overlooking San Francisco Bay.

Now here we are in 2016, watching and supporting however we can the largest ever gathering of Native Americans at the North Dakota Access Pipeline encampment. Many previous protests have targeted the sports world, particularly the Washington Redskins football team, which refuses to change its racist name. But tonight, the Cleveland Indians continue to display this equally racist symbol and millions of baseball fans are watching and millions of dollars are generated through this symbol. We need to do more than just turn off the TV. This really is Unf*#!ing Believable.

Addendum:

I'm checking in every now and again and commiserating with the Cubs fans (it's game 5). If the Indians win, which looks likely, I hope the pressure builds up that our national championship team has got to consign Chief Wahoo to the dustbin of history.

Postscript: The Cubs won!

Thursday, November 10, 2016

It's All Over Now, Party Blue

"The rulers are interested in keeping their subjects in darkness because otherwise the injustice, the arbitrariness, the immorality, the irrationality of their own rule will be altogether too easily exposed. So from the early beginnings of man [woman] an age old conspiracy by the few against the many has been organized and kept going, because unless they do this the few cannot keep the many in subjection."

—Isaiah Berlin, *Freedom and Its Betrayal*

I stayed up late enough on election night to know what the outcome would be Wednesday morning. So I wasn't shocked but deeply concerned for the people who are likely to suffer the most—and the soonest—if indeed Trump becomes the president in January (maybe he'll be in jail by then): undocumented immigrants; the young people protected under the Dream Act; Black Lives Matter activists; the water protectors at Standing Rock; the people on Medicaid. This sadness was tempered only by relief at my almost empty e-mail inbox: no more DNCC pleas of "last chance," "we're screwed," "don't delete this e-mail" from Barack, Michele, Nancy Pelosi, Elizabeth Warren, James Carville, Brad Schneider and on and on (the relentless release of these e-mails discouraged participation instead of eliciting it, but that's another story).

Today's story is that the Democratic Party establishment is first and foremost to blame for Trump's election and for the Republican takeover of Congress and state governments. Ever since the New Deal the Democratic Party has been leaning right towards this, our second gilded age, embracing neoliberalism as the path towards 1% rule. That's why they fought so hard to discredit Bernie in his run for the nomination: he hammered relentlessly on economic inequality that resonated with folks across the country. He was criticized by some on the left for not addressing more directly the issues of race as well as class, but I think he felt his only path towards the nomination was to discredit HRC where she was most vulnerable as a member of the neoliberal elite who has been instrumental in disenfranchising the working class.

Maybe if Bernie had been able to pit his populist message against Trump's so-called populist message more folks would have seen the latter not as their savior, their "blow-it-up-guy" but as the corporatist financier that he is. Maybe if Bernie, or some other progressive candidate, had been able to direct white people's anger towards the Republican elite as well as the Democratic elite there would be less of it directed at minorities and others just as disenfranchised as they think they are.

The flip side of these "maybes" is the fact that many of the people who voted for Trump are people who would have voted for him regardless of a more powerful progressive candidate. Statistics show that this country is split right down the middle in terms of party affiliation, and even with a candidate like Trump the rank and file Republicans are going to vote Republican come hell or high water. We know why the rich Republicans vote that way: it's in their best interests. Why so many whose interests are not represented by the Republican party is the question that many, most famously Thomas Frank, have been asking for years.

As much as I hate to acknowledge it, for fear of being labeled elitist myself (actually, I'm definitely white and privileged but not elitist), a vast group of people in this country, schooled by the Rush Limbaughs and Michael Savages and Bill O'Reillys, are ignorant, misinformed, and fear-driven by identity politics and cultural transformation. They are also the products of a country that prides itself on white Protestant individualism that encourages authoritarianism and discourages empathy (many of these folks are also fundamentalists, which makes it even worse). This is where the white nationalism comes into play upon which Trump fed and flourished. These folks' interests will not be served by Republican or Democratic elites: globalization, financialization, and automation have taken their jobs away and they won't be coming back. Their lives don't matter, either. When you're afraid, when you're hurting, when you're confused, find some other population even more vulnerable to blame: immigrants, blacks, Muslims, gays, etc. Then find someone endowed with the authority to build the wall, send them back to where they came from or strip them of their individual liberty: Donald Trump fits the bill.

I'm a Democrat only by registration so I can vote in primaries for local candidates. I voted for Bernie; I didn't vote for Hilary. That so much of our energy and attention has been invested in this campaign for the last year and a half is obscene. The fight for justice through the ballot box is rigged from the beginning: two parties that severely limit a choice of candidates; big money super PACS that bankroll those candidates; gerrymandering of election districts to wipe out the opposition; the electoral college (HRC won the popular vote); voter suppression, ad infinitum.

Neither will justice prevail by posting on Facebook. Many social media users were sucked into daily harangues with so-called "Friends" over who we were going to vote for, if we were going to vote, and what we should be doing if we didn't vote. How many times did you see someone announce that he or she was purging so and so from his or her friend's list because he or she didn't like his or her position on HRC? Or how many times did you seen someone announce "I'm not going to post anymore political comments" because all the anger and vitriol in which everyone is engaging is not only not going to change anyone's mind but that the sources upon which the anger and vitriol are based are unverified and often untrue. Then the next day they were back there with a post claiming that not only Wikileaks but also the director of the FBI were throwing the election to Trump.

I've been a grassroots organizer and activist engaged in social and environmental justice my entire adult life. I know how difficult it is to fight the machine: so do groups like Occupy and Black Lives Matter, as did La Raza Unida, the Black Panthers, and SDS. In his article in *Current Affairs*, editor Nathan Robinson ends his take down of the Democratic Party with the immortal words of Joe Hill: "Don't mourn, organize!" While I fantasize that once Trump gets bored having to be in the Oval Office every day and sit through cabinet meetings he'll abdicate (he'd have to take Pence with him), Joe Hill's exhortation is mandatory. There is no other way out.

Saturday, April 1, 2017

Your Book That No One Reads

"In general, I try to be very honest in my memoirs. If I lose a few friendships, so what? On the other hand, I sometimes say the best way to keep a secret is to publish it, since no one reads it. My books aren't indexed. So anyone who wants to know what I wrote about him has to read the whole thing."

That's Edmund White. I read this quip shortly after I published my memoir, *Culture Clash: Environmental Politics in New Mexico Communities*. It's only kind of a memoir, really more of a political analysis of what went on in the 1990s over control of natural resources in the land based communities of northern New Mexico. It qualifies as a memoir, I guess, because I was not only a journalist covering these events but an activist who lived in the communities and played a role as the battles ensued.

Unlike White, however, I didn't lose any friends over what I said in the book—I only went after enemies—but my opinion of them went south when I realized his second point, that they weren't going to read the book anyway. I had to nag my kids to read it (to his credit, one of them had a long conversation/critique with me about it). One of my closest friends apparently read it but then never said a word about it to me until I nagged her, too. Another one, whose book I was helping edit, has obviously never read it. Several others, whom I informed that it was coming out, never asked me about it again.

Then I published another book called *Stories From Life's Other Side: People Living on the Margins of Modern Day Society*. I wrote these stories over many years as I encountered the characters who gave birth to these tales of struggle, grit, and acceptance. Same story.

So does this indicate that people don't read or that people don't know how to be friends or that everybody is so self-involved that you can't really parse any meaning?

Yes, some of my friends and colleagues did read the books: several of them gave them good reviews in *Taos Friction*, *La Jicarita*, and *Enchantment* and several others told me they really enjoyed reading them (including John Nichols and Lucy Lippard). My thanks to all of you.

So what do I do now? Publish another book that no one is going to read?

Here it is.

www.ingramcontent.com/pod-product-compliance
Lightning Source LLC
Chambersburg PA
CBHW030433300426
44112CB00009B/983